# Contending for Truth

## Standing for Jesus in a Turbulent World

**Jim Cockburn**

malcolm down

PUBLISHING

First published 2022 by Malcolm Down Publishing Ltd
www.malcolmdown.co.uk

24 23 22 21 20 7 6 5 4 3 2 1



British Library Cataloguing in Publication Data
A catalogue record for this book is available from the British Library.

ISBN 978-1-915046-10-9



Cover design by Esther Kotecha
Art direction by Sarah Grace

Printed in the UK

# Contents

# Introduction

The year 2020 will long be remembered as the year in which the world faced a seismic change. For millions of people worldwide it meant death, pain and suffering as the Covid-19 pandemic spread devastation in its wake. Even in countries with sophisticated healthcare systems there was a fear that these systems would not be able to meet the medical needs of those who succumbed to the virus; in the United Kingdom, for example, we were asked to restrict our contact with others in order to '*save the NHS*'. In addition, many families suffered severe poverty, requiring the services of food banks and other charitable relief. There was a concern that poorer countries would not have the infrastructure to combat the effects of the virus; many people, particularly in urban areas, faced the unenviable choice of the health risk of breaking lockdown restrictions or starvation because they were unable to work.

There have been many other effects causing hardship and distress. So many families faced the pain of not being able to visit their loved ones in hospitals and care homes because of restrictions imposed, and very sadly they were not able to be with them as they passed away. Mental health issues have become more prominent as an increasing number of people have found it hard to cope with the isolation of lockdowns, fearing for their health and their livelihoods in a world where it seems that a small virus has taken control. Education systems have been thrown into chaos with school closures forcing already stressed parents to home school their children, and with students not being able to sit their examinations leading to interminable arguments about what grades they should be awarded.

And so the list could continue. Despite all the restrictions, however, Ella, my wife, and I enjoyed many aspects of the lockdown in the spring and early summer of 2020. Yes, we did miss meeting up with people, especially our grandchildren. We missed going to church but we enjoyed the live streaming of services and discovered Zoom as a way of keeping in touch with our home group and running evangelism and discipleship courses. We missed going to the theatre and football matches, and Ella missed doing the fortieth Great North Run, although she did a virtual challenge instead. We were due to go to Israel in March and indeed spend Palm Sunday in Jerusalem, but this was inevitably cancelled. The weather, however, was by and large lovely, and so we spent much time in the garden and going on walks in the country. It was so peaceful, and so when sitting in our garden enjoying the sunshine and the birds singing it was hard to believe that there was a global crisis going on around us.

For many of us, catching up on reading or 'binge watching' films and television series was a popular way of using our time. One of our sons, David, bought me for my birthday the DVD set of *Chernobyl*[1] which had me absolutely captivated. It tells the story of the devastating meltdown at the Chernobyl nuclear plant in 1986 in what was then the Soviet Union. This accident caused thousands of fatalities both in the local area and throughout Europe as radiation from the plant spread across the continent. The series recounts the story of the accident and its devastating effects, the cover up by the Soviet authorities and the struggle by nuclear scientists led by Valery Legasov to expose the truth. In the last episode Legasov very bravely made a blistering attack on the Soviet authorities at the show trial of those held to be culpable for the disaster. This is what he said in his denouncement of the Soviet state: *'When the truth offends, we lie and lie, until we can no longer remember that it is there, but it is still there. Every lie we tell incurs a debt to the truth. Sooner or later that debt is paid.* ***Lies!****'*

This action by Legasov made such an impact on me that it became one of the inspirations for this book. Here was a man who was determined to bring the authorities' attention to the truth that the disaster was

1. *Chernobyl* (Sky/HBO, 2019).

caused by design flaws in the system that were approved by the Soviet authorities themselves for cost-saving reasons. In a system fuelled by lies he decided to contend for the truth, despite the threats to his own life, in order to ensure that similar accidents did not happen again.

Tragically, just before this book was due to go to print, Russia mounted a full-scale invasion of the independent state of Ukraine. Ironically, Russian troops took control of the Chernobyl power station, perhaps with a view to blackmail the West. Lies were once again used as President Putin tried to justify what most of the rest of the world saw as an unacceptable act of aggression.

In the world of the 2020s, where lies and hatred are so overbearing, many people are looking for truth and purpose. Politicians and scientists have shown that they do not have all the answers. For Christians the ultimate truth is the Lord Jesus Christ and the good news that he brings.

Whatever 'new normal' scenarios emerge in the 2020s we do need men and women who will contend for the truth in Christ. Tom Holland is a secular historian who has a tremendous affinity for the Christian message. In an interview in October 2020 he expressed disappointment in the church for not setting forth the teaching of the Bible to explain why the world faces the crisis of the pandemic and what our spiritual response should be. He declared, '*The response of the churches was a kind of pallid echo of public health announcements*.'[2] The fact that we have someone searching for the truth and not having his needs met is an indication of how we desperately need more men and women to contend for the truth of the gospel in these very difficult days.

Despite the shortcomings of the church that Tom Holland pointed out, we do have many wonderful examples of those who are prepared to contend for the gospel. These men and women earnestly try to follow the examples of Jesus and Paul, and we, too, shall try to learn from these

2. Tom Holland, 'How Christianity Gained Dominion' (October 2020) https://www.youtube.com/watch?v=favILmUsVdg&t=2601s (accessed 8.12.21).

New Testament examples in Parts Two and Three. In Part Four we shall consider a few present-day contenders for the Lord, and again see what we can learn from each of them.

There is, however, a word of warning as we do that. In 2020, as a result of Black Lives Matter protests, we have seen a number of incidents of statue toppling on both sides of the Atlantic. These were statues of men associated with the slave trade or other unsavoury aspects of colonialism. The problem with literally putting people on pedestals by making statues to honour them is that all these people have flaws which may well cause offence to some group. Indeed, all of us have flaws, part of what the Bible calls sin. Even my inspiration, Valery Legasov, lied when he spoke at a meeting of the International Atomic Energy Agency and on that occasion covered up state responsibility for the Chernobyl disaster.

The same applies to the men and women put on a pedestal in this book. We can learn so much from them, as long as we remember that they (apart, of course, from Jesus himself) are all sinners saved by grace. Indeed, we can also learn from their shortcomings and failings, which they all humbly acknowledge.

May we all be willing to learn under God to contend for truth.

# Part One

## Lies, Hate, Truth and Love – a 2020 Perspective

# Chapter 1: Starting in China

It was in January 2020 that a young Chinese ophthalmologist, Doctor Li Wenliang, rose to prominence as the physician who released what was to be far-reaching information to the world. He reported that there were confirmed cases of coronavirus related to a seafood market in Wuhan, the Chinese city in which he worked. This information spread across the Chinese internet and came to the attention of the Wuhan Public Security Bureau. Li was subsequently interviewed and admonished for spreading false rumours and disrupting social order. He was made to sign a letter promising not to spread further rumours, otherwise he would be prosecuted.

Li returned to work a few days later, only to contract the virus himself, possibly from one of his patients whom he was treating for glaucoma. Li was taken into intensive care on January 12th 2020 and tragically died on February 1st. Li's treatment by the police authorities and tragic death led to outrage amongst the Chinese people. He was even likened by some to Valery Legasov, the Chernobyl whistleblower of 1986. Key quotes from the *Chernobyl* television series such as '*What is the cost of lies? . . . The real danger is that if we hear enough lies, then we no longer recognise the truth at all*' were posted on Chinese social media.[3]

Although an official government report withdrew the reprimand against Li and rebuked the police for the way they covered up the coronavirus outbreak, many felt that those higher up in the system should have also been reprimanded themselves for not dealing with the outbreak sooner. Critical messages against the Chinese government surged across the internet at a faster rate than censors could remove them. Numerous academics called for greater freedom of speech.

3. Ishaan Tharoor, 'China's Chernobyl? The coronavirus outbreak leads to a loaded metaphor' (*Washington Post*, February 12th 2020).

It is generally agreed that the Chinese government did not act quickly enough in dealing with the outbreak, although when it did, it introduced a very draconian lockdown in Wuhan, the epicentre of the outbreak. Likewise, it did not warn the rest of the world quickly enough of the imminent danger of the spread of the virus. It was perceived that the Chinese Communist Party under President Xi Jinping wanted to preserve its reputation in the eyes of the world (as the Soviet government tried to do in the aftermath of Chernobyl), as well as keeping control over its population.[4]

There was no way that President Ji was prepared to allow greater transparency and freedom of speech, as was called for by academics after Li's death. Instead, as the spread of the virus turned into a global pandemic, he increased the stranglehold of the party on the country, allowing no opposition to the party and its version of the truth. At the very end of the year, for example, a Chinese Christian journalist, Zhang Zhan, was given a four-year prison sentence for her reports from Wuhan, which in the words of the *Reuters* report '*painted a more dire picture of the pandemic epicentre than the official narrative*'.[5] This stranglehold included stronger restrictive measures forbidding Christians and members of other faiths from putting their God on a higher plane than the party.

Life in Wuhan was very difficult during the lockdown, but for many Christians it was an opportunity to seek God through prayer, Bible study and online fellowship with other believers. Pastor Huang Lei, leader of one of the churches in the city, ensured that the life of his church continued, albeit online. In an interview he declared:

---

4. It is now more strongly believed by Western scientists that the virus could have escaped from a laboratory in the Wuhan Institute of Virology, something that the Chinese government strongly disputes. See *The Economist*, 'Assessing the theory that Covid-19 leaked from a Chinese lab' (May 29th 2021).
5. BBC, 'Zhang Zhan: China jails citizen journalist for Wuhan reports' (December 28th 2020) https://www.bbc.co.uk/news/world-asia-china-55463241 (accessed 8.12.21).

> *The epidemic hasn't cut down our meetings. We have more than fifty groups. Almost all the groups are meeting via internet, praying, studying the Bible, sharing, witnessing, praising and worshipping . . . It's bringing us closer together.*[6]

Through this time of crisis, President Ji intensified his policy of Sinicisation that he began in 2015. The aim of this policy was to root out foreign influences on Chinese culture and life. In the case of the churches, this involved using Chinese symbols rather than foreign ones such as the cross, and ensuring that theology was aligned to Communist Party dogma. Since the death of Chairman Mao in 1976, life for Christians depended very much on local factors such as the degree of interference from local bureaucrats or intervention from the local police. Under Ji, however, there was now a new focus on religion from the highest levels of government.

We have been used to hearing stories of churches being demolished, crosses being removed from buildings and services being disrupted as part of the Sinicisation policy. Now that more services were being forced to be online as a result of the pandemic, a more insidious attack was beginning to take place against Chinese Christians: data surveillance equipment was being used to monitor their online activity. International Christian Concern reported that on Easter Sunday 2020, an online service being run by Early Rain Covenant Church in Sichuan was disrupted as armed police officers raided the homes of church members, removing a number of them and detaining them for prosecution. This was a case of private religious activity being penalised by the authorities.[7]

This particular church had faced persecution from 2018 when Pastor Wang Yi was arrested for publishing a letter criticising the state

6. Lindy Lowry, 'Chinese pastor from Wuhan: the virus can't stop us' (*Open Doors USA*, March 18th 2020).
7. 'Sichuan Church Members Detained During Easter Service' (International Christian Concern, April 13th 2020), www.persecution.org (accessed 15.12.21).

authorities for their attacks on organised religion. As a result, Wang was given a nine-year prison sentence in December 2019 on charges of '*operating an illegal business activity*' and '*inciting subversion of state power*'.[8] All of these charges were trumped up lies. The church faced further interference from the state in 2020. In one case, an elder of the church, Li Yingqiang, was detained by authorities for posting a tweet calling on believers to pray for Pastor Wang; he was told that the church was banned in Chengdou province and that he should leave the province.[9]

It is not only Christian churches that have suffered under the Sinicisation policy. Possibly about a million Uighur Muslims are believed to have been detained in re-education camps in the Xinjiang region of western China. In these camps, it has been alleged by eyewitnesses that detainees have been cajoled to renounce their faith and learn Mandarin Chinese, and have also suffered physical and mental torture, including in some cases forced sterilisation. The Chinese authorities deny these allegations, claiming instead that the camp members are receiving vocational training.

In a very revealing interview with the Chinese Ambassador, Liu Xiaming, in July 2020, Andrew Marr from the BBC challenged the ambassador about the treatment of Uighur Muslims. He showed the ambassador drone footage of hundreds of Uighur Muslims kneeling blindfolded and shaven, waiting to be put on trains. He was also shown a clip of a woman speaking about her experience of forced sterilisation.

In his responses, the ambassador tried to pretend that the drone footage could be of normal prisoner movement that takes place in any country, that Xinjiang was a very beautiful place where the Uighur population was rising, not falling, and that China would never indulge

---

8. Gina Goh et al., 'Religious Suppression in China' (International Christian Concern, July 2020).
9. Cara Bentley, 'Church elder interrogated in China for posting prayer about imprisoned pastor on Twitter' (*Premier Christian News*, October 12th 2020).

in ethnic cleansing. It was clear that he was using all sorts of implausible explanations for what was happening, including clearly vacuous and fallacious claims:

> *Uighur people enjoy harmonious life, peaceful, harmonious coexistence with other ethnic groups of people . . . We have a very successful ethnic policy. We treat every ethnic group as equal . . . There's no so-called pervasive massive forced sterilisation among Uighur people in China. It's totally against the truth . . . The government is strongly opposed to this type of practice.*[10]

Before the onset of the coronavirus outbreak, the Chinese population was enjoying greater prosperity than they had ever known, and it is likely that the rate of economic recovery after the pandemic will be significantly higher than in most other countries. Yet at the core of the Chinese State is a regime buttressed by lies, subterfuge and hatred towards those who are perceived to be opposed to its rule, including those who revere God more than they do the president.

What gives hope, however, is not just the survival of the Chinese church, but its phenomenal growth, in spite of – or even because of – persecution. Professor Fenggang Yang, Director of the Centre on Religion and Chinese Society at Purdue University in Indiana, estimates that there were 116 million Protestant Christians in China (compared with only 90 million Communist Party members), and that by 2030 there will be more Christians in China than any other country in the world.[11]

---

10. *The Andrew Marr Show* (July 20th 2020).
11. *Time* Magazine, 'Prison Sentence for Pastor Shows China Feels Threatened by Spread of Christianity, Experts Say' (January 2nd 2021).

# Chapter 2: Moving to the West – the United Kingdom

The World Health Organisation declared the outbreak of Covid-19 a pandemic on March 11th 2020. It was evidently not something that simply affected China, but rather was now having a global impact. People in Britain, for example, watched news footage in February from Northern Italy where the hospital system was swamped by those suffering from the disease and the country was put into a very restrictive lockdown. Britain was soon going to face its own Covid crisis with the first two cases being reported on January 31st, the first death from coronavirus on March 5th, and the first national lockdown regulations coming into force on March 26th.

Governments in western democracies are clearly not as authoritarian as the Chinese State, although as the virus spread there was the view that measures were being introduced without much debate. Certainly Boris Johnson, the British prime minister, introduced lockdown restrictions in March without bringing them before parliament. Although he was criticised for not acting quickly enough in March following the Italian experience, there was a degree of sympathy for the prime minister as this was a totally new and unexpected crisis for the government. Sympathy for him grew further when he was taken into intensive care in April suffering from the virus, with many Christians praying for his physical and spiritual wellbeing.

Although there was sympathy, there was also increasing concern that the government was not handling the crisis particularly well. Many felt that our civil liberties were being eroded. Serious restrictions were imposed. These interfered with basic aspects of life, such as earning a living, meeting family and friends, visiting family in hospitals and care homes, and being with loved ones at the end of life. Most people initially accepted these as necessary to preserve life, but as time passed there was a growing sense on the part of many that these were infringements on our basic freedoms.

One area of concern was the closure of churches and other places of worship. In the first lockdown, faith leaders agreed that centres of worship should be closed to prevent the virus from spreading; after all, there were reports coming out of South Korea of large church gatherings spreading the virus.[12] As restrictions eased throughout the country in the late spring and summer, on June 13th the government allowed churches in England to reopen initially for private prayer and then on July 4th for public worship. Strict rules were applied to ensure that the buildings were 'Covid secure' with limited attendance, social distancing, the wearing of face masks and a ban on singing all being applied. This was positive news, and churches began to make plans for reopening. There was a strong belief, however, amongst many Christians that the government had got its priorities wrong by allowing the hospitality and leisure sectors, important as they are to the economy, to reopen before churches.

Feelings that churches were not being treated fairly became more heated in the autumn as the country faced a second wave of the virus. A two-week lockdown was introduced in Wales on October 23rd that included a ban on public worship. Police intervened when churches tried to defy the ban.[13] A four-week lockdown was introduced in England on November 5th, and again churches were closed except for private prayer. The health arguments for closure were again to prevent the virus from spreading through large gatherings. It was now argued, however, that churches had worked hard to make their buildings and services

---

12. https://www.bbc.co.uk/news/world-asia-53803011 (accessed 15.12.21).
13. https://www.independent.co.uk/news/uk/home-news/wales-coronavirus-firebreak-lockdown-rules-police-church-illegal-service-b1370645.html (accessed 15.12.21).

'Covid secure', and that the scientific experts could produce no data to demonstrate that church services were a health threat.[14]

Marcus Walker, in *The Spectator*, emphasised that public worship was an essential human right: '*The worship of God is life-giving and transformational, it informs who we are at our very core. For those who believe, it is the very opposite of inessential – in the most literal meaning of the word "essential" – it is of our essence.*'[15]

It was argued that by determining whether churches should meet for public worship or not, the government was going well beyond its God-given remit. In the House of Commons lockdown restrictions debate, former prime minister, Theresa May, commented that while the government was making it illegal to conduct acts of collective worship for the best of intentions, it had established a precedent for a future government with the worst of intentions, and so there were unintended consequences.[16]

A small number of churches defied the restrictions and continued to meet, some in secret. One pastor told *The Observer* newspaper, '*We've been holding clandestine services since this lockdown began. It feels weird for us to act this way. People have said it feels more like an underground church in China.*'[17]

The message did finally get through to the government, and so in the third lockdown starting in January 2021, communal worship in churches and other places of worship in England was permitted, subject to Covid safety restrictions, with church leaders being allowed to decide for themselves as to whether they should open their churches or not. Unfortunately, Nicola Sturgeon, the First Minister of Scotland, still

---

14. Tola Mbakwe, 'Scientific advisor says no strong evidence proves church service ban will help with lockdown' (*Premier Christian News*, November 5th 2020).
15. Marcus Walker, 'If anything is essential, it's worship' (*The Spectator*, November 2nd 2020).
16. United Kingdom Hansard (November 4th 2020).
17. Harriet Sherwood, '"Let us disobey": Churches defy lockdown with secret meetings' (*The Observer*, November 22nd 2020).

failed to see the importance of worship and so Scottish churches were locked down again in January.[18]

The government faced criticisms in other areas. Promises were made with regard to the supply of protective personal equipment in hospitals and other frontline centres. They also promised to provide a 'world beating' track-and-trace system. In both cases the government found it exceptionally difficult to keep these promises. Although these were not downright lies, the government had made promises that it was not able to keep and had indeed 'overpromised and underdelivered'. The government consistently claimed that they were acting 'according to the science', and yet it became increasingly clear that there was no one 'scientific truth'. Different scientific bodies presented different models, predictions and scenarios, depending on the assumptions and data they were using.

As the year went on, the government faced increasing criticisms for parts of its policy. People were horrified at the death rate in care homes. The government had not given them the priority that they should have been given. Young people and their teachers felt let down by the Education Secretaries in both England and Scotland over the cancellation of exams and the awarding of grades. The government was accused of not having a strategy and making too many U-turns; perhaps one of the most blatant was the decision of the prime minister to introduce a full lockdown in November only days after dismissing the idea when it was put to him by members of the opposition. Indeed, it was later suggested that he was so angry at having to put the country into another lockdown that he blasted out in a rant on October 30th, '*No more lockdowns. Let the bodies pile high in their thousands*!' (expletive removed). He and Downing Street officials denied that he made this

18. A group of Scottish church leaders did manage to win their case in March 2021 at the Court of Session in Edinburgh when the judge Lord Braid declared that the Scottish government's ban on public worship was unlawful.

statement, although it is alleged that three people overheard the remark and confirmed that that was what he said.[19] Clearly lies are being told, on one side or the other.[20]

It would seem that the prime minister found it hard to learn from previous errors as he forced the country into a more restrictive lockdown at the beginning of 2021. Only a day after he claimed that schools were very safe and that primary school parents should send their children there at the start of the new term,[21] to the astonishment of the nation, he announced on Monday January 4th that all schools would be closed as from the following morning. Governments make mistakes, but there has been very little humility shown by saying that they were sorry when they had clearly got things wrong.

People were also horrified at the behaviour of Boris Johnson's special adviser, Dominic Cummings, during the first lockdown in March and April. His wife developed Covid symptoms, and having gone home to see how she was, he then returned to Downing Street. This was a clear failure to apply lockdown rules, the very rules that he had helped to devise. He then drove his wife and young child up to County Durham, in order that members of his family could help look after their son, which was probably a reasonable thing to do (although his main critics did not agree with that action). Cummings later developed symptoms himself. The family a few days later took a fifty-mile round trip to the historic market town of Barnard Castle on the pretext of checking that Cummings' sight was good enough to drive home. This latter

---

19. Gordon Rayner, '"Let the bodies pile high": what really happened on night Boris Johnson was accused of outburst' (*The Telegraph*, April 27th 2021).
20. Allegations of lies seem to have followed Boris Johnson throughout his public life, something on which there is a high degree of agreement, but seemingly overlooked when he was elected leader of the Conservative Party and then prime minister. One of his former Cabinet and Foreign Office colleagues, Rory Stewart, described him as '*the most accomplished liar in public life – perhaps the best liar ever to serve as prime minister*' in an interview on the BBC Radio 4 *Today* programme on November 5th 2020.
21.*The Andrew Marr Show* (BBC, January 3rd 2021).

action became the butt of many comedians' jokes. Cummings failed to apologise for his actions or show any humility. Furthermore, the prime minister refused to take any disciplinary action against him. Church of England bishops were amongst the most vociferous in condemning both Cummings for his actions, and Johnson for supporting him. They argued that the general public had made huge sacrifices to keep to the rules, while a senior official felt that he was free to ignore them.[22] There was certainly some substance in the bishops' arguments in this case. The question needs to be asked, however, as to why they had not spoken out with as much vehemence on the more important spiritual issue as to how we, as a nation, needed to repent and put our faith in Jesus as the only person who can offer real hope.

Towards the end of the year there was both bad news and a glimmer of hope for the country. Tragically, the number of United Kingdom Covid-related deaths crossed the fifty-thousand barrier on November 11th 2020.[23] In the same week, however, there was a ray of hope when it was announced that the pharmaceutical giant Pfizer had developed a vaccine that could begin to be rolled out before the end of the year. This is where science had really come into its own by being able to develop a vaccine in the space of only ten months. In fact the mass vaccination programme was able to start on December 8th. With this news people were now beginning to hope that things might return to a degree of normality in 2021.

Despite the good news about the Pfizer and subsequent vaccines, 2020 ended and 2021 started in very gloomy circumstances. Families were

---

22. Ed Thornton, 'PM's support for Cummings has lost our trust' (*Church Times*, May 25th 2020).

23. https://coronavirus.data.gov.uk/details/deaths (accessed 15.12.21). The number crossed the 70,000 barrier on Christmas Day and reached 100,000 on January 26th 2021. In the press conference that day, the prime minister offered his deepest condolences to all who had lost loved ones and took full responsibility for government actions, saying that the government had done all that it could to minimise death and suffering. This latter statement was, however, met with a high degree of incredulity.

only allowed to come together for one day for Christmas. The whole of the United Kingdom went into a lockdown in January affecting much of normal life, including non-essential businesses, schools, colleges and universities. A new mutant of the virus was rampaging initially throughout London (where the mayor declared a state of emergency) and the south-east, and then throughout the rest of the country. This mutant, along with others later discovered in South Africa, Brazil and India spread more quickly than the original virus, accelerating the rates of infections, hospitalisation and deaths across the country.[24] Given these new developments, there was reluctant agreement with the need for this lockdown.

24. The year 2021 also ended gloomily as a new variant, omicron, spread across the country with a very high rate of transmissibility.

# Chapter 3: The United States – the Pandemic in the Midst of a Presidential Election

The coronavirus has had a devastating impact on the United States with more than three hundred thousand deaths recorded by the end of 2020. This is an extraordinary figure given the immense resources and knowledge that the richest country in the world possesses. Lives were destroyed, hospitals found it hard to cope and the economy spiralled downwards. Initially, communities came together to support one another, but division and hatred seemed to intensify across the country. Even the issue of whether to wear a mask or not seemed to be a major source of division.[25] There was a general view that President Trump was not taking the virus seriously enough. Ironically, shortly after he declared, '*It is disappearing*', he himself ended up contracting it with fairly serious symptoms. With better medical help than most people could afford he seemed to recover very well, saying in an interview on Fox News on October 18th 2020, '*I beat this crazy horrible China virus.*' Despite what he had undergone, he still failed to encourage social distancing, with his political rallies being called 'super spreaders'.

There were arguments as to whether churches should be closed, but division amongst churches, even evangelical churches, was more extreme than in Britain. One of the most prominent evangelical pastors in the country, John MacArthur, defied state law by keeping his Los Angeles mega-church open during the pandemic, even daring the authorities to put him in prison so that he could preach the gospel there. He argued that it was important for the people of God to meet and worship

25. Lauren Aratani, 'How did face masks become a political issue in America?' (*The Guardian*, June 29th 2020).

together and that indeed the pandemic did not really exist, but rather there was a 'virus of deception'.[26] This, however, was not the general view among church leaders. Pastor D.J. Jenkins, also from Los Angeles, felt that although he greatly respected MacArthur, he had misused official statistics and thus distorted the truth and misled people. He said that he was praying that MacArthur would repent of the false witness he was bearing.[27]

The presidential election demonstrated the extent of the discord that was so prevalent in American society. The incumbent president, Donald Trump, was admired by many of his followers as the man who had '*made America great again*', according to his mantra from the previous election. He was seen by his followers to have brought prosperity back to many parts of the economy, protected jobs, shown strength in world affairs and stood for traditional values in areas such as abortion and marriage. His opponents, however, loathed him and saw him as a clown-like figure who communicated through tweeting, lacking substance in his statements. They accused him of dividing the country along racial lines, continually telling lies, for example about the pandemic or his tax returns, and having a past history of a sexually immoral life.[28]

His Democratic opponent, Joe Biden, was believed by his supporters to be a decent man who had a lot of experience as vice-president under Barak Obama, had seen personal tragedy in his life and had the qualities to bring the country back together. Although he was described as boring, many, especially suburban voters, saw that as being a positive quality after their experience of four years of what they saw as Trump's erratic behaviour. He did not seem to be as tainted with lies as the

---

26. Jaclyn Cosgrove, 'L.A. megachurch pastor mocks pandemic health orders even as church members fall ill' (*Los Angeles Times*, November 8th 2020).
27. https://www.premierchristianity.com/Blog/There-is-no-pandemic-Mythbusting-John-MacArthur-s-claims (accessed 15.12.21).
28. *The Washington Post* claimed on July 13th 2020 that Donald Trump had told over twenty thousand lies since taking office.

president was. There was, however, controversy over whether he and his family had gained from contacts in Ukraine and China, with possible damaging material found on a laptop belonging to his son, Hunter.

Christian leaders were concerned about who would be more likely to promote traditional Christian values and protect Christians who wanted to make a stand in defence of these values. Evangelicals have tended to support Trump. Indeed, according to exit polls as many as 80 per cent of white evangelicals may have voted for him in the 2020 election.[29] Nevertheless, in looking at the Christian faith of the two candidates, there was some strong difference of opinion amongst evangelical leaders. On his 'Desiring God' website, a leading evangelical preacher, teacher and writer, John Piper, explained why he could not vote for either candidate in the forthcoming presidential election.[30] He felt that one of the candidates (presumably Trump, although he did not name him) had certain qualities including '*flagrant boastfulness, vulgarity, immorality, and factiousness*' that are '*nation-corrupting and move out from centres of influence to infect whole cultures*'. Therefore, he could not vote for a man who had such qualities. On the other side, he believed that abortion policies allow the murder of children and as such are abhorrent, thus preventing him from voting for the other candidate who permitted such policies (presumably Biden).

An equally prominent evangelical leader, Wayne Grudem, came to a different conclusion and respectfully refuted Piper's arguments. He felt that Christians could live with Trump's character flaws but many would find it very difficult if laws were passed that promoted the LGBT agenda or used taxpayers' money to promote abortion facilities, which could

29. Elana Schor and David Crary, 'AP Vote Cast: Trump wins white evangelicals, Catholics split' (*AP News*, November 6th 2020).
30. https://www.desiringgod.org/articles/policies-persons-and-paths-to-ruin (accessed 15.12.21).

happen under a Biden presidency.[31] By and large, evangelical Trump supporters put forward rational arguments but some foolishly put forward 'words from the Lord' that he would win. His spiritual advisor, Paula White, ranted for his victory believing that angels were on their way to rescue him in a video that went viral.[32]

There were Christian leaders who supported Biden, who himself is a strong Roman Catholic, although he did not want to impose his church's teachings on abortion and same-sex marriage on others. Dr Joel Hunter, a former mega-church pastor and Republican voter, decided that he would vote for a Democrat candidate for the first time. His group 'Pro-Life Evangelicals for Biden' believes that the Republican Party was not supporting policies such as providing access to health care. He stated that lives were being threatened by failing to endorse such policies.[33]

The election battle was a bad-tempered affair. Pollsters had put Biden way out in the lead, but the reality was that it was very close at the end. Eventually, after a few recounts, the media declared that Biden had gained the required number of electoral college seats. Trump refused to accept the result, stating as early as election night that he had won. He stated that the election had been stolen from him due to electoral fraud, claiming that the postal votes had been rigged to favour Biden. The whole democratic process was being called into question as he began lawsuits in a number of states. Nevertheless, despite the fact that lawsuits were continuing, Biden remained calm until all the votes had been counted and he was declared the winner. Even into 2021, however, Trump would not accept that he had lost the election, stating that he would never concede defeat.

---

31. http://www.waynegrudem.com/a-respectful-response-to-my-friend-john-piper-about-voting-for-trump (accessed 15.12.21).
32. https://www.youtube.com/watch?v=gHsBIk1ZLr4 (accessed 15.12.21). The issue is not the existence of angels, but rather whether the Lord did give that particular word.
33. Kelly Valencia, '"I took a gamble": Evangelical leader who supported Trump in 2016 switches sides ahead of US election' (*Premier Christian News*, October 30th 2020).

It will, however, be a massive job to bring peace and unity to such a divided nation. Over seventy million voters cast their ballot for Donald Trump, and it will take much effort to heal their wounds. John Pitney, an American political scientist, was quoted as saying, '*Many Republicans and Democrats believe that the other side isn't just mistaken but evil.*'[34] This was seen most vividly and horrifically on January 6th 2021, the day that Congress was due to confirm the election of Biden as President. Encouraged by President Trump, whom they saw as their 'commander-in-chief', thousands of protesters rallied in Washington to 'save America' and 'stop the steal' of the election. The world was shocked as they saw pictures of rampage and looting inside the seat of the American government. Five deaths were reported during the riot. Trump eventually called upon the protesters to go home, saying that they were very special people whom he loved. Although he did not condemn their actions or apologise for the events that shook American democracy in that message, he did make a U-turn the following day, presumably under pressure, and condemned the lawless actions committed.

Hatred runs deep in American society, but it was the death of George Floyd on May 25th 2020 that brought this hatred to the surface in a way that would reverberate round the world.

34. Rory Carroll, 'Piecing America Back Together' (*The Guardian*, November 9th 2020).

# Chapter 4: Black Lives Matter and Identity Politics

Police were called to deal with a forty-six-year-old unemployed black man for allegedly using a counterfeit bank note to buy cigarettes. Officers handcuffed him and tried to put him in their car. Because he claimed that he was having difficulty breathing, they made him lie down on the ground instead. White police officer, Derek Chauvin, arrived on the scene and took charge of the situation by kneeling on George Floyd's neck for seven minutes and forty-six seconds, despite Floyd repeatedly crying that he could not breathe.[35] He lay motionless when he was put in an ambulance and was declared dead an hour later. The whole event was captured on video. Chauvin was eventually charged with second-degree murder and his three colleagues with abetting the murder.[36]

The death of George Floyd sparked mass protests in American cities and over sixty countries across the world. His death was taken to symbolise police brutality against African Americans in the States and similar brutality against members of ethnic minority groups in other countries, including Britain. The protests were largely peaceful, although they occasionally degenerated into looting and violence. The slogan that was most commonly used was 'Black Lives Matter', linked to a global network that aims to promote justice and freedom for black people.

When the term 'Black Lives Matter' became associated with protests in 2020, the reaction of many people was to say 'All Lives Matter', but that is a truism that is not particularly helpful. If it is the case that people of colour face mistreatment at the hands of individuals or discrimination at the hands of the authorities, then it is only right to bring their

---

35. It was mistakenly believed to be eight minutes forty-six seconds and so 8:46 became symbolic in many demonstrations.
36. Chauvin was found guilty of murder on April 20th 2021.

predicaments to the fore and take action to create a more just society. People of colour need to have the same opportunities for advancement as white people in all areas of life, including the job market. This is true in the church as well, and many churches have had to examine their practices to ensure that they welcome and meet the needs of people of all ethnic groups.

One symbol that has been used to support Black Lives Matter is to 'take the knee' during protests and also at the beginning of sporting events, such as premiership football matches. It has become commonplace for players and officials to bend their knees before play begins. People should, of course, have the freedom to 'take the knee' or not as they wish according to their beliefs. It would, however, take a fair bit of courage not to bend the knee in a public demonstration of solidarity. One person who decided not to take the knee before a premiership rugby match was England rugby player Billy Vunipola. In an interview on 'The Good, the Bad and Rugby podcast' in August 2020 he said, '*When we were asked if we wanted to "take the knee" or not, from what I saw in terms of that movement was not aligned with what I believe in by burning churches and Bibles. I can't support that. Even though I am a person of colour, I am more a person of Jesus.*'[37]

The view taken by Vunipola over 'taking the knee' reflects the issue many people will have: they support the concept that black lives matter, but they cannot support the organisation itself which is seen by many (rightly or wrongly) to be Marxist, anti-Christian, not in full support of the nuclear family and too supportive of LGBT issues. White privilege is a reality in both Britain and America, but there is a danger that by emphasising the term in a vitriolic way, people of different colours are placed in silos of hatred and distrust. They need instead to be integrated into society for the common good. Martin Luther King Jr in the 1960s

37. https://www.youtube.com/watch?v=a7xeuR3iDeU (accessed 15.12.21).

led African American protesters in bowing the knee in prayer and looked forward to when

> *My four little children will one day live in a nation where they will not be judged by the colour of their skin but by the content of their character . . . and one day right there in Alabama little black boys and black girls will be able to join hands with little white boys and white girls as sisters and brothers. I have a dream today.*[38]

King saw all people as being created in the image of God and longed for an integration of all into one nation. So far, his dream is far from being fully realised, but it is also not clear that the Black Lives Matter movement will necessarily take us in that direction.

The movement has called for a rewriting of history that has resulted in action such as the destruction of statues of former slave traders, the renaming of buildings such as the David Hume Tower in Edinburgh University (where the author had many undergraduate lectures, coffees and snack lunches), and encouraging schools to include more black history in the curriculum. Some of this approach can be seen as positive, but there is a danger that we no longer properly understand our past and instead end up with an unbalanced view of history that has moved to the opposite extreme. Trevor Phillips, former chairman of the Equality and Human Rights Commission and himself a product of the 'Windrush' generation, has argued for a balanced approach. In a well-argued essay in *The Times*, he wrote:

> *Censorship of the past is merely the warm-up for the crushing of dissent in the future. If we remove the reminders of where we have*

38. Martin Luther King Jr, 'I have a dream' (speech delivered on August 28th 1963).

> *been, we take away the signposts to the cul-de-sacs – fascism, communism, genocide – into which human greed, vanity and selfishness have taken us, and we will almost certainly take the same routes again.*[39]

We are seeing this crushing of dissent at the present time across society, even with regard to the changing use of language such as forbidding the use of traditional gender determined personal pronouns and changes to the definitions of men, women and marriage, so as not to offend the LGBT community.

There are serious consequences for those who disagree with the prevailing view. Cancel culture results in people with traditional views on topics such as marriage, gender or abortion being prevented from speaking at particular venues, such as university student unions. People have been vilified for saying things that seem to many to be common sense. J.K. Rowling, the celebrated *Harry Potter* author has been both vilified and cancelled for supporting a researcher called Maya Forstater, who had been sacked from her job for saying that men are men, women are women, and it is impossible to change sex. That is a traditional view, but there is a widely held belief both within and beyond the LGBT community that the traditional view is offensive to transgender people, and so in their opinion Forstater deserved to be fired and Rowling deserves cancellation and abuse.[40] Whatever side of the gender argument one is on, it is surely right, however, that nobody deserves the intolerant treatment that both women suffered. As Phillips argued above, dissent is being crushed.

Free speech is being damaged as people increasingly identify with groups based on ethnicity, gender, sexuality and religion. Each group

39. Trevor Phillips, 'When you erase a nation's past, you threaten its future' (*The Times*, September 19th 2020).
40. Maya Forstater won her appeal against dismissal in June 2021. J.K. Rowling has received death threats as well as continuing cancellation.

fights to overcome the oppression it has perceived to suffer from other groups, believing as it does so that it has some degree of superiority over other groups. Identity politics has taken over, and as a result free speech is stifled and hatred is intensified. Douglas Murray, in his book *The Madness of Crowds*, describes the divisive nature of identity politics, giving numerous examples of those who unwittingly in a comment '*nick the tripwire*' and find the intensive rage of a particular crowd storming against them.[41]

Along similar lines, Tim Keller, the renowned American preacher and writer, sent the following tweet that clearly and succinctly sums up society's picture of truth:

> *Two seemingly contradictory currents mark our society:*
> *(1) There is a denunciation of all claims of absolute truth.*
> *(2) Yet there is also a fanaticism in which one position or group is absolutely right, nothing is ambiguous, and divergent views should be destroyed.*[42]

41. Douglas Murray, *The Madness of Crowds* (Bloomsbury Continuum, 2020), pp. 244-245.
42. Timothy Keller (@timkellernyc, September 5th 2020).

# Chapter 5: The Role of the Media

The media play a major role in determining how as a society we see the truth, and in the United Kingdom the BBC plays a particularly prominent role as our national broadcaster.

Many groups, whether they be political parties, churches or supporters of particular values, however, feel that the BBC is not impartial and that there is a bias in its reporting. It is not that reporters and journalists tell deliberate lies, but rather that they show discretion in what aspects of a news story to report and what not to report. Robin Aitken, a Christian and former BBC journalist, wrote a book entitled *The Noble Liar*[43] in which he argued that, with the best of intentions and for the perceived good of society, the corporation had thrown in their lot with the liberal reformers and tended to ignore the arguments of those who were socially conservative. This would include ignoring traditional beliefs such as the truth of the Christian gospel and traditional views on marriage, divorce, sexuality, transgender and abortion. Even the veteran BBC broadcaster John Humphrys wondered about the reason for creating a new post of LGBT correspondent.[44]

As a result, specifically Christian news or aspects of news stories tend to be played down. One example of this was their extensive reporting of the tragic death of 'Black Panther' star Chad Boseman, at the young age of forty-two, from colon cancer. There was, however, no mention of his Christian faith. On their website the BBC included quotations from the speech that he gave to graduates at Howard University, his alma mater, in 2018, but omitting the very strong Christian references that he made in his speech.[45] For example, he said:

---

43. Robin Aitken, *The Noble Liar* (Biteback Publishing, 2018).
44. John Humphrys, *A Day Like Today* (William Collins, 2019), p. 361.
45. https://www.bbc.co.uk/news/world-us-canada-53955912 (accessed 15.12.21).

> *Sometimes you need to feel the pain and sting of defeat to activate the real passion and purpose that God predestined inside of you . . . God says in Jeremiah, "I know the plans I have for you. Plans to prosper you and not to harm you" . . . When God has something for you it doesn't matter who stands against it. God will move someone who is holding you back away from the door and will put someone there who will open it for you.*[46]

We have seen how seriously (and rightly so) the BBC has taken the persecution of Uighur Muslims by the Chinese government, but they have not given very much coverage of the persecution of Christians in China and elsewhere. Expressing his concern for the Christians cruelly persecuted in predominantly Muslim countries such as Pakistan, John Pontifex, Head of Media for Action for the Church in Need, lamented the fact that such people are ignored by the BBC saying, '*If their voice is not heard by the media, by the BBC in particular, what hope have they of getting justice and a restitution of what is rightfully theirs?*'[47]

Far more influential, however, than the press or the broadcasters in influencing the public perception of the truth is the insidious power of social media. Netflix released a documentary in 2020 entitled *The Social Dilemma* in which a number of former designers from companies such as Facebook and Google laid bare the practices of these corporate giants that are able imperceptibly to change our behaviour. Tristan Harris, one of the main protagonists in the film, made a number of chilling statements, including:

> *Never before in history have fifty designers, twenty- to thirty-five-year-old white guys in California, made decisions that would have an impact on two billion people. Two billion people*

46. https://www.youtube.com/watch?v=RIHZypMyQ2s (accessed 15.12.21).
47. https://www.youtube.com/watch?v=ATw_JGl5opY (accessed 15.12.21).

> *will have thoughts they didn't intend to have because a designer at Google said, 'This is how notifications work on that screen that you wake up to in the morning.' . . .The system biases towards false information which makes companies more money, as truth is boring . . . Social media amplifies exponential gossip and exponential hearsay to the point that we don't know what's true, no matter what issue we care about . . . If we don't agree on what is true, or there is such a thing as truth, then we're toast.*[48]

The censorship power of the social media giants can be disproportionately felt by relatively small organisations with traditional, socially conservative agendas. In their newsletter of October 9th 2020, Voice for Justice UK, a Christian organisation promoting, amongst other things, the adoption of a biblical approach to sex, marriage, gender and abortion, reported that their Twitter account and those of three other socially conservative organisations had been suspended. In the newsletter it was suggested that this action was possibly the result of an attack by an LGBT biased organisation that had complained to Twitter. What is clear is that Twitter has the power to silence those who disagree with the prevailing orthodoxy, thus limiting free debate and a pursuit of truth.

48. *The Social Dilemma* (Netflix, 2020).

# Chapter 6: The Origin of Lies and Hatred

Looking at the world of the 2020s, we see the power of lies and hatred. It is even worse when we consider the many countries where there are human rights abuses. In a leader article, *The Economist* newspaper reported that eighty countries worldwide have regressed in their approach to issues of democracy and human rights during the pandemic.[49]

Christians in many countries have found it difficult during the crisis, but perhaps none more so than those living in the cruel regime of North Korea. The Korea Future Initiative produced a damning report on how Christians and members of other faith groups are brutally treated by the North Korean authorities by means of imprisonment, sadistic torture and starvation.[50]

We could of course catalogue many examples of worldwide human rights abuses. The question we need to ask from a Christian perspective, however, is whether biblical teaching can shed any light on the origins of the evil that dominates our world.

In John chapter 8 we read of Jesus discussing his claim that he had come from God with those Jews who were trying to kill him. They claimed that they were children of Abraham and so belonged to God, but Jesus refuted their claim, arguing that Abraham never tried to kill someone who had come from God. Instead he told them who their real father was:

49. 'Torment of the Uyghurs and the global crisis in human rights' (*The Economist*, October 15th 2020).
50. Hae Ju Kang, Suyeon Yoo and James Burt, 'Persecuting Faith: Documenting religious freedom violations in North Korea' (Korea Future Initiative, October 2020).

> *You belong to your father, the devil, and you want to carry out your father's desires. He was a murderer from the beginning, not holding to the truth, for there is no truth in him. When he lies, he speaks his native language, for he is a liar and the father of lies.*[51]

Jesus made it clear that the father of lies is Satan. Indeed this goes back to the story of the serpent who tempted Eve in the Garden of Eden. The first man and woman were given great freedom in the garden, but they were told that there was one tree from which they could not eat the fruit. Satan in the guise of the serpent distorted what God had said, saying to Eve, '*Did God really say, "You must not eat from any tree in the garden"?*'[52]

This was not what God had actually said, and so the serpent tried again by questioning God's word: '"*You will not certainly die," the snake said to the woman. "For God knows that when you eat from it your eyes will be opened, and you will be like God, knowing good and evil.*"'[53]

Through the father of lies, sin came into the world, as people wanted to be like God. Lies and hatred have continued ever since as humanity has tried to take the place of God and rebel against his standards. Satan is continuing to tempt us to live lives that are opposed to God. Perhaps what God has been teaching us through this crippling pandemic is that we cannot control our own destinies, despite how clever our politicians and scientists are; it is only God who is ultimately in control. It is God who is calling us back out of our rebellion to trust in him through faith in Jesus Christ.

And we need to do it before it is too late. As God proclaimed to the prophet Isaiah:

---

51. John 8:44
52. Genesis 3:1
53. Genesis 3:4-5

> *Woe to those who call evil good and good evil, who put darkness for light and light for darkness, who put bitter for sweet and sweet for bitter.*[54]

That is a picture of our rebellious society that has turned God's standards upside down. Such a world needs a saviour.

54. Isaiah 5:20

# Chapter 7: Truth and Love

In many ways this portrait of the world in 2020 has been very bleak, with an emphasis on what is not right about it. There is much, however, that is good and beautiful about our world. Although, in theological terms, the world has fallen and so is a broken place filled with broken people, it is still true that we have been created in God's image, following on from Adam and his sons.[55] This means that we have God's mark stamped on us with his characteristics, such as compassion, rationality and creativity as part of our (albeit sinful) human nature.

When the coronavirus came to Britain, there seemed a determination on the part of the population at large that we would work together to defeat it. In many areas there was a strong sense of community, reminiscent of the dark days of wartime. There was a genuine concern for neighbours as people did what they could to support the vulnerable, especially those who were shielding for medical reasons and those who were feeling isolated. Frontline workers in the NHS and care homes worked tirelessly to care for those who were taken ill as a result of the virus, often putting their own lives at risk, and some tragically losing their lives in service. Poverty, particularly child poverty, became an increasing concern as the economic consequences of the pandemic bit into families' finances. Food banks tried to meet people's needs, and there was much generous giving to support them.

Compassion was shown in countries throughout the world as people struggled to meet their basic needs amidst the disruption to normal life, caused by the spread of the virus. It has been the already struggling poor who have inevitably been hit most by the disease and ensuing lockdowns. Faith groups, charities and other non-governmental organisations have

55. Genesis 5:1-3

provided much-needed relief in some of the most difficult regions of the world.

One of the men in the frontline of the fight against the coronavirus is Dr Francis S. Collins, Director of the National Institutes of Health in the United States, who, in his own words, has spent '*almost every waking hour, seeking to accelerate the development of better diagnostic tests, therapeutics that will save the lives of those infected, and vaccines that will prevent future infections*'. In September 2020, he was presented with the 2020 Templeton Prize for Science and Religion. At his acceptance ceremony he gave a very inspiring speech, in which he mentioned how he became a Christian as a young doctor by listening to his patients and mentors who had a genuine faith and by realising that the evidence from science seemed to cry out for a creator.

> *God must be an amazing physicist and mathematician. But would he or she actually care about me? The major world religions seemed to say yes – but why should I trust that? And then I met the person who not only claimed to know those answers, and to know God, but to be God. That was Jesus Christ. I had thought he was a myth, but the historical evidence for his real existence was utterly compelling – including his life, death, and – yes, even this – his resurrection. And as the truth of the New Testament sank in, I realised I was called to make a decision. In my twenty-seventh year, I could simply not resist any longer. With some trepidation, I knelt in the dewy grass on an October morning somewhere in the Cascades, and I became a Christian.*

He had hoped, at the beginning of the pandemic in 2020, that the American community would come together to fight the virus. That seemed to happen initially, but now there seemed to be more division than ever. He called for three things to happen. Firstly, he sought a return to truth and reason that had got lost, as a result of social media. Secondly, he wanted people to address the spiritual void in their lives that had set them adrift and live according to the standards set forth by Jesus in the Sermon on the Mount. Thirdly, he called on people to love one another to overcome hatred.[56]

If we are going to overcome lies and hatred, we need to follow what Collins laid out in his speech. We need people who will contend for truth, and in particular people who realise that ultimately Jesus is the truth and desire to follow him. We also need to realise that because Satan is the father of lies, it is a spiritual battle that we are fighting. As Paul wrote: '*For our struggle is not against flesh and blood, but against the rulers, against the authorities, against the powers of this dark world and against the spiritual forces of evil in the heavenly realms.*'[57]

In the rest of the book, we shall see how Jesus, Paul and a range of people in the modern world have been involved in that battle to promote truth and love.

56. All quotes from speech given by Francis Collins, 'In Praise of Harmony' (September 25th 2020).
57. Ephesians 6:12

# Part Two

## Jesus is the Truth

# Chapter 8: Jesus Proclaims His Identity

Jerusalem was crowded for the annual Passover Festival as people gathered to celebrate their ancestors' release from slavery in Egypt. There was, however, further tension this year as Jesus of Nazareth, whom many had seen as the long-promised king, was on trial for his life. The Jewish authorities saw him as a threat to the religious status quo and as a blasphemer against God. They wanted the Roman governor, Pontius Pilate, to put him to death. Pilate could not work out what all the fuss was about as he engaged Jesus in conversation. He asked Jesus whether he was a king or not, to which Jesus replied, '*You say that I am a king. In fact, the reason I was born and came into the world is to testify to the truth. Everyone on the side of truth listens to me.*' Pilate replied by asking the rhetorical question, '*What is truth?*' not knowing what to make of this staggering answer.[58] Pilate went on to abdicate his responsibility for justice; he allowed the Jewish religious leaders and the mob they controlled to have their way, and sentenced Jesus to a cruel death.

What Jesus said to Pilate was absolutely amazing, but what John recorded in an earlier chapter of his gospel was even more stunning. At the beginning of chapter 14, Jesus consoled his disciples about his forthcoming death. He told them that there were many rooms in his Father's house and that he was going to prepare a place for them. Thomas, one of his disciples, asked what might be considered a very obvious question, '*Lord, we don't know where you are going, so how can we know the way?*' It was at this point that Jesus made his mind-blowing claim, '*I am the way and the truth and the life. No one comes to the Father except through me. If you really know me, you will know my Father as well. From now on, you do know him and have seen him.*'[59]

58. John 18:37-38
59. John 14:1-7

There are clear messages that come out from Jesus' statements in this passage.

1. We do not have to fear death, because there is life after death and Jesus has gone to prepare a heavenly place for us and will come back and personally take us there.
2. He is the way to God and our heavenly home. Indeed, he makes it clear that it is only through himself that we can arrive there. Following other religions or great leaders will not bring us the life with God in heaven that Jesus offers.
3. He is the embodiment of all truth, and so if we want to seek truth, ultimately we need to seek Jesus. Likewise, if we are contending for truth, we are contending for Jesus.
4. He is the source of life for all eternity. Without Jesus, we are spiritually dead.
5. His divinity comes through very strongly. As the Son, he is in a deep loving relationship with his heavenly Father. He claimed that if we want to see what God is like, we should look to Jesus. He made this even clearer when he said in verse 11 of that chapter, '*Believe me when I say that I am in the Father and the Father is in me*'.

John recorded in his gospel a number of similar 'I Am' claims that Jesus made. In chapter 6, for example, Jesus was able to feed a huge crowd of five thousand men, and probably many times more women and children, with only five loaves and two fish. Indeed, they even had twelve basketfuls of bread left over. After such a miracle, the crowd wanted to make him king so that they could have regular supplies of food to meet all their needs. Jesus had to explain to them that he was offering them something much more than bread to fill their stomachs: '*I am the bread of life. Whoever comes to me will never go hungry, and whoever believes in me will never be thirsty.'*[60] What he was offering was living bread that would fill their deepest needs forever. By 'eating on' him we would be satisfied throughout eternity for as he said, '*I am the living bread that came down from heaven. Whoever eats this bread will live forever. This bread is my flesh, which I will give for the life of the world.*'[61] In this, he was also pointing forward to his death when he would sacrifice his flesh to save the world.

In John chapter 10, Jesus made two claims about himself. The first was '*Very truly I tell you, I am the gate for the sheep.*'[62] He made the invitation to his sheep, namely ourselves, that if we enter through him we shall be saved and that we shall find life in all its fullness. He also claimed, '*I am the good shepherd; I know my sheep and my sheep know me – just as the Father knows me and I know the Father – and I lay down my life for the sheep.*'[63] In these verses we see Jesus as being that loving, caring shepherd who personally knows, leads and protects his people, even to the point of death.

We then read in chapter 11 of John's gospel that Jesus was told that his good friend Lazarus lay seriously ill. By the time Jesus arrived, Lazarus had been in his tomb for four days. Martha, one of Lazarus' sisters, came out to greet Jesus, but with a rebuke implying that if Jesus had come earlier Lazarus would still be alive. Jesus reassured her that Lazarus would, in fact, rise again. Martha did not fully understand this, believing that Lazarus would rise at the last day, not in the immediate future. Jesus then made a claim that Christians, in the face of death, have found so reassuring, '*I am the resurrection and the life. The one who believes in me will live, even though they die; and whoever lives by believing in me will never die.*'[64]

60. John 6:35
61. John 6:51
62. John 10:7
63. John 10:14-15
64. John 11:25-26

What a claim and what a promise! Jesus has power over death, and that whoever puts their trust in him will be raised to new life. Death is not the end! Jesus knows what we are going through when we face death, either our own or the death of our loved ones, and he grieves with us. When Mary, the other sister of Lazarus, came to greet Jesus, he saw that she was weeping and he too wept. The story of Lazarus did not end in sadness, however, because when Jesus shouted to him from outside the tomb, '*Lazarus, come out!*'[65] that is exactly what took place. The amazing happened: Lazarus came out from the tomb alive and Jesus demonstrated that he was indeed the resurrection and the life.

John recorded a claim of Jesus that had a strong Old Testament reference. In John chapter 15, Jesus said, '*I am the true vine, and my Father is the gardener.*'[66] Again Jesus was giving an absolutely clear declaration that he was divine and that God was his Father. In the Old Testament, Israel was seen to be the vine expected to produce good grapes, but alas it was a disappointment.[67] That is why Jesus called himself the true vine, because he produces good fruit, in contrast to the people of Israel. He wants his people, the Church, to be part of the vine and to be bound up with him and each other. Thus he declared, '*I am the vine; you are the branches. If you remain in me and I in you, you will bear much fruit; apart from me you can do nothing.*'[68] Remaining close to Jesus we can bear much fruit. If, however, we try to live our lives in our own strength without him, we can achieve nothing. This is so important for us as we strive to contend for truth.

Earlier in this book, we looked at an incident where Jews were trying to kill Jesus because they felt that the claims that he was making about himself were blasphemous. This story is recorded in John chapter 8. The dispute began as a result of Jesus' claim when he said, '*I am the light of*

65. John 11:43
66. John 15:1
67. See, for example, Isaiah 5:1-2
68. John 15:5

*the world. Whoever follows me will never walk in darkness, but will have the light of life.*'[69] In the Genesis creation account God said, '"*Let there be light," and there was light.*'[70] Here, Jesus now proclaimed that he was the light, that people should follow him to escape the darkness of their lives and come to the source of all life and truth. It was no wonder that his opponents wanted to kill him.

At the end of that same chapter, Jesus further angered his opponents by saying that Abraham had looked forward to his coming. The infuriated Jews declared, '*You are not yet fifty years old . . . and you have seen Abraham!*' to which Jesus replied, '*Very truly I tell you . . . before Abraham was born, I am!*' At this, the Jews could take no more and picked up stones to kill him. Jesus, however, slipped away.[71]

Why were they so angry at Jesus' statement, a statement that to us does not make much grammatical sense? They realised that by declaring, 'I am', Jesus was claiming that he had always existed and that he had not been brought into existence through birth as Abraham had been. He was claiming a divine, heavenly existence. It would also remind his Jewish opponents of the incident when God told a very reluctant Moses that he had to go to Pharaoh to tell him to release the Israelites from slavery. When Moses asked God who he should tell his Israelite compatriots was sending him, he was told, '*I AM WHO I AM. This is what you are to say to the Israelites: "I AM has sent me to you."*'[72]

It was not only John who proclaimed the deity of Christ; the other gospel writers also did this. An example of this is the story of how Jesus forgave and healed a paralysed man, which Matthew, Mark and Luke all recount.[73] The room that Jesus was teaching in was so crowded that the only way that his friends could bring the paralysed man to Jesus was

69. John 8:12
70. Genesis 1:3
71. John 8:57-59
72. Exodus 3:14
73. Matthew 9:2-8, Mark 2:1-12, Luke 5:18-26

through the roof. Jesus then shocked those in the room, particularly the teachers of the law, by telling the man that his sins were now forgiven. The teachers believed that Jesus was committing blasphemy; only God could forgive sins. Jesus, however, had got to the fundamental root of the man's problem that he, like all of us, needed to have his sins forgiven. To show everyone that he had authority from God, he said to the man, '*I want you to know that the Son of Man has authority on earth to forgive sins . . . I tell you, get up, take your mat and go home.*'[74] To everyone's utter amazement, the man got up and walked out of the house. Jesus had dealt with both the man's spiritual and physical needs, and showed that he himself was divine.

The title that he used in the above story is 'the Son of Man', and this is a title that he used to refer to himself in each of the gospels. It might be thought that this title referred to his humanity in the same way the title 'the Son of God' referred to his divinity. Jesus was certainly fully human. The title 'Son of Man', however, meant much more than referring to the fact that he was fully human. Those Jews who knew their Scriptures, and who were listening to him, would clearly understand that the Son of Man was a divine figure referred to in a vision given to Daniel.

> *In my vision at night I looked, and there before me was one like a son of man, coming with the clouds of heaven. He approached the Ancient of Days and was led into his presence. He was given authority, glory and sovereign power; all nations and peoples of every language worshipped him. His dominion is an everlasting dominion that will not pass away, and his kingdom is one that will never be destroyed.*[75]

---

74. Luke 5:24
75. Daniel 7:13-14

The Son of Man had divine authority, would be worshipped by all nations and would control an eternal dominion. Jesus was making staggering claims about himself. Some critics will argue that he was a lunatic, a man absolutely deluded in his view of himself when he made these claims. Yet madmen do not proclaim the sort of wise, deep sayings that Jesus taught, show the sort of love that Jesus showed, or perform the miracles that Jesus did, including rising from the dead. Nor was he simply a very good man who showed people how to live their lives. Good men do not claim to be God incarnate.

We are left with the conclusion that Jesus was exactly who he said he was, God's beloved Son.

# Chapter 9: Jesus Proclaims the Kingdom of God

Very early on in Mark's gospel, Jesus made one of his staggering pronouncements, '*The time has come . . . The kingdom of God has come near. Repent and believe the good news!*'[76] What did this mean for his listeners? The Jews were waiting for their Messiah, the Anointed One, their long-promised king to come and rescue them and set them free. Jesus seemed to be telling them that their wait was now over. The time had come close and their long-awaited king was here. How were they to respond? They had to turn from their sins and believe the gospel that he was bringing. The kingdom was not yet fully established, but it was near because the king had come.

The Jewish people looked back to the great King David and his son Solomon, and expected a king who would drive their enemies out, give them freedom and make their nation great again. This promised king would be of the line of David. Through the prophet Nathan, God had made this promise to David, '*Your house and your kingdom shall endure for ever before me; your throne shall be established for ever.*'[77] Jesus was the promised king coming from the line of David.[78]

Jesus, however, was not to be the sort of king that the Jewish people expected. As we have seen, after Jesus fed the crowds with five loaves and two fish, they wanted to crown him as king, but he had to tell them that he would feed them *spiritually* so that they would be *eternally* satisfied. As he later told Pilate, '*My kingdom is not of this world. If it were, my servants would fight to prevent my arrest by the Jewish leaders. But now my kingdom is from another place.*'[79]

76. Mark 1:15
77. 2 Samuel 7:16
78. Matthew 1:1-17
79. John 18:36

Jesus showed how different his kingdom would be. It would not be established through military might, for he said, '*Love your enemies and pray for those who persecute you.*'[80] Rather, it would be established by people responding to his word and allowing his heavenly Father to bring growth. In the parable of the sower, those who are seduced by Satan, or who are put off by trouble and persecution, or enticed by wealth and concerned with the worries of this world, will not enter the kingdom. Those who would be accepted would be '*like seed sown on good soil, hear the word, accept it, and produce a crop – some thirty, some sixty, some a hundred times what was sown*'.[81]

Furthermore, those who belong to the kingdom are not necessarily those who might be expected to be there. Matthew recorded an incident when Jesus was being questioned by the chief priests and elders about where his authority came from. Jesus refused to answer. He then told them a parable about a man who asked his sons to go and work in his vineyard. The first son said that he would not go, but then changed his mind and decided to go as he was asked. The second son said that he would go but, in fact, did not bother going. When asked which of the two did what his father wanted, his listeners said that it was the first son. Jesus then made a statement that would startle and indeed horrify them.

> *Truly I tell you, the tax collectors and the prostitutes are entering the kingdom of God ahead of you. For John came to you to show you the way of righteousness, and you did not believe him, but the tax collectors and the prostitutes did. And even after you saw this, you did not repent and believe him.*[82]

80. Matthew 5:44
81. Mark 4:20
82. Matthew 21:31-32

The least respected members of society had repented, in other words changed their minds like the first son, in response to the teaching of John the Baptist. On the other hand, the religious leaders refused to do that. It was evident that Jesus had a deep, loving compassion for the marginalised in society.

It was inevitable that Jesus would meet opposition as he proclaimed the kingdom and contended for truth. His kingdom was so different from what people expected. The ways in which he dealt with opposition are interesting. He sometimes refused to give a direct answer, especially if he believed that his listeners would simply pour scorn on it. Often, being the brilliant teacher that he was, he would ask them another question in order to make his opponents think for themselves, as in the case above.

On other occasions, he was very direct in dealing with his opponents. In Matthew chapter 23, he proclaimed woe seven times against the Pharisees and the teachers of the law for their blatant hypocrisy. For example, he cried,

> *Woe to you, teachers of the law and Pharisees, you hypocrites! You are like whitewashed tombs, which look beautiful on the outside but on the inside are full of the bones of the dead and everything unclean. In the same way, on the outside you appear to people as righteous but on the inside you are full of hypocrisy and wickedness.*[83]

It would be hard to be more direct in condemnation. To Jesus, what was important was what we were like in our hearts as people, and not the outward shows that we might put on to impress others.

It was this opposition that led to Jesus being taken, unjustly tried, tortured and left to die a gruelling death hanging on a Roman cross. He

83. Matthew 23:27-28

hung under a sign that Pilate insisted was placed on the cross. It read '*Jesus of Nazareth, the king of the Jews*'. People, seeing this poor figure hanging there, would scoff at the idea that this man could possibly be the king of the Jews, the one who said that he would destroy the temple and build it again three days later. If he was who he said he was, why did he not come down from the cross and save himself?[84]

Yet, it was through this cruel death that God was carrying out his plan to usher in his new kingdom, with Jesus not as a dying king, but as a risen king who had rescued his people from the deadliest enemy of all – sin.

84. Mark 15:29-32

# Chapter 10: Jesus Proclaims His Mission Call – the Answer for Our Broken World

Jesus proclaimed that he had come not only to preach, teach and heal, but even more importantly, to die upon the cross in obedience to his heavenly Father. He proclaimed the kingdom of God, but this kingdom would not have come to fruition had he not borne the sins of the world on his shoulders on the cross.

A revealing exchange took place between Jesus and Peter, one of his closest disciples, at what turned out to be the midpoint of Mark's gospel record. Jesus asked his disciples who people thought that he was. He received various responses including John the Baptist, Elijah and one of the prophets. Jesus then made it personal and asked the disciples who *they* thought that he was. Peter, always willing to give an answer, cried out, '*You are the Messiah*.'[85] This sounded like a brilliant answer and you would imagine that Jesus would be so pleased that Peter understood who he really was. In the following verse, however, Mark recorded something very strange: '*Jesus warned them not to tell anyone about him*.'[86]

Why would Jesus not want the disciples to tell people who he was? You would think that this would help in the proclamation of the kingdom. Perhaps he was concerned that the crowds following him would be too immense for him to handle. A more likely explanation, however, was that although the disciples might now be coming to a clearer understanding of who Jesus actually was, they had not really understood the full implications of his mission call.

This is evident in Mark's following verses: '*He then began to teach them that the Son of Man must suffer many things and be rejected by the*

85. Mark 8:29
86. Mark 8:30

*elders, the chief priests and the teachers of the law, and that he must be killed and after three days rise again.'*[87] Jesus taught them very clearly on this occasion, and on a number of other occasions, that he was going to suffer, be put to death and rise again. Peter's almost unthinking response to this was that there was no way that he would let anything happen to his Master, and he even went as far as to rebuke Jesus. So serious was Peter's misunderstanding that Jesus had in turn to rebuke him very strongly saying, '*Get behind me, Satan! . . . You do not have in mind the concerns of God, but merely human concerns.*'[88]

Peter was not ready to tell people about Jesus because he did not really understand that the kingdom of God could only really be established by the death of Jesus on the cross. That was God's plan, something that could not be envisaged in the minds of humans. He had some understanding, but he did not yet have the full picture.

The cross was very much on Jesus' mind. Just after Jesus rebuked Peter, he said to his disciples and the crowd who were hanging on, '*Whoever wants to be my disciple must deny themselves and take up their cross and follow me. For whoever wants to save their life will lose it, but whoever loses their life for me and for the gospel will save it.*'[89]

These are very demanding words. His listeners were very aware of the cruelty of crucifixion as they would often see prisoners being forced to carry their crosses on their way to this barbaric death. Jesus was now expecting his disciples to carry their own crosses in order to follow him. After all, that was what he was going to do. When he went to his death on the cross, he was denying his own comforts and wants, and instead he was following the will of his heavenly Father in service to others. His disciples, who may or may not literally take up a cross, were expected to do likewise. They were to put the will of God and the service of others

87. Mark 8:31
88. Mark 8:33
89. Mark 8:34-35

before their own desires. Otherwise, they would lose their souls, despite how successful they might appear to be in the eyes of the world.

Jesus knew what he had been called to do. He knew that he was to serve by giving up his life for the sake of others. As he said to his disciples, '*For even the Son of Man did not come to be served, but to serve, and to give his life as a ransom for many.*'[90] In other words, kingdom life did not mean lording it over others, but rather living a life of service. Jesus himself was the prime example of this; he had not come to be served, as was his due, given his position, but rather to serve.

Furthermore, his service was absolutely unique, as he was going to give his life as a ransom for many. The purpose of his death was to buy freedom for his people, by paying a ransom for them. Jesus, the altogether innocent Son of God, was going to take our place on the cross and pay the punishment for our sin. The physical pain would be horrific, literally excruciating (a word derived from the pain of crucifixion), but so would be the spiritual side of his suffering when he was completely separated from his heavenly Father with whom he had had perfect communion. The whole wrath of God was poured out on him as he hung there in our place, and through this act the amazing love of God was poured out on humanity. This was the fulfilment of God's rescue plan for the human race as foretold by the prophets hundreds of years before. As Isaiah said:

> *Surely he took up our pain and bore our suffering, yet we considered him punished by God, stricken by him, and afflicted. But he was pierced for our transgressions, he was crushed for our iniquities; the punishment that brought us peace was on him, and by his wounds we are healed. We all, like sheep, have gone astray, each of us has turned to our own way; and the LORD has laid on him the iniquity of us all.*[91]

90. Mark 10:45
91. Isaiah 53:4-6

Jesus then, of his own accord, followed his Father's will, and so was tried, tortured and hung on the cross between two criminals. Even in that situation he showed wonderful compassion, praying for his torturers who were gambling for his clothes: '*Father, forgive them, for they do not know what they are doing*.'[92] As he hung there he knew that, for the purpose of his perfect sacrifice for humanity, he was separated from God, and cried out, '*My God, my God, why have you forsaken me?*'[93] Then having paid our debt for us, he declared, '*It is finished!*'[94]

The debt was paid, but that of course was not the end of the story, as Jesus had told his disciples that he would rise again after three days. And it happened! Jesus' body, which had been destroyed, was raised to life three days later. God raised Jesus from the dead, thus declaring his victory over sin, Satan and death. He appeared on a number of occasions to his followers, explaining to them that his death and resurrection were all part of God's plan. In his gospel, Luke recorded part of Jesus' teaching, saying, '*This is what I told you while I was still with you: everything must be fulfilled that is written about me in the Law of Moses, the Prophets and the Psalms*.'[95] He then went on to tell them that, because they were witnesses to what had happened, they had to be at the forefront of spreading the word to all nations. They were not going to be on their own, however: far from it, he would send his Spirit to empower them.

What relevance then does the life of Jesus have today in our world that is so fearful amidst the coronavirus pandemic, and so dominated by evil and lies? If what we have discovered about Jesus is absolute truth, then he himself is the answer.

At the beginning of the pandemic, Professor John Lennox wrote a very helpful little book, *Where is God in a Coronavirus World?* As part

92. Luke 23:34
93. Matthew 27:46
94. John 19:30
95. Luke 24:44

of his answer to the question in his title, he talks about '*two crowns*'.[96] The word 'coronavirus' is derived from the Latin word for crown, '*corona*', because this tiny virus looks like a crown. It has caused fear and chaos spreading its dominion throughout the world. Lennox points out, however, that, in the gospel records, there was another crown, a crown of thorns placed on Jesus' head at his crucifixion. It is the one who wore that crown that can bring hope to this coronavirus world. The first crown shows how broken our world is, but the second one shows how we can be reconciled to our Creator. The first crown has brought so much suffering to the world in the 2020s, whereas the second crown, the crown of thorns, demonstrates the love of God who entered into the world to bear that suffering for us. Lennox is suggesting that God is using the coronavirus as a loud megaphone, calling the world back to him that we might belong to his kingdom.

As we have seen, Jesus constantly proclaimed his kingdom, calling us to repent and believe. We need to have a desire to give our lives over to the king. Jesus made clear the attitude we should have if we want to enter the kingdom, when he said, '*Truly I tell you, anyone who will not receive the kingdom of God like a little child will never enter it*'.[97] A little child is absolutely dependent on his parents or guardians for everything in life. Likewise, we have to realise that, because of our sin, we are not in control of our lives, a lesson that the coronavirus has clearly taught us. Rather we need to submit to the one who can provide salvation and direction for our lives – the one who is the Truth.

---

96. John C. Lennox, *Where is God in a Coronavirus World?* (The Good Book Company, 2020), pp. 48-49.
97. Mark 10:15

# Part Three

## A New Testament Role Model Contending for Truth: The Apostle Paul

# Chapter 11: Changed by the Grace of God

Imagine visiting the great city of Ephesus in Asia Minor in the middle of the first century, say about AD 54. Whatever the reason for your visit, you have heard of strange happenings associated with a Jew called Paul and your interest is aroused. Each day this unassuming man who, from his demeanour, looked as if he had been through physical hardships, even beatings, spoke to and debated with a large crowd in the lecture hall of Tyrannus. He was no great orator in the Greek tradition, but he held the attention of his audience as he spoke to them about the one true God and the Messiah that he had sent as Saviour and Lord.

He explained that the man Jesus was the long-promised Messiah and that he had come to establish his kingdom, not through military might but by dying upon a cross – and not only by dying, but by rising again from the dead. Paul contended that Jesus did this to show God's love for us and to bring us into his kingdom, not by our good works, but by God's grace which we can receive by faith. His speaking seemed to have the desired effect, as his contemporary biographer, Luke, recorded, '*This went on for two years, so that all the Jews and Greeks who lived in the province of Asia heard the word of the Lord*.'[98] As people heard and responded to the message of this man, and then as they moved on in their travels, they would spread the word of the Lord.

This Jewish man, Paul, claimed to be a missionary to the Gentiles (non-Jews) proclaiming the truth of the Lord Jesus Christ. Yet if we were setting up an appointments panel to choose who would be the best person to take the message of Jesus to the Gentiles, Paul would probably come close to the bottom of the list. Why? Because when the Christian message of Jesus rising from the dead began to spread, Saul of Tarsus,

98. Acts 19:10

as he was then known, was violently opposed to it. When Stephen, one of the first followers of Jesus, was stoned to death, Luke recorded, '*And Saul approved of their killing him.*'[99] From that point on, the Jerusalem church began to suffer terrible persecution with Saul at the centre of it, with his aim of violently destroying the heretical message of these believers. These believers had every reason to be afraid of this man.

So how does the image of Saul, the cruel persecutor of the church, fit in with the man who preached the Christian message to such great effect in Ephesus? Something must have happened to transform his life so completely. The answer is that Jesus appeared to him in a striking way as he was travelling to Damascus in pursuit of believers there. A light from heaven flashed around him, even brighter than the sun as he was to proclaim later in a trial before the authorities.[100] Jesus asked him a very piercing question, '*Saul, Saul, why do you persecute me?*'[101] In other words, he was not only persecuting the followers of Jesus, but he was persecuting the Lord himself. There was no escape; Saul must have realised that he was doing something terribly wrong against Almighty God himself. He was at that point blind and could do nothing for himself, and so he was taken to Damascus where a believer called Ananias (no doubt very nervously) met with him and placed his hands on him so that he could once more see. Now, however, he would see things very differently. He was baptised, thus identifying with his new Lord and all of his followers. Shortly afterwards, he went to the desert in Arabia where the Lord himself would teach him. No doubt, he would develop an understanding as to how all his deeply held beliefs, going back to the roots of his Jewish religion, were fulfilled in the Lord Jesus, the Messiah sent by God to all nations. He would learn that he, Saul of

99. Acts 8:1

100. Acts 26:13-14. In this account, Paul tells Agrippa that his companions *all* fell to the ground as a result of the blinding light, thus ruling out the theory that Paul had had some seizure.

101. Acts 9:4

Tarsus, the zealous Pharisee, later called Paul, would be used by God in taking this message to both Jews and Gentiles.

Paul understood how little he deserved to be forgiven by God for the wrongs that he had committed against his Lord. This acceptance by God for who he was, despite his sinfulness, would be a great motivating force, as he contended for truth, serving his new master. He would later write to his follower Timothy these words:

> *I thank Christ Jesus our Lord, who has given me strength, that he considered me trustworthy, appointing me to his service. Even though I was once a blasphemer and a persecutor and a violent man, I was shown mercy because I acted in ignorance and unbelief. The grace of our Lord was poured out on me abundantly, along with the faith and love that are in Christ Jesus. Here is a trustworthy saying that deserves full acceptance: Christ Jesus came into the world to save sinners – of whom I am the worst.*[102]

Paul experienced the abundant grace of God – mercy that he knew he did not deserve, as he was the worst of sinners. And if that had happened to him, he contended that all sinners could be saved by Christ Jesus.

Paul's life was markedly changed from being a top-notch Pharisee, whose pedigree, zeal and legal righteousness could not be surpassed, to becoming a contender for Christ, the one he had persecuted. This transformation affected his attitudes and his behaviour. In the words of David Wenham, he had to 'unlearn' a number of things, including his belief that Jesus was a false prophet who deserved execution, his zealousness for the Jewish law, his aversion to sinners and Gentiles, his confidence in his own righteousness and his proclivity to use violence to gain his ends. Instead he had discovered that Jesus had miraculously risen from the dead and that he was divine, that he, Paul, was called to

102. 1 Timothy 1:12-15

take the love of God to those Gentile sinners he had despised and that he had to follow his master Jesus in a self-sacrificial way.[103]

This does not mean to say that he had become perfect. Far from it, as he knew his faults and weaknesses. Indeed, he stated in the seventh chapter of his letter to the Romans:

> *I do not understand what I do. For what I want to do I do not do, but what I hate I do. And if I do what I do not want to do, I agree that the law is good. As it is, it is no longer I myself who do it, but it is sin living in me.*[104]

Paul realised that there was a battle going on in his life, and although he knew that his sins were forgiven as a result of the sacrifice that Jesus made on the cross for him, sin still stuck to him making him do the things that he knew were wrong. If Paul faced this battle, we know that we too as Christians constantly face the same sort of battle.

Yet there is hope for us, because we can say as Paul said at the end of that chapter, '*What a wretched man I am! Who will rescue me from this body that is subject to death? Thanks be to God, who delivers me through Jesus Christ our Lord!*'[105] We have victory and deliverance through Jesus!

Paul was zealous for his Lord, but life was not easy for him as he contended for truth. Indeed he was warned about this at his conversion. Ananias who, as we saw earlier, laid hands on him was told by God, '*I will show him how much he must suffer for my name.*'[106] Paul certainly did suffer. In writing to the Corinthian church, he listed a catalogue of hardships that he had been through for the sake of his Lord. These included spending time in prison, receiving the thirty-nine lashes, being stoned, being shipwrecked, experiencing danger wherever he

---

103. David Wenham, *Did St Paul Get Jesus Right?* (Lion Hudson, 2010), pp. 37-38.
104. Romans 7:15-17
105. Romans 7:24-25
106. Acts 9:16

went, knowing deep hunger and thirst, and being cold and naked.[107] In all this, he did, however, know the strength and reassurance of the Lord. A few verses further on he was able to write that the Lord said to him, '"*My grace is sufficient for you, for my power is made perfect in weakness." . . . That is why, for Christ's sake, I delight in weaknesses, in insults, in hardships, in persecutions, in difficulties. For when I am weak, then I am strong.*'[108]

Let us now look at how this man, totally transformed by the grace of God, contended for his Master.

107. 2 Corinthians 11:23-29
108. 2 Corinthians 12:9-10

# Chapter 12: Paul Contends for Christ

As Paul visited towns and cities in his journeys around the Mediterranean, there was a common pattern to his activities. He would get himself established in his occupation of tent making and start preaching in the local Jewish synagogue. As a Jew, he was encouraged by his fellow-Jews to do this.

Luke recorded that in the synagogue in Psidian Antioch, Paul was asked by the synagogue rulers to bring a message to the people. They probably wished that they had not asked! Paul began his message by rooting it in what God had done in the past for the people of Israel. He continued by explaining that God had sent Jesus, a descendant of King David, as their Saviour King. In line with the words of the prophets, the Jewish rulers did not recognise Jesus, but rather asked Pilate to have him executed. Although he had been put in a tomb, God raised him from the dead and he appeared to his followers. Paul urged his listeners to consider what Jesus had done: '*Therefore, my friends, I want you to know that through Jesus the forgiveness of sins is proclaimed to you. Through him everyone who believes is set free from every sin, a justification you were not able to obtain under the law of Moses.*'[109] In other words, Jesus could set them free from sin, something that trying to adhere to the law of Moses could never do. He also warned them to pay heed, lest they perish.

Paul and his companion Barnabas were invited to speak again the following week, but some of the Jews took exception at what they were saying and the interest shown in their message, and had them driven out of the city. Paul and Barnabas were not deterred, but went on to the next city, '*filled with joy and with the Holy Spirit*'.[110]

---

109. Acts 13:38-39
110. Acts 13:52

Paul had this experience again and again: preaching Jesus as the Messiah in the synagogue and then meeting opposition from the Jews. Many of the Jews could not see that the man hanging on the cross was God himself and that his coming, death and resurrection were foretold in their own Scriptures. After being rejected by his own people, Paul would move on to the Gentiles to preach to them. That is why we found him in the lecture hall of Tyrannus in Ephesus. The message, however, was always the same: Jesus is the Messiah who has come to rescue us; he is the risen Lord and only by God's grace and through faith in Jesus can we be accepted by God.

In his letters, Paul constantly proclaimed the deity of Jesus, as God's Messiah (the Christ) sent to rescue us and as his Lord. For example, in his greetings to the churches in each of his letters, he grouped God the Father and the Lord Jesus Christ together as members of the godhead. Writing to the Ephesians, he greeted them by proclaiming, '*Grace and peace to you from God our Father and our Lord Jesus Christ*', and then going on to give praise saying, '*Praise be to the God and Father of our Lord Jesus Christ, who has blessed us in the heavenly realms with every spiritual blessing in Christ.*'[111] One can sense his amazed excitement as he writes that we who are Christians are 'in Christ' and that we have received from heaven every spiritual blessing. God the Father and our Lord Jesus Christ are bound together and have bestowed on us blessing after blessing, including peace with God from the bountiful riches of his grace.

To those who had any doubt about the deity of Jesus, Paul spelled it out very clearly in his letter to the Colossians:

1. Jesus is the image of the invisible God: if we want to know what God is like we can see him in the person of Jesus.

111. Ephesians 1:2-3

2. Jesus was involved in creation, along with God the Father, and furthermore, all things were created for him.
3. He is sovereign over all things, holding the whole of creation together.
4. He is the first born of the dead, having been raised to life by the Father, with the promise that his church, of which he is the head, will be raised to new life.
5. There is no doubting his divinity as all the fulness of God dwells in him.
6. He has brought sinners into reconciliation with God by shedding his blood on the cross.[112]

For Paul, the Christian faith either triumphed or fell on the truth or otherwise of the most significant event in history: the resurrection of Jesus. Writing in his first letter to the Corinthians, he declared that if this central truth were to be found after all not to be true, and that there was no promise of a resurrected life for believers, then '*we are of all people most pitied*'.[113] In other words, their faith would be absolutely worthless. Paul, however, continued with the word 'but'; every time we see the word 'but' in Paul's letters we need to sit up and take notice, because he is going to say something astonishing. In this case he said, '*But Christ has indeed been raised from the dead, the firstfruits of those who have fallen asleep*.'[114] For him, it was absolutely true that God had brought Jesus back to life from the grave, as firstfruits, a precursor to the resurrection of all believers from death. Those in Christ can share his resurrection experience! This includes receiving a new resurrection body that will not decay, a body that is '*raised imperishable*', '*raised in glory* and '*raised in power*'.[115]

112. Colossians 1:15-20
113. 1 Corinthians 15:19
114. 1 Corinthians 15:20
115. 1 Corinthians 15:42-43

But how was Paul so sure that Jesus had risen from the dead? The answer is that he looked at the evidence, and he described that evidence earlier in 1 Corinthians 15. '*Christ died for our sins according to the Scriptures*.'[116] Jesus did not just swoon on the cross; he certainly died, and the Romans of all people knew when somebody was dead or not. Then he appeared to a number of his followers, including Peter and the other disciples. In fact, '*he appeared to more than five hundred of the brothers and sisters at the same time, most of whom are still living, though some have fallen asleep*'.[117] What he was saying to his readers in that statement was, 'If you do not believe me, there are enough eyewitnesses still alive that you can interrogate.' Finally, he claimed that the risen Lord Jesus had also appeared to him, referring presumably to his Damascus road experience.[118]

But there was still more than that! Paul wanted believers to know that Jesus was coming back again, this time not as a baby in a manger, but as a triumphant king who was going to establish his eternal kingdom once and for all. To the Thessalonians he wrote:

> *For the Lord himself will come down from heaven, with a loud command, with the voice of the archangel and with the trumpet call of God, and the dead in Christ will rise first. After that, we who are still alive and are left will be caught up together with them in the clouds to meet the Lord in the air. And so we will be with the Lord forever.*[119]

Paul said that to encourage the believers, but also as a warning that we should be ready for the Second Coming of Christ.

---

116. 1 Corinthians 15:3
117. 1 Corinthians 15:6
118. 1 Corinthians 15:8
119. 1 Thessalonians 4:16-17

# Chapter 13: Paul Contends for Eternity and Christ-like Living

Paul was always finding himself in difficulty. One prominent example was in the city of Philippi, when a crowd was stirred up against Paul and his companion Silas, because he had expelled an evil fortune-telling spirit from a slave girl, thus losing her owners considerable potential income. False charges were made to the city magistrates against Paul and Silas: '*These men are Jews, and are throwing our city into an uproar by advocating customs unlawful for us Romans to accept or practise.*'[120] Paul and Silas were certainly not doing that, but nonetheless, they were beaten and securely chained in prison. If that had happened to any of us, we would be very angry and wanting to call our lawyer. Yet these two staunch believers were spending their time in prison praying and singing hymns to God.

A stupendous miracle then happened: a violent earthquake blasted open the prison doors and shook the prisoners' chains off them. The prisoners had been set free! The jailer was beside himself when this happened, and was about to kill himself by the sword to prevent the Roman authorities from doing that, the standard punishment for losing prisoners. Paul reassured him that there was no need to do that as the prisoners were all still there. The jailer then came in trembling and fear before Paul and Silas, and asked a question that was to affect the whole of eternity for him, '*Sirs, what must I do to be saved?*', to which they replied, '*Believe in the Lord Jesus Christ, and you will be saved – you and your household.*'[121] Paul and Silas declared to the jailer that it is through having a personal faith in Christ that you can receive eternal life. They

120. Acts 16:20-21
121. Acts 16:30-31

spent much time that night explaining the gospel to the jailer and his family, and then baptised them.

The following morning, Paul and Silas spoke to the magistrates who were brought to the prison, berating them for illegally beating and imprisoning them. They were Roman citizens and so should not have been punished without a fair trial. The magistrates were alarmed in case *they* were punished for the miscarriage of justice. Why, however, did Paul and Silas not bring up the issue of their citizenship earlier rather than going through a flogging and false imprisonment? Paul must have felt that God had a greater purpose that would have been fulfilled by his imprisonment. God used Paul's imprisonment and the earthquake to bring the jailer and his family to belief in the Lord Jesus Christ and salvation. These words spoken to the jailer have had an amazing effect on the lives of many people seeking salvation down through the centuries.

In his letters, Paul repeatedly emphasised the need to have faith to receive the salvation that God has offered us by his grace. We need to be saved or rescued from '*the present evil age*'[122] controlled by Satan and to which we are kept in bondage by our sinful nature. In his letter to the Ephesians, Paul described the human situation as being '*dead in your transgressions and sins*'.[123] Then we see again Paul's use of the word 'but', which is intended to make us sit up and take notice. '*But because of his great love for us, God, who is rich in mercy, made us alive with Christ even when we were dead in transgressions – it is by grace you have been saved*'.[124] Even though we were spiritually dead without any relationship with God at all, God made us alive with Christ – we share in his resurrection. And it shows his great love for us, that God did this by grace, demonstrating mercy that we did not deserve. And how do we accept this mercy? It is in the same way as Paul explained to the Philippian jailer, '*For it is by grace*

122. Galatians 1:4
123. Ephesians 2:1
124. Ephesians 2:4-5

*you have been saved, through faith – and this is not from yourselves, it is the gift of God – not by works, so that no one can boast.*'[125] In other words, it is by believing on the Lord Jesus Christ. Notice that Paul emphasised that it is certainly not by doing works – we cannot earn our salvation by trying to live a good life, as our sin is too terrible.

This applies to all of us, no matter how good we think we are, because as Paul made clear in Romans 3:23, '*for all have sinned and fall short of the glory of God*'. As a result of our sinful natures, we cannot make ourselves righteous or acceptable before God. God, however, does promise righteousness to those who have faith in him. Continuing his argument in Romans chapter 3, Paul declared, '*This righteousness is given through faith in Jesus Christ to all who believe.*'[126] Because God, however, is a just, holy God who abhors sin, a sacrifice had to be made for our sin. Paul explained it thus: '*All are justified freely by his grace through the redemption that came by Christ Jesus. God presented Christ as a sacrifice of atonement, through the shedding of his blood – to be received by faith.*'[127] We were reconciled to God through Christ's sacrifice on the cross.

One can argue of course that if we receive salvation solely by the grace of God through faith, with good works having no place, then we can live our lives in any way that we want, not worrying about sin. After all, sin has been taken care of! He answered that charge with strong irony at the beginning of Romans chapter 6: '*What shall we say, then? Shall we go on sinning so that grace may increase? By no means! We are those who have died to sin; how can we live in it any longer?*'[128]

The charge was made that if we increased our sinfulness, then we could receive even more grace from God. There is perhaps some logic in that argument, but it does not fit in with the idea of a transformed life living for Jesus. Paul would have nothing to do with that contention, as

125. Ephesians 2:8-9
126. Romans 3:22
127. Romans 3:24-25
128. Romans 6:1-2

he saw that in Christ we are dead to sin, and so we should not desire to live in sin any longer. If we have shared with Christ in his crucifixion, how dare we desire to go on sinning?

So, what about good works – what is their place? As we saw in his letter to the Ephesians, Paul made it clear that our salvation was certainly not by works, and so we have no cause to boast. In the second chapter of that letter, after Paul expounded what God has done for us by his grace, he wrote a short sentence to explain what we have been saved for. '*For we are God's handiwork, created in Christ Jesus to do good works, which God prepared in advance for us to do.*'[129] We are certainly not saved by doing good works, but rather we are saved *to do* good works. Even then, it is all of God by his grace. God has created us through his redeeming act of saving grace to be in Christ as his handiwork, and the works he wants us to do have all been set out in advance.

Once we realise our position in Christ as dead to sin and self, we can begin to live *for* Christ and *in* Christ in the different ministries to which he has called us. Paul knew that from his own experience. In writing to the Galatians, he was able to say how he lived his life for God. '*I have been crucified with Christ and I no longer live, but Christ lives in me. The life I now live in the body, I live by faith in the Son of God, who loved me and gave himself for me.*'[130] What a wonderful set of truths that applies to all of us who are Christians. We ourselves no longer live, but it is Christ who lives in us, and we are living by faith in him. All of that is possible because of the sacrificial love of the Lord Jesus.

That we should live Christ-like lives was self-evident to Paul, and he gave us lots of commands and exhortations that we should follow. It was important to Paul, however, that his readers understood *why* we should desire to live godly lives. Sinclair Ferguson, the Scottish theologian, explains it in terms of '*gospel grammar*', in that '*divine indicatives*' always

129. Ephesians 2:10
130. Galatians 2:20

precede '*divine imperatives*'. In other words, statements about what God has done, is doing or will do always come before what our response should be.[131] God's graceful provision of grace lays the foundation for our Christian living in following his commands.

An example of this is in Paul's letter to the Romans where, in the first eleven chapters, he gave a majestic exposition of grace, justification by faith, being crucified with Christ, being raised to new life in Christ and so much more! In these eleven chapters Ferguson calculated that out of 315 verses only seven were commands.[132] Paul comprehensively laid the groundwork of God's grace before starting to give commands in the first two verses of chapter 12:

> *Therefore, I urge you, brothers and sisters, in view of God's mercy, to offer your bodies as a living sacrifice, holy and pleasing to God – this is your true and proper worship. Do not conform to the pattern of this world, but be transformed by the renewing of your mind.*[133]

Likewise, in his letter to the Colossians, Paul instructed his readers how they ought to live in line with the gospel. He reminded them again of their position in Christ, with the same emphasis as in Romans chapter 12, before telling them where they had to set their hearts and minds. '*Since, then, you have been raised with Christ, set your hearts on things above, where Christ is, seated at the right hand of God. Set your minds on things above, not on earthly things.*'[134] If it is true that we have been raised with Christ, our hearts and minds should be set where he is seated – in heavenly places at the right hand of God. If our hearts and minds are set there, we are more likely to have attitudes and actions pleasing to

131. Sinclair B. Ferguson, *Devoted to God* (Banner of Truth Trust, 2016), p. 33.
132. Sinclair B. Ferguson, *Devoted to God*, p. 39.
133. Romans 12:1-2
134. Colossians 3:1-2

him. Therefore, we should put to death the evil practices belonging to our old selves and '*clothe ourselves with compassion, kindness, humility, gentleness and patience*'.[135]

How, though, can we take off these evil practices and put on these wonderful qualities? Surely we cannot just work ourselves up to being more compassionate, kind, humble, gentle and patient; we would just fail! In his letter to the Galatians, Paul had a similar list of excellent qualities, '*love, joy, peace, forbearance, kindness, goodness, faithfulness, gentleness and self-control*', which he called '*the fruit of the Spirit*'.[136] It is God's Holy Spirit who will work within our lives to transform our minds, help us to be rid of evil practices and help us to put on Christ-like qualities. Paul knew that from his own experience.

135. Colossians 3:12
136. Galatians 5:22-23

# Chapter 14: Paul Contends Against Opposition

Paul realised that his ministry would lead to him ending up in chains, imprisoned for his Lord. This was certainly the case when he arrived back in Jerusalem from his missionary travels. False charges were brought against him by Jews from Asia Minor, resulting in a riot and an attempt on his life. He had to be rescued by the Roman authorities. The soldiers gave him the chance to speak to the crowd, and Paul fearlessly gave his testimony about how the Lord had met him on the road to Damascus. The crowd seemed to listen to him until he made a statement that made them see red. Luke recorded that Paul proclaimed, '*Then the Lord said to me, "Go; I will send you far away to the Gentiles."*' Immediately the crowd shouted, '*Rid the earth of him! He's not fit to live!*'[137] The hatred that these Jews had for the Gentiles soon rose to the fore, and they bayed for Paul's life.

Paul was taken before the Jewish High Priest and Sanhedrin where he was given nothing like a fair hearing, and indeed the Roman commander took Paul away for his own safety. Paul remained in the hands of the Roman authorities for about two years and had a number of hearings involving Governor Felix, Governor Festus and the Jewish King Herod Agrippa. In his hearings before these powerful men, Paul consistently and fearlessly shared his testimony and the word of the Lord. For example, he was not afraid to talk to Felix about '*righteousness, self-control and the judgement to come*',[138] which brought fear to Felix's heart.

Paul stood his ground throughout these hearings, knowing that his Lord was standing with him. It was his right as a Roman citizen to appeal to the highest authority in the Empire, Emperor Nero himself, and this set him on his journey to Rome.

137. Acts 22:21-22
138. Acts 24:25

Paul also contended against opposition in the letters that he wrote. Paul was consistently concerned about those who would infiltrate the church with a different message, '*a different gospel – which is really no gospel at all*',[139] and thus take believers away from their devotion to Christ. Paul was concerned for the purity of the gospel, and warned in very strong words that his brothers and sisters in Christ should be on their guard against those who would lead them away.

He was particularly concerned about Judaizers, those who argued that belief in Christ was not enough for salvation, but rather it was necessary also to follow the ritual practices of the Jewish law, including circumcision for males (and so they were often called the circumcision group[140]). Their message was very much 'Jesus plus' to earn salvation, which was of course completely contrary to the message that he had received from the Lord, that salvation was a gift by God's grace, received through faith alone. He was quite blunt in his denunciation of them, wishing that '*they would go the whole way and emasculate themselves*',[141] or warning that the Philippian church should '*watch out for those dogs, those evildoers, those mutilators of the flesh*'.[142]

It was the Galatian churches that concerned Paul most over this issue, as '*evidently some people* [were] *throwing* [them] *into confusion and . . . trying to pervert the gospel of Christ*'.[143] If Judaizers were trying to seduce the Galatians to renounce the gospel and take on Jewish rituals, Paul reminded them of Abraham, the father of the Jews who believed God and who was justified by faith. Abraham, and those who succeeded him living by faith, would receive blessing from the Lord. The doctrine of justification by faith was not some new invention by Paul, but went back to God's dealings with Abraham! If, however, you insisted on trying to

139. Galatians 1:6-7
140. As, for example, in Galatians 2:12, Titus 1:10.
141. Galatians 5:12
142. Philippians 3:2
143. Galatians 1:7

earn salvation by observing the law, you would be cursed. '*For all who rely on the works of the law are under a curse, as it is written:* "Cursed is everyone who does not continue to do everything written in the Book of the Law."'[144] It is impossible to live to that standard.

Paul, however, declared that there was an answer. '*Christ redeemed us from the curse of the law by becoming a curse for us, for it is written: "Cursed is everyone who is hung on a pole."*'[145] We can receive blessing that we do not deserve, because Christ, the altogether sinless one, became sin for us.

Paul was prepared to use forceful language against his opponents and to believers who were drifting away. All that was said, however, was said out of love – love for Christ, love for the gospel and love for Christian believers. He ended his powerful letter to the Galatians by saying, '*The grace of our Lord Jesus Christ be with your spirit, brothers and sisters. Amen.*'[146]

144. Galatians 3:10
145. Galatians 3:13
146. Galatians 6:18

# Chapter 15: Paul Contends in Prayer

Prayer was absolutely central to Paul's life; his communion with God through the Holy Spirit was the powerhouse that drove his life. As we visualise him on his long journeys over land and sea, we would see him spending much time talking to his Master. Sitting in prison, preparing to write his wonderful letters, he would have many hours of prayer.

Listening to God was a vital part of his prayer life. When Paul arrived in Corinth, he did not have a very easy time of it, with the Jews being particularly abusive towards him. Although many Gentiles responded to his message, he perhaps felt fearful about his work in that city. God spoke to him clearly in a vision, saying, '*Do not be afraid; keep on speaking, do not be silent. For I am with you, and no one is going to attack and harm you, because I have many people in this city.*'[147] It is just as well that Paul listened to this reassuring message, as he went on to spend a year and a half in that very cosmopolitan city contending for Christ and building up the church there.

As we read his letters, we sense the close partnership he had with his readers, as he prayed that God would meet their needs, especially their spiritual needs. What a tremendously long prayer list he must have had! For example, in writing to the Philippians, he said with great feeling, '*I thank my God every time I remember you. In all my prayers for all of you, I always pray with joy because of your partnership in the gospel from the first day until now.*'[148] He prayed with joy and thanksgiving.

So, what did Paul pray for when he prayed for these different churches? It is interesting to note what Paul did *not* emphasise in his prayers. Alistair Begg points out in his very helpful examination of

147. Acts 18:9-10
148. Philippians 1:3-5

what Paul prayed for, entitled *Pray Big,*[149] that he very rarely prayed over health matters. Nor did he pray in the rather vague, weak way we often pray saying, 'Be with . . .' As Begg noted, '*Paul prayed big prayers because he believed great things.*'[150]

In praying to the Ephesians, for example, he gave thanks for their faith and love. '*For this reason, ever since I heard about your faith in the Lord Jesus and your love for all God's people, I have not stopped giving thanks for you, remembering you in my prayers.*'[151] And he was doing this without ceasing! But he wanted more for them. He prayed that they might have wisdom and revelation to know God better. He prayed that their eyes would be opened further to know the hope to which they had been called, along with the gloriously rich inheritance that they had been promised. He prayed as they lived their lives that they might know God's incomparably rich resurrection power.[152]

Yet, he still asked for more. In the third chapter of his letter he prayed:

> *And I pray that you, being rooted and established in love, may have power, together with all the Lord's holy people, to grasp how wide and long and high and deep is the love of Christ, and to know this love that surpasses knowledge – that you may be filled to the measure of all the fullness of God.*[153]

O, to know Christ's love like that and to be filled with all the fullness of God!

These requests are on a much higher plane than the prayers we tend to offer. It is of course not wrong to pray for day-to-day things, such as for our daily bread as in the Lord's Prayer, or for health matters,

149. Alistair Begg, *Pray Big* (The Good Book Company, 2019).
150. Alistair Begg, *Pray Big*, p. 8.
151. Ephesians 1:15-16
152. Ephesians 1:17-20
153. Ephesians 3:17-19

because God cares about these requests as well. Paul, however, more than anything wanted his readers to know Christ in all his fullness. And it was all for the glory of God!

> *Now to him who is able to do immeasurably more than all we ask or imagine, according to his power that is at work within us, to him be glory in the church and in Christ Jesus throughout all generations, for ever and ever! Amen.*[154]

154. Ephesians 3:20-21

# Chapter 16: What Might Paul Say to Our Churches Today?

There is so much more that we could say about Paul, but in concluding this section, it is worth thinking about how Paul might relate to our churches in the 2020s. Again, he would have a lot to say, but let us just consider three messages.

The first would be to preach Christ crucified. This was his central message, and although it might seem '*a stumbling-block to Jews and foolishness to Gentiles,*'[155] this was the means by which God demonstrated his love and grace to a world in need of rescue. This has to be the message that our world needs, and so if we preach that we must repent from our sins and turn in faith to the crucified and resurrected Christ, we are preaching a message that meets people's deepest needs. Powerfully and lovingly preaching that message to a world that is in fear as a result of a raging pandemic will be more effective to those who are seeking truth than what Tom Holland called in our introduction '*public health lectures*'.

A second message that Paul would want to share with our churches would be to maintain biblical standards. Many of our churches today, in the face of declining numbers, have sought popularity by watering down the gospel so that it reflects the standards of the world. Such churches, in a bid to be more inclusive, have accepted that there might be many ways to God rather than only by the grace of God through faith in Jesus. Likewise, if the world has developed a new morality with regard to sexual ethics that accepts a wide range of sexual practices, many churches have felt that they should similarly accept these practices rather than the biblical view that sex is a gift from God that should be maintained within monogamous heterosexual marriage. Yet, church attendance has

155. 1 Corinthians 1:23

still declined, particularly in those churches that are trying to rebrand in the image of modern society. Paul would be horrified that churches were following the way of the world, rather than following the teachings of the Bible.

Paul gave this instruction to Timothy whom he left in charge of the church in Ephesus:

> *But as for you, continue in what you have learned and have become convinced of, because you know those from whom you learned it, and how from infancy you have known the Holy Scriptures, which are able to make you wise for salvation through faith in Christ Jesus.*[156]

That instruction must also be taken on board by today's church leaders – in other words, continue to contend for truth as contained in the Scriptures.

A third and vital message for today's churches must be to rejoice and pray. As we have seen, that was part of Paul's lifeblood – a living relationship with his Lord through prayer. In our churches today, we too must contend in prayer. As Paul commanded the Thessalonians: '*Rejoice always, pray continually, give thanks in all circumstances; for this is God's will for you in Christ Jesus*.'[157] That is also God's will for us today.

156. 2 Timothy 3:14-15
157. 1 Thessalonians 5:16-18

# Part Four

# Modern Contenders for Truth

# Chapter 17: Andy Bannister

On the Zoom screen was a man in his forties explaining to a young lady how twenty years ago he took his lovely new wife out to an Italian restaurant for a romantic candle-lit dinner for two. He went on to say that towards the end of the evening, he leaned over the table to give his wife a kiss (as young romantics do). Suddenly, his wife leapt back and shrieked, '*You're on fire! You're on fire!*' He explained that it was not his rugged charm that she was describing, but rather the fact that his hair gel had been set alight by the flame of the candle and that he now had a two-inch flame on the top of his head! His wife acted quickly, taking a carafe of water and pouring it over his head. He was soaked and smelled of burning hair. Needless to say he has never been back to that restaurant. His marriage did, however, survive the incident.

Why would anyone relate that embarrassing episode to a large audience watching on Zoom? It was like an interview on some television magazine programme. This was, however, an interview followed by a talk at a university Christian Union evangelistic meeting with about sixty students who had 'zoomed' in to watch the event. The theme of the event was looking at the issue of whether science had disproved God. The man in question was Dr Andy Bannister, director of the Solas Centre for Public Christianity, based in Dundee. The story had no real link with the theme (not even to demonstrate the combustibility of hair gel!), but rather it acted as an ice-breaker to create a rapport with his audience before he started his talk. Despite his academic qualifications and deep knowledge of his subject, he was an ordinary human being who has made embarrassing mistakes.

At breakneck speed, Andy spoke for fifteen minutes on how there was no contradiction between a belief in God and the practice of science. Although he went at a fast pace, his speech was vibrant, his explanations were clear and his slide presentation provided excellent examples to back up his arguments. For example, he showed a slide of Leonardo da Vinci's *Mona Lisa*, and asked the question as to why Leonardo painted that portrait. Scientists, he argued, could carry out a whole battery of tests on the paints and the frame to show *how* the portrait was painted, but they could not answer the question as to *why* Leonardo painted that particular lady. Andy's point was that science had its limits. It was not the case, as the late eminent atheist physicist, Stephen Hawking, declared, '*Science has trumped over everything.*' Andy quoted the Nobel Prize-winning biologist, Peter Medawar, who wrote:

> *That there is indeed a limit to science is made very likely by the existence of questions that science cannot answer, and that no conceivable advancement of science would empower it to answer . . . I have in mind questions such as: 'How did everything begin? What are we all here for? What is the point of living?'*[158]

Science pointed to there being a creator or a designer, but it is only when we look to Jesus do we see what the creator is really like and how he intervened in the world. Andy used as an illustration the lunar astronaut Neil Armstrong's words from space in 1969: '*It suddenly struck me that that tiny pea, pretty and blue, was the Earth. I put up my thumb and shut one eye, and my thumb blotted out the planet Earth. I didn't feel like a giant. I felt very, very small.*' Andy pointed out that God showed his love for these very small people by stepping on to that tiny blue pea in the person of Jesus, that we might know what the creator God was like and that we might have life. He ended by quoting Jesus, '*I have come that they may have life, and have it to the full.*'[159]

158. Peter Medawar, *The Limits of Science* (Oxford University Press, 1988), p. 59.
159. John 10:10

Andy had prepared a brilliant presentation on the subject, but the next bit of the evening was totally unrehearsed: he had to answer a series of questions sent in by students, covering issues related to science and Christianity. Here his deep knowledge of his subject and his communication skills really came to the fore. He was able to give clear, yet profound, answers to the questions he was given, using scientific sources to back up his answers.

When, for example, he was asked about the 'Big Bang' he brought in both the atheist physicist Fred Hoyle and the Genesis account. Fred Hoyle coined the term 'Big Bang', but hated the concept because he rigidly believed that the universe had always been there; a 'Big Bang' implied that there was a beginning, and also pointed to a creator outside the system. Andy emphasised that a 'Big Bang' required a 'Big Banger' to create the universe, to light the blue touch paper and bring life into existence. Thus he related the 'Big Bang' to the Genesis creation story. '*And God said, "Let there be light," and there was light.*'[160] A 'Big Bang' if ever there was one!

One question that was asked, which was a bit different from the others, was whether Christianity was simply a crutch, or whether it was a real help in life. Andy pointed out that a crutch could of course be very helpful if you had a broken leg. People, however, who argue that Christianity is *only* a crutch are often saying that it has no truth value, but it may be psychologically comforting. Andy gave the illustration of jumping from a plane; a parachute would provide psychological comfort, but you really want to know that it works. Those who see Christianity as only a source of psychological comfort are ignoring the reality of the evidence for the Christian faith. Covid has swept many 'certainties' away from us, but Andy was able to say from his own experience that Jesus is the rock upon which you can build your life, and he will not be swept away, but would always be there, whatever else happens in your life.

160. Genesis 1:3

This was an excellent session from Andy, full of powerful academic arguments, put forward in a way that would relate to students. Most of all, however, Andy came across as someone who had Jesus at the centre of his life, with a desire that others come to know Jesus for themselves.

I have been able to find out more about how Andy contends for truth through Zoom interviews with him, reading material that he has written and checking out the Solas website.

## Starting on the road to future ministry

Andy was brought up in south London in what he describes as '*a good Baptist home*'.[161] He enjoyed church and the youth group, but he realised that it was not his own faith that he was experiencing, but rather that of his parents. It was at a Crusaders (now rebranded as Urban Saints) youth camp at the age of twelve that he really felt the gospel connect with him. At the end of one evening meeting, he felt strongly led to respond to the altar call, and he gave his life to Jesus. That was his first public declaration that he was going to follow Jesus. From then, he started to work out the implications of the decision that he had made.

At school, he met up with two or three other Christians and together they started a Christian Union. They managed to get some friends along to talk about the big questions of life. One of the lessons that Andy learned at this point that would have important bearings for his future ministry was asking the right questions. As Andy expressed it, '*If you pitched the question right, you can get a conversation going round gospel issues.*' This was to be an approach that he would use later in his life in sharing the gospel with others, and in teaching others to share the gospel. Also in these formative years, Andy took an interest in stand-up comedy, which has borne much fruit in his Christian ministry; his writing is full of humorous references, and his quick wit is evident as he leads sessions or answers questions from his audiences.

161. Indeed, he quipped on being asked about his Christian upbringing, '*You don't need to be a Baptist to go to heaven, but why take chances?*'

After he left school, rather than going to university he deferred his place and spent a year working for the Oasis Trust. Andy was part of a Frontline Team that had been sent to work in a church in Sunderland, where he was heavily involved in leading children's and youth work. As Andy explained, this was a real turning point for him:

> *It was a great year to learn more about myself and about God. When you're young and sent to another part of the country away from home, you basically need to learn to rely on God, because you very quickly realise that you haven't got the experience to do any of the things that they want you to do. So, I learned how to pray desperately.*

During his time in Sunderland, he came into contact with the local branch of Youth for Christ (YFC), and felt really led by God to return to London to set up a YFC branch in his home area, to meet the needs of young people there. This would mean giving up the university place that he had deferred and trying to find a job to support himself financially as he served the Lord in YFC. He ended up working for St George's Hospital Medical School running medical conferences and events, a post that sustained him for five years. For Andy, this was very much the providence of God at work, as he was not particularly well qualified for the job, but he learned so much about running an organisation and mounting events, skills that would be of paramount importance in his future ministry. At the same time, he was able to set up a new branch of YFC and do the Christian youth work that he felt called to do.

In 1997, Andy gave up his hospital job to start full-time paid Christian work. A group of churches in south-east London wanted to work with their local schools, and so wanted to appoint a schools' worker. It was his responsibility to make contact with secondary schools and find opportunities to get in to take lessons and assemblies, start lunch-time clubs and create links with the churches. Andy loved this job, but, as he said, it was not easy.

> *When you are faced with a thousand young people aged eleven to eighteen at nine o'clock on a Monday morning, and you are told not to go too strong on the 'God thing', otherwise you will not be allowed back, but you want to be authentic, and you only have five minutes, you learn very, very fast.*

This is where he learned to communicate in five-minute chunks, a skill that many years later he used in creating five-minute short-answer videos for Solas. He also learned to contextualise his presentation of the gospel, tailoring presentations to the particular needs of listeners in different situations.

It was also in 1997 that Andy's interest in Islam began to materialise. Jay Smith came to lead a seminar one weekend at their church on relating to Muslim friends and neighbours. Jay offered to take Andy to Speakers' Corner where each Sunday afternoon, from the top of a ladder, Jay debated with Muslims about the truth of Christianity. Andy went along with Jay, but was a bit surprised when he realised that Jay was carrying two ladders, only to be told that one was for Jay and one was for him. Reluctantly, he climbed the ladder to be faced with a barrage of questions from the Muslims down below. He found, to his horror, that he was not able to answer their questions, because, as he realised, he knew neither enough about his own faith or about the faith of his protagonists. After much soul searching, often in the middle of the night, he was determined to put this right, and so he bought and read lots of books on Christian apologetics so that he understood the basis of his faith.

He returned to Speakers' Corner a month later, with lots of reading to help him answer the questions of his Muslim friends, only to discover that they had come up with a whole barrage of new questions which again he found very difficult to answer. Andy, however, refused to give up, and so he read more books and over the next few months returned to Speakers' Corner for more debate and dialogue, growing in confidence all the time.

This experience had profound effects on Andy. He developed a passion for apologetics and publicly defending his faith, which would underpin his future ministry. He also saw again the power of questions, something that he first realised in the school Christian Union. As he stood on the ladder, he knew that not only did he have to answer the questions thrown at him, but that he could fire questions at those down below to make them consider what they believed, in the light of the claims of Christ. He also realised that he had a love for Muslims and wanted to reach out to them. All of this together, along with promptings from his wife Astrid whom he married in 1998, laid on Andy's heart that he should do further study, and so in the year 2000, he applied to go to London Bible College (now called London School of Theology).

Andy chose London Bible College for his studies because it had an excellent Department of Islamic Studies. After three years of undergraduate study, he started a year-long masters' course in Islamic Studies. He was doing so well on this course, relishing his research and producing such high-quality material, that he was invited to do a PhD instead. He had told Astrid that this course of study would only last three years; in effect it lasted seven years (albeit on a part-time basis). Altogether Andy was a student in London from 2000 to 2010.

## From Oxford to Dundee via Canada

When Andy started going out with Astrid in 1997, she told him that she believed that God had called her to go out to live and work in Canada. In one sense this was something that Andy did not really want to hear, as he was, in his own words, '*the most parochial Brit you could ever hope to meet'*. By this point in his life, he had not even left England, let alone the United Kingdom, and was terrified of flying. He kept ignoring the idea of going out to Canada, but Astrid kept praying, and indeed prayed for ten years that God would move Andy to take the momentous step of transferring out to Canada.

As well as working on his doctoral thesis, Andy got involved in the Ravi Zacharias International Ministries (RZIM) team at its European headquarters in Oxford. Ravi Zacharias, the founder of RZIM, has since his death been the centre of controversy over issues of sexual abuse and exploitation. Andy has been horrified about the revelations that have been brought to light, but he is also quite clear that in the years when he had dealings with both Zacharias and the team there was no indication of any of these horrific problems.

In 2007, he was invited to assist Amy Orr-Ewing, director of the Oxford Centre for Apologetics, in a debate on the Premier Christian Radio show *Unbelievable?* hosted by Justin Brierley.[162] Amy went back to the team in Oxford, telling them that Andy was someone that they should contact as he would be an excellent addition to the team. Andy joined their team of associate speakers and took part in a number of events for them.

In 2008, Andy was sitting at a meeting in Oxford where a colleague was talking about ministries in different parts of the world, and, in particular, spoke about how active the work was in Canada. As Andy described the experience, '*The best analogy I can think of is that it felt like God had put a laser beam right into my brain and said, "Oi, Bannister! You need to listen to this."*' What the Canadian team seemed to be doing sounded very exciting and fitted in with Andy's passions, and of course it was what Astrid's prayer had been for ten years. Andy went home and told Astrid, and she dropped her coffee mug in astonishment, as

162. This apologetics programme of debates between Christians and non-believers continues to run on Premier Christian Radio, along with a very popular podcast.

this was the first time that he had shown any interest in Canada. Andy followed this up by reaching out to the Canadian team; they took him on, not simply as a speaker, but as their new director. In June 2010, he and Astrid moved out to Toronto.

They spent six fruitful years in Canada. He developed the ministry and built up the team as he criss-crossed the country on different speaking engagements, trying out new ideas as he did so. He found that the Canadians took to him because of his British accent. They loved conversation, and so dialogue events were an important means of reaching out to them. When having dialogue with Canadians, he learned the importance of listening; provided he did that, he would earn respect and would get a good hearing.

As in any mission situation, sometimes his listeners were convinced, while others had yet to be persuaded. Andy learned patience in his ministry, realising that you do not always reap what you sow on the same day, or even in the same week. God often uses multiple contact points in bringing in a harvest, similar to what Paul described to the church in Corinth, '*I planted the seed, Apollos watered it, but God has been making it grow. So neither the one who plants nor the one who waters is anything, but only God, who makes things grow.*'[163]

One example of that was from an email that he had very recently received from a former RZIM Canada colleague.

> *Back in 2014, we had done a mission in Calgary up in the middle of Canada. I got talking to a student after one of the events and spent a lot of time with him. This student actually stayed drinking coffee one night with four of us on the team until about one o'clock in the morning, asking questions, question after question. And then of course you move on and you never hear again. The student had got in touch with my friend to tell him that three*

163. 1 Corinthians 3:6-7

*months ago he had become a Christian and that he had just got baptised last weekend. That is such an amazing answer to prayer from a mission that had taken place seven years before. The Lord was still at work. Other people were obviously involved over the years, but it was such a privilege to have played some part in his journey.*

Andy and Astrid also had two children in Canada, Caitriona and Christopher, and by 2015 they felt that God was nudging them back to the United Kingdom, partly to be closer to the children's grandparents. They had expected to go back to Oxford to be involved with RZIM there, but God had other plans. David Robertson, at that time a very influential Free Church of Scotland minister who also headed up the Solas organisation, phoned Andy and asked him if he would like to become director of Solas in his place. Andy initially turned David down, but then found that doors in Oxford were closed, while David remained persistent in trying to persuade him to lead Solas. As a result, he realised that God was calling him to Dundee, and so in 2016 the family left Canada for Scotland to face a new challenge.

## Solas

The title of the organisation that Andy came back to Britain to lead is intriguing; it is not an acronym but rather a Gaelic word meaning 'light', giving it a vision of the light of the gospel spreading throughout the land. It is also a very clever play on words, linking it to the five 'solas' of the Protestant Reformation: '*sola gratia*' (by grace alone), '*sola fide*' (by faith alone), '*solus Christus*' (through Christ alone), '*sola scriptura*' (by scripture alone), '*soli Deo gloria*' (for the glory of God alone). It is a name that Andy likes, because it is a good conversation starter:

> *'Who do you work for?'*
> *'I work for an organisation called Solas.'*
> *'Solas, what does that stand for?'*
> *'It doesn't actually stand for anything, but it means . . .'*

The emphasis within Solas is very much evangelism and apologetics (or pre-evangelism). On its website,[164] its mission statement is very clearly stated as: '*Solas persuasively communicates the transforming truth of who Jesus is and empowers others to do the same*.' In a video on the same page of the website explaining the purpose of Solas, Andy very powerfully proclaims,

> *We live in such a post-Christian culture that we are encountering people now who have no conception of what the gospel is. They're not resistant to it – they just don't know what it is. Our challenge as Christians is how we convey the gospel into the halls of power, into the public square, into the market place, into education and media in such a way that it engages people.*

Pre-lockdown, Andy would travel to take part in different events at the request of universities, local churches, and even to remote villages in the Scottish Highlands, where perhaps nobody else would go to take part in such events. These events are usually evangelistic, but he sees the vital importance of incorporating training within the programme. Andy has enthusiastically described the importance of training thus:

> *Imagine what it would be like if we could get every Christian in the UK, confident, relaxed and feeling able to share their faith in Christ with their peer group in a way that was natural, winsome and wasn't scary. Think of the impact for the kingdom and how*

164. https://www.solas-cpc.org/about/ (accessed 16.12.21)

*God would use that. That's a big, bold, audacious goal. If Solas could just be a tiny part of that, it would be terrifically exciting.*

Of course, during lockdown it was not possible to go to university campuses or to church events, and so like so many churches and organisations, Solas attended events online, such as the university event previously described. Indeed, in 2020, Andy participated in a major online mission run collaboratively by almost all of the Scottish Christian Unions, and felt very privileged to speak to a large number of non-Christian students. Similarly, just before Christmas 2020 he was due to speak at a Ministry of Defence site near Bristol, but because of lockdown he could not travel to it. Instead, the Christian groups at a number of sites came together to put on a major online event, thus allowing him to speak to several hundred personnel.

Solas has also used webinars to discuss topics that may be of interest to both Christians and non-Christians alike. The idea is that participants are able to watch a discussion streamed live for about thirty minutes followed by thirty minutes of question and answer with participants posing questions using a 'pigeonhole' website. An example of such a webinar took place just before Easter 2021 when Mike Licona, associate professor of theology at Houston Baptist University, was interviewed by Andy on the question 'Did Jesus really rise from the dead?'[165] Andy of course was not a neutral interviewer, and so was able to ensure that Mike used the results of his massive historical research to demonstrate the truth of the resurrection in an accessible, yet still academically plausible, way. This included asking Mike about what the resurrection meant for him personally. The question-and-answer session afterwards was similarly well led by Andy, again allowing Mike to share his expertise with those watching. Andy finished the session by gently suggesting that

165. https://www.youtube.com/watch?v=3Rq2qVJz4-g (accessed 16.12.21).

those who were still searching should get hold of Mike's book on the resurrection,[166] or some similar volume on the subject.

The Solas website is a wonderful treasure chest of resources that can be used to deepen the understanding of Christian believers on particular issues, as well as sharing them with those who are not yet Christians. Of particular value for sharing are the short-answer videos on particular questions. Questions are at the heart of Andy's ministry. Does God actually exist? Why is there suffering? Do all religions teach that God is a God of love? Can we have forgiveness without God? Why would a loving God send people to hell? What would God say to Boris Johnson? These, and others, are questions that many people love to ask, and are given short, clear responses by Andy and other presenters in videos lasting five or six minutes. They can then be used as a catalyst for further discussion with individuals or groups.

## Communicating Christian truth

After his first rather miserable experience of debating at Speakers' Corner, Andy resolved to become more sure of his faith and thus follow the words of Peter, '*Always be prepared to give an answer to everyone who asks you to give the reason for the hope that you have.*'[167] To help him do this he started to devour books on Christian apologetics. Alister McGrath gives a simple definition of what otherwise might seem a very complex discipline, '*Apologetics is about persuading people that Christianity makes sense.*'[168]

McGrath argues that there are three tasks that an apologist has to carry out.[169] The first is to *defend*, which requires answering questions that people might have about Christianity. The second task is to

166. Michael R. Licona, *The Resurrection of Jesus: A New Historiographical Approach* (IVP Academic, 2010).
167. 1 Peter 3:15
168. Alister E. McGrath, *Mere Apologetics* (Baker Books, 2012), p. 71.
169. Alister E. McGrath, *Mere Apologetics*, chapter 1.

*commend* the Christian faith; in other words, to show its attractiveness to those who are seeking, in being both internally coherent and more compelling than alternative worldviews. The third task is to *translate* the Christian message to the culture of the audience, many of whom will have no understanding of biblical terminology. In the same way that Jesus used agrarian-based parables to reach his audience, twenty-first century apologists need to give relevant, appropriate examples to ensure that the audience appreciates the full truth of the gospel that is being presented.

Apologetics is a central plank in Andy's ministry, both in his speaking and his writing. It is something that he has described as pre-evangelism, as, for it to be completely effective, it has to be linked to calling individuals to make a personal commitment to the Lord Jesus Christ. It can be very easy for individuals to assent intellectually to rational arguments without actually taking that necessary step of faith. It may be the case that people do not realise that they need to 'believe in' (or better still 'believe into', signifying a movement of the will) as well as 'believing that'. A Jewish scribe once approached Jesus asking him what the greatest commandment was. When Jesus told him the two greatest commandments, the scribe seemed very pleased and showed intellectual understanding. Jesus said to him, '*You are not far from the kingdom of God*.'[170] He was not far, but he had not yet taken that step of faith to follow Jesus and enter the kingdom. So many people are intellectually close to the kingdom, but need to repent and make a personal commitment to Jesus. Where that is the case, this needs to be explained to them.

Or it may be the case that people accept the arguments, but they believe that the cost of following Jesus is too great, as was discovered by the rich young ruler. He approached Jesus to find eternal life, but he was

170. Mark 12:34

not prepared to put Jesus before his wealth.[171] We need to continue to pray for such people that they will ultimately see that Jesus is the pearl of great worth.[172]

The university mission Zoom call, discussed at the beginning of this chapter, is an excellent example of how Andy carried out the tasks of the apologist by defending Christianity against the attacks of science. He commended the Christian faith as being able to answer the 'why?' questions of life better than alternative philosophies such as the belief that science has all the answers. By using examples such as space travel or even a parachute, he translated the tenets of the faith into contemporary culture. In his presentation, he also called upon his audience to move beyond science to see the love that God has for the world. God showed his love by entering into history in the person of Jesus, who gave up his life for us on the cross that we might have life. He explained that the invitation that Jesus offers us '*is unique to Christianity, the invitation that God makes in Jesus Christ, not just to know that there is a Creator who designed this wonderful universe, but the invitation also in Jesus Christ that we can get to know that Creator and Designer personally, in a relationship as he intended with him*'. He was asking his audience to consider beginning a relationship with God through Jesus.

In his communication of the truth, Andy loves dealing with questions. The question-and-answer sessions enable him to get to the issues that people are struggling with. As we have seen above, people are interested in issues related to Christianity and science, but since the beginning of the pandemic, he has sensed a greater interest in other issues. People are thinking more about the meaning and purpose of life and dealing with issues related to depression and loneliness, as well as current concerns around the environment or sexual identity.

171. Matthew 19:16-29, Mark 10:17-30, Luke 18:18-30
172. Matthew 13:45-46

Andy also loves using questions to start a conversation, and this is one of the key strategies he uses in training Christians. He presented a webinar in July 2020, entitled 'How to Talk About Jesus Without Looking Like an Idiot'.[173] At the beginning of the webinar, he gave the example of a rather angry student who approached him at the end of an event accusing Christians of being 'anti' all sorts of people and issues, including women. Andy asked the young man what was wrong with being anti-women. The student answered that it was just wrong to discriminate against people on the basis of gender. Andy kept on asking why to the answers the student was giving. The student was getting increasingly frustrated at not being able to give an adequate response to Andy's questioning. Andy finally gave his answer that discrimination was wrong because all people are made in the image of God and so are entitled to respect and dignity; therefore Christians are not 'anti-women'. The conversation then became calmer and more fruitful.

He went on to explain in the webinar, reasons for asking questions when having a conversation with non-Christians. They first of all expose people's motives and assumptions; in other words, why they take the position they do with regard to faith. Questions can help to create a conversation, rather than just imposing your views on people. They also force people to think out what they really believe. Finally, questions can help the Christian in the conversation by taking the pressure off and not having to do all the work! Helpful questions include, '*What do you mean by that*?', '*Why do you think that*?' and especially for those who seem to have no interest in the gospel, '*Have you ever wondered . . .* ?'

Andy gave an example of how he turned a question round when he was asked by a friend in a cafe if he thought that abortion was wrong. He redefined the question by asking his friend if it was ever all right to take the life of a wholly innocent person. His friend replied that taking

173. https://www.solas-cpc.org/how-to-talk-about-jesus-without-looking-like-an-idiot/ (accessed 16.12.21).

such a life was never justified, which meant that they could then have a more open conversation about the nature of life in the womb, and the fundamental arguments against aborting innocent lives. As we saw earlier in the book, this was the way that Jesus often dealt with questions.

In his speaking, Andy comes across in a clear, engaging, coherent way that commands the respect of his audience. From his training as a teenager in stand-up comedy, he is able to throw away one-liners to very good effect. The same is true in his writing. He is able to write lucidly with compelling arguments and excellent illustrations in a way that will hold his readers' attention. It is not often that we consider books on apologetics or theology as 'page-turners', but Andy's writing comes into that category. It is his use of humour that really grabs his readers.

His use of humour is evident in his book *The Atheist Who Didn't Exist or the Dreadful Consequences of Bad Arguments*.[174] His chapter headings very clearly show his humorous leanings: 'The Loch Ness Monster's Moustache', 'The Aardvark in the Artichokes', 'The Lunatic in the Louvre', to mention just three. His text is littered with one-liners. For example, when suggesting some of the things that might be going wrong in your life, he ends with '*Oh, and you're a Bradford F.C. fan*'.[175] Even his footnotes are full of humour. Most of us when reading books do not bother too much about the footnotes, but you cannot afford to miss an Andy Bannister footnote for the one-liner gems they often contain. When making a fairly serious point about Sigmund Freud's views about God, he attached a footnote that said, '*His wife also revolutionised women's undergarments with the invention of the Freudian Slip*'.[176]

Humour has allowed him a vehicle that encouraged people to read his books and understand the serious points that he was making. His

174. Andy Bannister, *The Atheist Who Didn't Exist or the Dreadful Consequences of Bad Arguments* (Lion Hudson, 2015).

175. Andy Bannister, *The Atheist Who Didn't Exist*, p. 17.

176. Andy Bannister, *The Atheist Who Didn't Exist*, p. 239. He learned the use of the comedy footnote from reading books in his teenage years by Douglas Adams and Terry Pratchett who found that they could apply a comedic pause by using footnotes.

eye-catching chapter headings lead into serious points, particularly about the incredulous nature of many of the arguments of atheists such as Richard Dawkins, Sam Harris and the late Christopher Hitchens, who since about 2006 have been called the 'New Atheists'.

Throughout his book, he does the work of an apologist in defending, commending and translating Christian truth. In his final chapter, however, he emphasises that the crunch question is not so much 'Does God exist?' but 'What is God like?' and that we can see what God is like in the person of Jesus. For Andy, as it was for the New Testament writers, it is Jesus who brings hope that '*everything that is broken, including us, can be mended*'.[177] He calls his readers to put aside the bad arguments of the atheists and '*give Jesus a careful, considered look*'.[178]

## Islam

We have touched on Andy's fascination with Islam, which began when Jay Smith spoke at a seminar in Andy's church in 1997, leading to rather disappointing performances in debates, or perhaps heckling matches, with members of the Muslim community. It was at this point that Andy got into Christian apologetics in a serious way, as well as developing a burning desire to learn more about Islam. Therefore, as we have seen, he chose to study at London Bible College because of its strong Islamic Studies Department, coming out with a PhD in 2010.

The title of his PhD thesis was 'An Oral-Formulaic Study of the Qur'an', looking at how the oral environment of Arabia at the time of the prophet Muhammad influenced the text of the Qur'an. Andy used databases developed by scholars at Haifa and Leeds Universities, which had every word of the Qur'an labelled and identified. Andy then

177. Andy Bannister, *The Atheist Who Didn't Exist*, p. 232.

178. Andy Bannister, *The Atheist Who Didn't Exist.*, p. 232
To see a concise summary of poor arguments used by atheists, refer to his post entitled 'How to Avoid Being a Village Atheist' on his personal website https://www.andybannister.net/ (accessed 16.12.21).

developed computer software around the databases to scan the Qur'an at high speed to search for patterns. Some time after he had completed his thesis, he teamed up with academic friends to develop 'Qur'an Gateway' (similar to 'BibleGateway', a digital tool used by Christians to explore the Bible). Andy saw the providence of God at work bringing together his interests in philosophy, theology and Islam along with his computing skills, and thus enabling him to carry out this major research project.

Of course, Andy has not undertaken all this research and developed his gateway to promote Islam, but rather so that he could understand this faith better and ultimately show Muslims how Christianity is so different from Islam. God has given him the skill to be able to present Jesus to Muslims without embittering them. This is so important in our culture when there are regular news items of Muslims being enraged about alleged actions against their faith. For example, in March 2021 a religious studies teacher was suspended from his post at Batley Grammar School for showing a class a cartoon of the prophet Muhammad. Noisy protests were held outside the gates of the West Yorkshire school with the local Muslim community demonstrating their anger at the teacher's unwise, although not illegal, action. The headteacher felt that he had to apologise to the community, and the teacher has been forced to go into hiding for his life.

Yet Andy has been able to say that he has not ever been accused (to his knowledge) of Islamophobia. Although he fundamentally disagrees with Islam as a faith, he has a great respect for those who adhere to that faith, and believes that we need to learn to live with people who have different beliefs. As he has written,

> *Somehow we need a way to get on despite our differences, to learn not to be threatened by those who hold very different beliefs, but to see these as an opportunity to learn. Perhaps the way to solve some of the tensions in our world is not by eradicating confidence*

> *and conviction, but by promoting kindness, especially towards those whose views do not harmonise with our own.*[179]

In February 2021, he was asked by a church in Blackburn to take part in an open forum on Christianity and Islam. After his presentation, lots of hands went up, with members of the Muslim community keen to ask questions. Without trying to be provocative, Andy was able to present clearly what he believed were the differences between the two faiths, and in particular what Jesus has done for us. In other situations, Andy has been able to start the conversation by asking the Muslim what he believes, and by using subsequent questions the conversation can flow quite easily. All of this is discussed in an atmosphere of mutual respect.

Many people believe that Christianity and Islam are very similar; after all, their adherents both worship just one God, and so it must be the same God that they worship. In Andy's eyes, however, nothing can be further from the truth. Although both faiths believe in one God, the Christian God has certain characteristics in terms of having a personal relationship with his people, being known by his people, especially through the person of Jesus, being holy, being love, and having suffered for his people. Allah, on the other hand, does not seem to have these characteristics as portrayed in the Qur'an, although he is seen to be all-powerful. Likewise, in terms of attaining salvation, Muslims need to follow Allah's commands if they hope to receive rewards in paradise. In complete contrast, the Bible makes it clear that we cannot do anything ourselves to rebuild our broken relationship with God, but rather that God himself took the initiative by sending his Son to die on the cross and take our punishment upon himself.

179. Andy Bannister, *Do Muslims and Christians Worship the Same God?* (Inter-Varsity Press, 2021), p. 31.

## Conclusion

Andy is very gifted in many ways as a speaker, a writer, an organiser, and an academic researcher. The organisation that he leads is growing, and has been able to take on additional staff. The vision that Andy has for Solas is to take it nationwide so that it has a greater impact across the country, in both evangelism and training Christians.

Gifted as he is, he realises that it is not just his skills, strategies and techniques that make a difference; God has to be at work to change lives, and so prayer is of paramount importance. For him, Jesus is at the centre, and it is his Lordship that drives everything and can change everything. He believes that the gospel has something to say in every situation.

He has a passion to make Jesus known, and so he gets excited about people coming to know Jesus, growing in him and telling others about him. Andy is very hopeful about the spread of the gospel in the future, as people open up to sharing their faith with others. Let us leave the last words to Andy.

> *We need more Christians to be equipped and less fearful of sharing their faith at home, at work and at school. That gets me excited to think what that would look like, because there is a spiritual hunger out there, and people are open to spiritual conversations. If we can get more people to open their mouths and talk naturally, they would be surprised. We live in a secular society, and it is tough, but it is perhaps not as tough as we sometimes think. I meet some Christians who think that it is hopeless, but it isn't.*

# Chapter 18: Michael Bushby

When you meet Michael Bushby, one of the first things that strikes you about him is his absolutely genuine smile. He has a warmth and a caring concern for others that come across straightaway. In many ways, Michael is just an ordinary guy; he is not the product of a university education and does not have a string of letters after his name. In his 'day job' he worked for Nexus, which operates the Tyne and Wear Metro, and having been a train driver for a number of years, he became a train crew assessor and instructor.

Part of his warmth comes from his origins in the north-east of England, but the depth of his love for others comes from his steadfast commitment to the Lord Jesus Christ. He has a deep desire to see others, and particularly unchurched men, come to a real faith in Christ. It is his love for Jesus that motivates him and gives him a fulfilling purpose in life.

I first came to know Michael through Christian Vision for Men, a national organisation with many local branches trying to reach men with Christian truth. My involvement in helping to lead a group in mid-Northumberland brought me into contact with Michael who has been the regional director for the north-east. Through hearing him give his testimony, I was very much aware that he was someone who lived for the Lord and contended for truth. Using Zoom, I was privileged to have a couple of lengthy conversations with him, where I was able to learn more about this humble servant of the Lord. I was also able to have conversations with Steve and Nigel, two men who know him well and who have been influenced by him.

## His early years

Michael grew up on a tough council estate in Gateshead in the 1960s.

There was very little money in the family as his father was a heavy drinker, smoker and gambler, and, as a result, often left the family short of cash. Tragically, he subjected Michael's mother to domestic violence. As Michael explained,

> *As kids, we saw quite a lot of wicked things happening in the house, evil things. My dad would quite often come in in drunken states and smash the house up because he had been to the bookmaker's and lost all of his money. We witnessed my mum being assaulted, and that was sad to see, and it certainly had a negative impact on my mental health and wellbeing. I still remember these images to this day. Psychologically it probably led me to go off the rails a little bit.*

Despite all the harm that his dad caused, Michael still loved him, and grieved for him when he died of Covid in 2020. His mum had died of breast cancer about fifteen years before, another sad event in his life.

His first job on leaving school was in a butcher's warehouse, doing a very hard physical job unloading beasts from the abattoir into the warehouse. Each evening, after a long day, he would come home covered in blood. Michael, however, had in his mind that he would like to obtain further qualifications, and so after a year in the warehouse, he enrolled in college with his mother's support. At the same time, he started to think about a career, and believed that serving in the police would be right for him.

He decided to move away from the north-east '*to leave all the horrors behind of childhood and upbringing*', and so he went to London and joined the Metropolitan Police. In many ways, he enjoyed success in his job, but he admitted to chasing women, drinking heavily and spending too much time enjoying the high life in nightclubs and casinos. The most challenging aspect of the job he found was in dealing with death, and, in particular, informing loved ones that somebody had died in tragic circumstances. Eventually the job dominated his life so much that he could not escape from it.

Michael felt the need to have a career break and to move back to the north-east. He obtained a good post on the Tyne and Wear Metro in 1988, as a revenue control inspector. In 1991, he started the rigorous training required to be a train driver, and qualified two years later. In fact, he was the first driver to drive a train on the Sunderland extension when it opened in 2002. It was during this time back in the north-east that he settled down, married Maria in 1987, and later had two daughters, Jennifer and Helen.

## Coming to faith

In 1993 a major episode occurred that was to change Michael's life forever. By that time, he was working on the Metro as a train driver and one day, one of his colleagues, Bob Arkley, spoke to him about his faith. Bob had had a difficult past; in many ways it was a past that was very similar to Michael's, but he had decided to give his life to Jesus and his life had been absolutely transformed. Michael was drawn to the love and contentment that Bob displayed in his life, and so when Bob invited him along to church he went along gladly.

Michael accompanied Bob to his church, the North East Christian Centre in South Shields, which was a predominantly charismatic fellowship. It seemed to Michael that everyone in the fellowship approached him and made him very welcome, showering him with love and kindness. For Michael, this was very much going to be the beginning of a new chapter in his life. He tells the story as follows:

> *The pastor came up to me and said to me, 'Would you like to become a Christian? Would you like to know this Jesus? Would you like to have your life turned around?' I did not hesitate. I*

> *looked at that church, I looked at the people, and I could see contentment, joy, happiness, peace and love. I thought that if that is what knowing Jesus does to you, I wouldn't mind inviting Jesus into my life. And that night I accepted Jesus as my personal Lord and Saviour. I laid everything before him, I repented of my past and prayed the 'sinner's prayer'. And Jesus came into my life in a very powerful way. That love, that joy, that contentment I could see in the church I experienced for myself. I was just filled with peace, filled with the Holy Spirit, filled with the life of Jesus.*

That night he came home a different man, and Maria, his wife, could see that he was quite changed. He told her his story, and she was absolutely delighted. There was, however, to be even further experience with the Lord that evening. As he lay down in bed that night, for about a split second he experienced his body bathed in light, as if a bolt of electricity had gone through him. As Michael himself put it, '*That was proof to me that I had found the Saviour. I really had seen the light that night.*' When facing difficulties in years to come, Michael would always refer back to that light which he experienced on the evening of his conversion.

Michael's conversion story was dramatic, perhaps much more so than for most others who become Christians. This was the way, however, that God chose to work in his life to prepare him for future ministry and suffering. All the elements of his difficult upbringing, his realisation that his experiences in London brought no real satisfaction, and the provision of a career with Tyne and Wear Metro where he was able to meet such a contender for the faith as Bob, were part of God's wonderful plan for his life. Added to all of these was a vibrant, loving fellowship who demonstrated the fruit of the Spirit that Paul described in his letter to the Galatians.[180]

---

180. '*Love, joy, peace, forbearance, kindness, goodness, faithfulness, gentleness and self-control*' (Galatians 5:22-23).

After his conversion experience, Michael began to share his new faith with others, including his workmates. People, as often is the case with a new convert, scoffed and mocked a bit, usually in jest, but they could see that Michael had changed. He was not particularly bothered by the mocking, because he knew that his experience was real. Furthermore, by the grace of God, he never had to face outright opposition that would have prevented him from speaking, and so he continued to share his faith in a quiet, subtle way.

He grew in his faith and in his knowledge of the Lord, and took opportunities to serve him where he could. He became a member of Christ Church, an Anglican fellowship in Felling. In 2008, he also began voluntary work as a City Centre Chaplain in Newcastle. This service allowed him to get alongside people in their workplaces and to provide a listening ear to them, particularly in times of need such as bereavement. In this way he was able to share God's love with others. He has been strongly supported in this by the Metro management, and indeed he has consistently been made welcome in Nexus House, the Metro headquarters, as they saw that he was able to provide a duty of care to their employees.

## The challenge of cancer

Michael's life, however, was going to be shaken off course in a major way in May 2013 when he was diagnosed with Stage 4 non-Hodgkin's lymphoma, which at this point was very widespread through his system. He was told by his consultant that it could not be cured, and although it could be treated through chemotherapy and immunotherapy, the cancer would still be there. When anybody hears that news, it is a major shock, and it was the same for Michael.

He underwent six months of intense chemotherapy, which he found to be quite debilitating, making him weak and quite sick. He was even forced into an isolation unit for a week because his immune system was extremely low. This was followed by an immunotherapy programme with the aim of keeping him in remission for longer. During these difficult treatments, Michael held fast to his faith, because he believed ultimately that God's ways are best.

There was a point, however, when Michael was told that the chemotherapy treatment was not working and that it would have to be upgraded. This is how Michael described his feelings when told this news and what he ended up doing:

> *I became very angry, angry with God, angry with life, and just wondered what the point was. Looking back, I clearly did the wrong thing, because it caused a lot of heartache and stress to my family. I left the hospital, jumped on the number 56 bus and went to a pub in Gateshead. I sat there just wallowing in self-pity, feeling really down about life, thinking, 'What's the point? I don't want to go through this treatment. I'm just going to die anyway. They told me that I can't be cured, and so let's just finish it.' I sat in the pub, got drunk and then came back home.*
>
> *I went upstairs, got a pair of skipping ropes, walked into the garage, slammed the garage door shut and decided that I was going to hang myself. I had made my mind up. I was finished with life and I was just going to take my own life. Looking back, I thank God that my daughters saw me going into the garage, and that they and my wife were braying frantically at the garage door, begging me to come out, telling me not to be so stupid, telling me how wrong it was. I just heard God's voice through my family. That made me look at the situation. I can't put my family through this pain – they were already going through enough pain already, and I didn't want to compound it by killing myself. I didn't want to leave them. I came out of the garage and apologised to them.*

> *Naturally, I gave them all a hug and told them I loved them. I did break down crying.*

Michael was brought down into the pit by his illness, taking his anger out on God and causing his family a massive amount of heartache. For that, he had to seek forgiveness, and then try to re-evaluate where his life was going. In seeking God he prayed, '*Whatever time I have left, I just want to give my life to you. I just want you to use this bit of life I have left and that some good would come out of this.*' In doing this, he was reconsecrating his life to the Lord. He just wanted to do more for the kingdom. In Michael's own words: '*At that instant, the fear of death left me and the fear of cancer left me. I suddenly found peace and that no matter what happened, God was in control.*'

He continued with his treatment, and he is still living with cancer. Yet he is living his life in God's strength, trusting that the Sovereign God will protect and provide for him until he finally takes him to his heavenly home. His favourite Bible passage is Psalm 91, which gives him great comfort. It begins:

> *Whoever dwells in the shelter of the Most High will rest in the shadow of the Almighty. I will say of the* LORD, *'He is my refuge and my fortress, my God, in whom I trust.'*[181]

He has been able to share his cancer experience on many occasions. For example, in a Radio Newcastle interview in August 2021, he was able to say, '*My Christian faith was a massive help to me when I was diagnosed.*' He was able to explain that this enabled him to live one day at a time.[182]

## Christian Vision for Men

When I spoke to Steve about Michael, his first reaction was to exclaim,

181. Psalm 91:1-2
182. Radio Newcastle, *Gilly Hope Show* (August 23rd 2021).

'*What a guy!*' Steve had been in and out of prison throughout much of his life, but he now feels that his life has been transformed since he gave himself to the Lord, through Michael's influence. Steve is a member of the Gateshead branch of Christian Vision for Men, which Michael established in 2014. Steve describes the meetings held in a local pub as being '*awesome*', and even when the meetings were forced to go online because of Covid restrictions, he continued to look forward to them so that he could '*have the joy of meeting with like-minded guys*'. Steve finds Michael a real inspiration.

Over the past few years, Christian Vision for Men has been the most important part of Michael's ministry. He longs to see more men coming to Jesus, and, as such, he shares the vision of the CVM organisation, which wants to stem the decline in male church attendance and Christian involvement. As the CVM website declares, '*We need to create an environment that makes the Christian faith accessible to the average UK man and church a place worth hauling themselves out of bed for*.'[183]

Michael has a particular concern about suicide rates amongst men, understandable given his own experience of attempting suicide. In 2019, the male suicide rate in England and Wales was 16.9 deaths per 100,000 of the male population; the corresponding female suicide rate was 5.3 deaths per 100,000. In other words, over three quarters of suicides were males.[184] For Michael, the gospel had to provide the answer to men's inner longings, and he knew that Jesus could meet men's deepest needs.

CVM would be the vehicle that Michael would use to develop men's ministry. In 2014, he was asked to be area coordinator, and so the Gateshead meetings started as Men's Curry Nights. Regular evening meetings were held in a Wetherspoon's pub, with on average about twenty to twenty-five men attending (indeed sometimes well over thirty men came along), enjoying each other's company in relaxed

183. https://www.cvm.org.uk/why-mens-ministry (accessed 16.12.21).

184. Office for National Statistics, *Suicides in England and Wales: 2019 registrations.*

surroundings and listening to a speaker's testimony. Michael and his team also organised social events with day trips to different places. The result was that men did get to hear the gospel, and a number responded by becoming Christians. With their newly found faith, they started reaching out to others.

Michael was still working full time on the Metro and, of course, he still had his cancer. He had, however, made his promise to God that he would allow God to use him for the sake of the kingdom in whatever time he had left. In 2016 he was asked to become regional director for the north-east. This required him to go out on the road visiting men's groups to encourage them in their work, as well as speaking in churches to persuade them to develop their men's ministries. He was even interviewed on BBC Radio Newcastle to share with a wider audience the work of CVM in the region.

Despite the restrictions of the pandemic, Michael has continued his work with CVM using the medium of Zoom. As we saw from Steve's comments, men continue to look forward to these meetings.

## Other ministries

While still playing a leading role in CVM, Michael has broadened his interests and has become involved in other ministries. He has, for example, been greatly influenced by Richard Trotter, the director of Reaper Ministries International; indeed, it was Richard who pointed him in the direction of CVM. In 2019 Michael became a trustee of Reaper Ministries International. The charity works closely with churches in developing countries to help them develop their ministries, including providing free education to children from poor communities.

Michael has a particular heart for the Good Hope School project in Lilongwe, the capital city of Malawi, established by Reaper Ministries in 2008. This is a Christian primary school providing free education for about six hundred children. Funding comes solely from donations, which means that resources are very tight. For example, pupil teacher ratios are very high, with currently forty-two pupils per teacher. Buildings are in a state of disrepair and other resources need to be upgraded.

Reaper Ministries are also involved in helping a range of vulnerable people in Malawi, including the victims of domestic violence, through a ministry called Hope for the Hopeless, established in 2019. The work of this ministry was highlighted in a television news broadcast on *Zodiak News* in Malawi in January 2021. The news item covered the tragic story of Marietta whose violent husband had chopped off her hands and left her struggling to look after her family with her disability. Hope for the Hopeless were able to provide supplies and emotional support to Marietta. Domestic violence is very much on the increase in Malawi, and the charity aims to show the love of Jesus by providing much-needed support to victims.

As a trustee, Michael spends a great deal of time in support of Richard Trotter and the ongoing work of the charity. He has, for example, been able to recommend suitable candidates for a prayer ministry; these prayer warriors commit themselves to praying for the charity as prayer ambassadors. He is also involved in finding sponsors for the charity to raise much-needed funds to meet the desperate needs of the people whom they are trying to help.

Prayer is central to Michael's life. He has seen many answers to prayer, not least in his own life. Prayer, however, is not restricted to his own locality, but rather it has a global dimension. He prayed for a lady in Pakistan called Shazia, who had been bedridden with cancer, but after prayer, she has been able to get up and get on with her daily business. Another lady from Pakistan called Shaheen had suffered from terrible stomach pains for over seventeen years. Again, she has been healed as God answered the prayers of Michael and others.

Michael has for some time organised monthly prayer meetings, originally meeting in person, but now on Zoom. The meetings started with six men, but they have grown and include people from all over the world, now meeting fortnightly. A great delight for Michael is that one of his old school teachers comes to the meetings.

Very much aware of his cancer and how God had helped him through his illness, Michael has sought opportunities to help those who were suffering in a similar way. Through Lymphoma Action, he joined their buddy scheme to support others who had the same illness. After undergoing training in Birmingham, he became a support buddy in 2016. As a result, he has been able to get alongside others, empathising with them in their illness. Although Lymphoma Action is not a specifically Christian charity, he has been able to show the love of God in action. This has been particularly vital during the pandemic when sufferers would otherwise feel completely isolated.

At the time of writing, Michael is seeking the Lord's will to undertake other areas of service. Since the beginning of the first lockdown in March 2020, he has had to shield because of his medical condition. By April 2021 his time of shielding was due to end, but by that time Michael felt that it was not right for him to return to work. He and his wife Maria prayed about it one day in April and amazingly, twenty minutes after they had finished praying, he received a phone call from his manager at work asking if he had considered the possibility of retiring from work on the grounds of ill-health. This was a wonderful answer to their prayers. Michael and Maria did, however, have to show patience over this matter, and he admitted that it was a worrying time. It was not until July 22nd, ten weeks later, after praying about it again, that he received another phone call saying that his request for early retirement had been accepted. Furthermore, by the grace of God, his retirement would be on maximum pension, which would allow him the expenses that he would need for travelling to places like Malawi and Pakistan for the sake of the gospel.

## Conclusion

Michael Bushby is a man with a real passion for Jesus, desiring to live for him and sharing his love with others. By getting alongside other men, he is able to contend for the truth of the gospel. His ministries with Christian Vision for Men, Reaper Ministries International, the City Centre Chaplaincy and Lymphoma Action have all been used by God, often in ways of which Michael is not aware. Even his actions of kindness towards others, such as mowing the lawns of elderly neighbours, demonstrate his deep love for God and his love for other people.

Nigel Moore, who serves with Junction 42, a Christian ministry that works with offenders, spoke very highly of Michael. Nigel very much appreciates his '*ability to connect, inform and communicate as well as his overall leadership qualities*'.

In his workplace, his services were greatly valued. On his retirement in August 2021, his managers spoke appreciatively of his work on the line and as a chaplain in an article on the Nexus website. Head of Metro Operations Delivery, Kevin Storey, said:

> *We are all going to miss Michael and we wish him well for the future. He has given outstanding service to the Tyne and Wear Metro over the last three decades. As a Metro driver he has mentored many trainees over the years, and he managed all of that after beating cancer and returning to work. Michael's role as a chaplain has also been of huge support to us. He's provided colleagues with pastoral care when they needed it, showing great warmth, compassion, and empathy. He'll be a big miss.*[185]

One of his former colleagues wrote to him, describing him as '*a Metro legend who will be sorely missed*'.

---

185. https://www.nexus.org.uk/news/item/metro-chaplain-michael-bushby-retires-after-30-years-service (accessed 16.12.21).

His life, as we have seen, has not been easy, from his tough upbringing through to his experience with cancer. He is of course still living with cancer and yet, because of his hope in Jesus, he has no fear of it. He has learned lessons, which he has found useful to share through the pandemic experience: not to take things for granted, that life is fragile but nonetheless it is a gift from God, and that we can see new opportunities from God in whatever circumstances we find ourselves.

Michael has a huge network that he keeps in touch with, informing them of upcoming events, as well as sending them encouraging texts and videos. One particular video that he sent out was a personal message from himself. It was set in Beamish Woods, a beautiful place that Michael often goes to in order to '*get lost with God*'. It is a place where he can follow the words of the Lord in Psalm 46, '*Be still, and know that I am God*'.[186] Michael tells his listeners about the good news of Jesus who came to earth, lived among us, died on the cross for us and rose again and that '*all who call upon the name of Jesus shall be saved*'. He reflects that life is not always easy, but that Jesus wants to live that life with us: '*I came through cancer myself and am still living with cancer. I know that when I lay my life down, I have been promised eternal life because I gave my life to Jesus*.' Finally, he quietly presents a challenge to his listeners, which sums up his ministry as he contends for truth, '*We all live with choices. What choice are you going to make today? Are you going to die lost or are you going to live in eternity with Jesus as your Saviour?*'

186. Psalm 46:10

# Chapter 19: Barbara Connor

Barbara Connor and I both come from the same town in Central Scotland, Grangemouth, known for its oil refinery with large cooling towers, and described in my primary school geography lessons as a 'boom town'. For all the prosperity, however, my recollection from the 1960s through to the mid-1970s was that spiritually the town was at a low ebb. There were a number of churches, but very few where somebody could find out about how to become a Christian and grow spiritually in their Christian lives. God, however, had not forgotten Grangemouth, and particularly its young people; he reached out to the young people in the town in different ways, although apart from two or three exceptions, it was not through the churches.

The starting point was when Norman Reid, a young science teacher, was appointed to lead the chemistry department in the town's high school. As well as being an excellent teacher, Norman was a committed Christian, and was keen to see the rather languishing Scripture Union group (as Christian Unions tended to be called in Scottish schools) becoming a vital force in the school. Weekly meetings were held, with the aim of presenting Christianity as fun, although with a more fundamental aim of introducing young people to Jesus Christ. Over time the meetings expanded to include a Saturday night evangelistic club, house meetings and various trips, as well as linking in with camps and conferences. This had an effect on a number of school students, and I for one saw real-live Christianity for the first time, and it was through Scripture Union that I became a Christian.[187]

187. For more detail on how the author came to faith, please refer to Jim Cockburn, *All by Grace: 21 Years of Christian Headship* (Onward and Upwards Publishers, 2017), pp. 21-24.

Norman's work with young people grew beyond the school, and out of it was born what was called the Grangemouth Fellowship. This was basically a Christian fellowship for young people across the town, where they could explore and grow in their faith. There was a wide range of activities, with a strong emphasis on discipling young people. When they came to faith, they were encouraged to be of service within the activities of the fellowship. For example, Saturday morning children's clubs were run to reach children for Jesus, and the teenage Christians were trained to be involved in serving in the clubs. In this way, Christian young people learned from a fairly early age what it meant to serve God and to pray for the extension of his kingdom.

Some good work with young people took place in a couple of the churches. The Brethren assembly attracted a large number of children and young people, and some of them got involved in Grangemouth Fellowship activities. A Baptist church was planted and met in a community centre, and Norman and his wife Gill became active members of this fellowship. A number of the Grangemouth Fellowship young people made this their local church, and again were involved in serving the Lord particularly in children's work, including summer holiday clubs.

One of the key young people in all of these activities was Barbara Connor, who first came to high school and joined the Scripture Union group in my last year at school. It was wonderful to see her develop as a Christian, and many people commented that she was mature beyond her years. Not only did she have a love for the Lord, but she also had strong leadership skills and a passion for others to come to know Jesus and become his followers. She very much bought into the philosophy of training and service that was such a key part of the Grangemouth Fellowship strategy, and what she learned then would underpin much of her future ministry in working with children and young people across the world.

After Ella and I left Grangemouth in 1977, we did not have much personal contact with Barbara, apart from her regular ministry newsletters that we received in later years. Therefore it was a real privilege for me to meet up with her on Zoom, seeing her in her home in Malaga, to discuss the material for this chapter. It was good for me to hear that despite her worldwide travelling, there still remained a Grangemouth accent!

## The preparation years

Barbara, like the rest of her family, had always gone to church, but it was at the age of twelve that she became a Christian through a Sunday school holiday camp run by the Brethren assembly. From that point on, she became very serious about following Jesus, and although she lived in many ways a normal teenage life, she refused to be drawn into the smoking, drinking and drugs culture of some of her peers, knowing that that was not the lifestyle that Jesus wanted her to follow. Her stand for the Lord did have an effect on others, including members of her own family. Her mother became a Christian when Barbara was about fourteen, partly through Barbara's influence and partly through the influence of a colleague at work. Her father became a Christian about a year later.

The Brethren assembly was a source of good Christian teaching for Barbara in her early days as a Christian, and George Wilson and Beth Easton had a strong influence on her and other young people. It was, however, through the school Scripture Union group, the Grangemouth Fellowship, and the newly planted Baptist church that Barbara was able to develop her ministry skills in working with children and young people. As a teenager, she was given responsibility for leading children's activities and young people's Bible studies. She also helped to plan major events like summer missions. All of these experiences had a major impact on Barbara's life. Thinking about that time in the 1970s she was able to say:

*I feel very privileged when I look back now. For the past forty years I have been part of a ministry whose highest value is believing in the spiritual capacity of children and youth, that children and youth can know God, hear his voice and serve him; this for some people is still quite radical. Yet I can look back on that experience in my own life where people believed in us and released us to lead things, give teachings and preach in church when we were still young teenagers.*

Barbara had a great love for languages, and was very gifted in language learning, and so, in 1977, she went to Glasgow University to study French and German. She attended Christian Union meetings, but she did not feel that was her main ministry; her calling at that time was to go back to Grangemouth at weekends and be involved in children's and youth ministry there. She continued in the leadership role that she had begun in her young teenage years.

As a languages student, she was required to have a year abroad in order to be immersed in the language and culture of a particular area. In 1979 she spent a year in northern France and was heavily involved in a church which did a lot of local evangelism and put a great deal of emphasis on intercessory prayer. Barbara learned a lot working with that particular church. She also, for the first time, came across Youth with a Mission (YWAM or in French, Jeunesse en Mission), and helped them on short-term outreaches, which she continued to do during future summer vacations. Barbara was used by the Lord to reach people during this time in France, although at the time she was not always fully aware of what happened to the seed that she was sowing. For example, in 2008 she met a YWAM France leader who told her that she had played a major part in him becoming a Christian in 1979; it was almost thirty years later that Barbara discovered how God had been at work in this man's life.

She returned to complete her degree in Glasgow and graduated in 1981. Knowing that she would be working with young people, she took a teacher training course at Jordanhill College in Glasgow to train as a secondary school languages teacher.[188] It was, however, going to be three years before she actually started teaching in Scottish schools, as she was first of all going to go abroad to work with YWAM.

## YWAM and KKI

YWAM, the organisation that Barbara started working with, was founded in 1960 on the basis of a vision that a young American student, Loren Cunningham, received from God. As he read his Bible one night, he saw waves crashing on the world's continents, ultimately covering the continents. He later wrote: '*I caught my breath. Then, as I watched, the scene changed. The waves became young people – kids my age and even younger – covering the continents. They were talking to people on the street corners and outside bars. They were going house to house. They were preaching.*'[189] This vision came to fruition as YWAM was founded and started to train young people to go into different communities worldwide to share the gospel of Christ. Since then, hundreds of thousands of young people have done missionary service with YWAM in over 180 countries. Barbara was one of these young people.

In 1982 she moved to Austria, where she taught English as a foreign language, and worked part-time with YWAM in Austria and France. After two years of part-time service, she worked full-time taking part in a fourteen-month school of evangelism. This involved a variety of experiences, including receiving training in Lausanne, outreach in Burkina Faso and the Ivory Coast, mobile team ministry travelling to serve local churches all over France and supporting them in their local

188. Indeed, Barbara used to tell people from the age of eight that she wanted to be a French teacher, even before she started to learn languages at all.
189. https://ywam.org/about-us/history/ (accessed 17.12.21).

evangelism, and outreach in different parts of Europe. Barbara gained so much from this work, including her African experiences, which would stand her in good stead as her ministry developed in future years.

This period was also a very fruitful time, with people hearing the gospel and responding in faith. Similar to the case mentioned above of the YWAM France leader, sometimes it was not until many years later that Barbara saw the full extent of what God had actually done. For example, in 2019 she was involved in a tree-planting project in Senegal when a lady in her fifties, who was on the camp with her daughter, asked to speak to Barbara. The lady explained that she remembered Barbara from her time in the Ivory Coast in 1985, and how Barbara led her to commit her life to the Lord following an open-air performance. The girl at the time was only fifteen, and here she was back meeting Barbara with her daughter thirty-four years later, and still going on in her faith.

In 1985, Barbara returned to Scotland for two years, when she taught in schools in Stirling and Falkirk. She believed that God very graciously gave her these jobs, at a time of high teacher unemployment. She still felt the calling, however, to undertake Christian ministry in Europe.

During the school summer holidays, Barbara went back to Europe to be involved in outreach activities in France and Austria. By 1988 she was ready to work full-time with YWAM in Austria, initially running discipleship training programmes in the mountain regions, before moving to the capital Vienna where she was involved in working with traditional churches, most of which were Catholic. The emphasis of much of the work was in bringing together born-again Christians from different church traditions to understand each other and grow together in their faith. The aim, as Barbara expressed it, was '*to see people really radical for following God*'.

It was during this time in Austria that she started working with the King's Kids International (KKI) movement within YWAM. KKI started in 1976, and its foundation is the Scripture verses given by Moses to the Israelite nation in Deuteronomy 6:6-8:

*These commandments that I give you today are to be on your hearts. Impress them on your children. Talk about them when you sit at home and when you walk along the road, when you lie down and when you get up. Tie them as symbols on your hands and bind them on your foreheads.*

In 1976, Dale and Carol Kauffman were working on a YWAM discipleship training programme in Honolulu. They felt led to work with the children of the members of the programme to teach them the ways of God, that they might listen to his voice and serve him. They then took them out in their van to put into practice what they had learned. The children spoke to people in the streets through the programme they had prepared. One lady approached Dale and fell down on her knees, saying, '*The children are so pure, I'm so dirty. Please help me!*' She gave her life to the Lord. That was not the end, however, as one boy from the group approached Dale and said, '*Dale, this is the first one.*' He was right; amazingly, other adults were falling on their knees to commit themselves to the Lord, as they heard the gospel from these children and young people.[190]

This small but dramatic event was the beginning of a ministry that would again span the globe, with hundreds of thousands involved in KKI outreaches and projects. The fundamental aim of KKI is to love and obey God in the belief that children and young people have the spiritual capacity to know God, hear his voice and follow his leading.

Many lives have been transformed through the ministry of KKI over the years. One person who was heavily influenced by KKI in her early Christian life is the theologian Amy Orr-Ewing, whom we saw in chapter 17 working alongside Andy Bannister in Oxford, where she was the director of the Centre for Apologetics. She wrote this about her experience with KKI as a teenager:

190. https://kki.global/who-we-are/history/ (accessed 17.12.21).

> *As the teenage years kicked in, I became involved with a ministry of YWAM, which was called King's Kids. We went all over the world doing performing arts and evangelism in the summer holidays. The leaders were absolutely phenomenal Christians who believed that children and young people could minister in the power of the Holy Spirit. In 1991, shortly after the collapse of Communism in Eastern Europe, a team of us went to the Czech Republic. Thousands were on the streets of Prague and we were performing on Charles Bridge and Wenceslas Square. As a fifteen-year-old I was given the opportunity to share testimonies and preach the gospel in the open air to these crowds.*[191]

This was the sort of work that Barbara was involved in with KKI, initially in Austria and later in other parts of Europe and in Africa. Children, young people and families were mobilised to spread the gospel through open-air events using drama, music and dance. Lots of people attended these events, enjoyed the high-quality performances and listened to the testimonies of the young people as they shared their faith. For some this was the first step in thinking about the claims of Christ and God's offer of salvation, whereas for others it was the time where they decided to commit their lives to the Lord.

These were exciting times for Barbara and the teams that she was working with. Unfortunately, she became seriously ill in 1989, with a combination of pleurisy and whooping cough. The Austrian doctors were becoming increasingly concerned, as she did not seem to be responding to their treatment, and so it was felt that she should go back to Scotland for more specialist care. Her Scottish doctors realised that nobody had diagnosed the whooping cough and so she had not received medication for that particular illness. She seemed to recover, and so she went back to Austria in 1990, but unfortunately she became very ill again. At that point she decided to relocate to Scotland.

191. https://kki.global/who-we-are/testimonies/ (accessed 17.12.21).

Although she had hospital appointments every three weeks, she did not allow her illness to stand in the way of her ministry. She involved herself in the Principles of Child and Youth Ministries (PCYM) training school and became the national leader of KKI in Scotland. Over the next seven years she led a number of mobilising events with children, young people and families reaching out to people with the gospel across the United Kingdom, Europe, Africa and America. This included leading outreach teams at the 1992 Barcelona and 1996 Atlanta Olympics.

The work that she was leading at this time based in Scotland, but travelling overseas, had grown out of the work that she had done in Grangemouth twenty years before. In working with children, she believed very strongly that she should not in any way be manipulating them. Norman Reid had given the advice that we should make it as hard as possible for children to become Christians; it was so easy for children to pray a prayer of commitment to please the leader. If it were a genuine working of the Spirit, children would respond without any undue pressure being put on them. Barbara followed that through by encouraging children to go home and pray that prayer on their own and then come back and let her know whether they had prayed it or not.

Discipling children and young people was fundamental to Barbara's ministry. She had seen too many new converts, including some of her own school friends, start off with enthusiasm, but then slip back due to '*the worries of this life and the deceitfulness of wealth*' as Jesus predicted in his Parable of the Sower in Matthew chapter 13. As she herself said, '*That shaped my desire to be very involved in discipleship, helping people to grow for the long haul in following God.*'

Also, when she ran discipleship training programmes, which tended to be taken by people in their twenties, and talked about issues such as the need to forgive others or how to hear the voice of God, she would hear too many people say, '*I wish that I had learned this earlier.*' This made her refocus and put a greater emphasis on discipling children and young people from an earlier age, to lay important foundations that would help them grow in the Lord and serve him.

## Contending for truth in Africa

Although from 1990 to 1997 Barbara was officially based in Scotland, she spent an increasing amount of time in Africa. She was invited to start KKI in Southern Africa, and so she went out there in 1993 with some students to do some pioneering work, initially for six months, followed by an eighteen-month stint in 1995 and 1996.

By 1998 she felt that she could not really justify being based in Scotland and spending so much time in Africa, and so she decided that it was right for her to relocate to Cape Town in South Africa. She was there for a further nine years. Her health was still an issue over all these years in Africa, and indeed her doctors in Scotland had not wanted her to make that first trip in 1993. Nevertheless, Barbara decided to trust God in leading her to Africa. Looking back, Barbara is amazed at what God enabled her to do given her serious lung condition.[192]

The 1990s were exciting times in South Africa. The apartheid era came to an end when Nelson Mandela, the former anti-apartheid revolutionary, became president in 1994, replacing F.W. de Klerk in the first multiracial general election. This was the beginning of a new era for South Africa. Barbara experienced this during her shorter stays from 1993 to 1996 and her more permanent stay from 1998 to 2007. She looks back at these years as her '*best ministry years*'.

In her first visit to South Africa in 1993 to pioneer the work there, Barbara took an international, multiracial team of young people from ten European countries, along with South African families. This team would model the KKI principles of listening to God and believing in the spiritual capacity of young people to reach out to others. Children,

192. Barbara's illness is officially bronchiectasis, where the airways of the lungs become widened, leading to a build up of mucus and an increased vulnerability to infection.

young people and families toured the country, holding open-air events to share the gospel. These events attracted large crowds who would hear the testimonies of the young people and see God at work through his Holy Spirit transforming lives.

Although these were exciting times of change for South Africa, they were also dangerous times. The end of the apartheid era could have resulted in a blood bath for the country, but amazingly that did not happen, as Christians prayed for peace and reconciliation in the country. Although there were sporadic outbreaks of violence, overall the transition from the de Klerk era to the Mandela era was generally peaceful. The team in 1993 spent much time in prayer for the country as they did their tour and, through it all, God protected them. On one occasion, they had the chance to visit Soweto, the huge township adjoining Johannesburg that had hit the international headlines in 1976 as a result of a massive violent protest against apartheid that became known as the Soweto Uprising. The team prayed about the invitation that they had been given; the answer that God gave them was that they should continue with their planned ministry programme. As Barbara put it, '*We were not there to be Christian tourists.*' God had warned them that they should not go to Soweto, which was just as well, because on the day they were due to go, there was a large riot there, and they would have been caught up in it.

Barbara did much work with churches in that initial visit through leading seminars on the spiritual capacity of young people. She was able to see a massive change in attitude over time as a result of her work. The South African culture suggested that children should be seen but not heard, but Barbara presented the concept of the spiritual capacity of young people as a biblical principle. The Dutch Reformed churches, in many ways very traditional, fairly quickly grasped the concept of children and young people hearing the voice of God and praying and speaking in church. This was because they had a strong biblical foundation, and so they responded well to biblical examples such as Samuel as a child hearing the voice of God, David fighting against Goliath, or the young Timothy going on mission with Paul.

Seeing and hearing children involved in praying for the nation also had a very powerful effect on the churches in the country. Barbara and her colleagues set up 'Daniel prayer groups' in the 1990s, following Daniel's practice of praying at three set times in the day.[193] Children and young people interceded in these groups for their nation and other nations of the world. There were hundreds of such groups established over the country. Also, as churches saw the power of children and young people praying, there was an increased impetus, too, amongst adult church members to be involved in praying for their nation and other countries.

Barbara and her colleagues were also able to take teams of Southern African young people on mission to other countries, even as far away as China. An example of this was during the Atlanta Olympics in 1996, when a team of African young people flew to the United States to share their faith during the Olympics. This included some very poor young people, who had very little in terms of this world's wealth. They found it amazing that God had provided for them to fly in a plane (with special headrest covers provided by the airline saying, '*Welcome King's Kids South Africa*') to the richest country in the world to tell people about Jesus. During this trip, they linked up with African-American churches, and they sought forgiveness from the black Americans for their forefathers' involvement in the Atlantic slave trade. Although white slave traders played a heinous role in the trade, black people in Africa were involved in enslaving and selling members of their own race, similar to the experience of Joseph who was sold by his brothers into slavery; this reference to Joseph motivated the young people to seek forgiveness from African Americans when they went to Atlanta. This was very much God's grace at work.

---

193. Daniel 6:10

The teams that Barbara worked with were all multiracial, a new experience for South Africa. It was important that different ethnic groups and nationalities were seen to be working together, as these teams would be role models for young people in the new South Africa. Many parents were so glad that their children were given the opportunity to work together in these multiracial teams. The teams were, of course, a reflection of God's absolutely inclusive love for people of all races, classes and backgrounds. There is no favouritism based on colour in the kingdom of God.

During her time in Southern Africa, as well as mobilising teams of children, young people and families for outreach, Barbara wanted to ensure that young Christians were discipled so that they grew in their knowledge of God and thus served him more effectively. She wrote curriculum materials for what she calls '*the emerging generations*', a practice that she recalled started with the materials that she wrote in Grangemouth back in the 1970s. Training others to work with children and young people took up an increasing amount of time, but she felt that it was important to pass on to others what God had taught her in order for the kingdom to grow.

There was one other African country that Barbara and her teams worked in, and that was Senegal in West Africa. Planting Together started in 2011 (a few years after Barbara had relocated to Europe) and was part of an intergovernmental project to plant 'a great green wall' across Africa from east to west, from Djibouti to Senegal. This huge wall of trees (fifteen kilometres thick and stretching over seven thousand kilometres) aims to prevent the Sahara Desert from advancing and devouring the northern villages of sub-Saharan Africa. Over a number of summers, Barbara has led multinational teams on this crucial environmental project. Typically, the teams would come together in an orientation camp, learning from God and thus preparing themselves to serve others, before travelling to their tree-planting areas. The teams would also be involved in children's ministry, sports ministry and friendship evangelism, and doctors and dentists on the teams would set up clinics to help deal with health problems, with some people walking for two days to receive treatment.

The local Senegalese communities very much appreciated the work of the teams. Senegal is predominantly a Muslim country, and this was an opportunity to share the love of Jesus with people of a different faith. One meeting that Barbara felt was very much of God was with a local marabout in 2016. This man was a Muslim holy man who also practised witchcraft for healing and foretelling the future. After team members had a three-hour-long conversation with him, he said, '*I believe that God ordained this meeting between us. When you come back, please come and speak with us again*.' Sure enough, the 2017 team met the marabout, but this time they went to his home and met with members of his family as well. Barbara wrote in her November 2017 prayer letter: '*This was kind of surreal! As they sat there, drinking their glasses of fermented goat's milk with mint spices, our team members had the opportunity to speak about Jesus with this prominent and influential Muslim family . . . The men all pulled out their mobile phones to record every word that was said*.'

## Leadership development

By 2007, Barbara felt that God was calling her to leave Cape Town to go back to Europe. This was hard as she had fifteen years of wonderful memories and, furthermore, she did not have a clear vision as to which country she should be settling in. She felt a bit like Abram who had left Haran on God's calling without really knowing where he was going.[194] In 2008, she settled in Malaga in Spain, where her former colleagues, Stephe and Rite Mayers, were working to establish a leadership training centre. When Barbara was based in Scotland, she and Stephe set up YWAM's first Leadership Development Course (LDC) in Ayrshire in

194. Genesis 12:1

1994. They were going to develop these courses further in Malaga in the coming years.

Leadership Development Courses multiplied across the globe in the years following that first one in Ayrshire. The aim is to train current leaders to evaluate their own leadership journey and be better equipped to develop future leaders. Barbara sees clearly the need for leaders to '*finish well*', as there are so many examples from the Bible and the present day of leaders who had started well but for various reasons have slipped from God's standards. Hundreds of leaders have benefited from these courses in over twenty countries.

Part of the original vision for LDCs in 1994 was the establishment of a Leadership Retreat Centre where leaders can come and learn from God how he wants their leadership to develop. That was not possible at the time, but Stephe and Rite were now given the vision to establish a centre in Malaga, and Barbara was with them when it opened in October 2008.

The centre had made a great impact on hundreds of leaders who had been hosted there, giving them an opportunity to reflect and learn. In 2018, however, it was decided to close the centre after ten years of very fruitful operation. There was a demand for LDCs to be run in different countries, but if leaders such as Barbara and the Mayers were travelling to expand the work internationally they could not sustain the work of the centre. Barbara explained it in words of Scripture they had received in terms of pruning: '*If we cut off some branches here, it will allow multiplication internationally.*' With the closing of the centre, Barbara had more freedom to travel to support courses elsewhere, until the global pandemic intervened.

As a result of the restrictions on travel imposed by the pandemic in 2020 and 2021, there were fewer opportunities to run 'in person' LDCs. Courses were, however, still held using video-conferencing, and so as a result of this technology, it was possible to continue with a programme of leadership development. Barbara also delivered coaching sessions, where she encouraged people to set goals for themselves and work out strategies to move towards these goals. These sessions have brought great blessing to many people. One example of a testimony of the power of coaching came from a missionary in the Balkans who wrote:

> *Several families in our team had faced situations of crisis or loss in 2019 and this plunged the whole team into a slightly traumatic time of transition. My coaching sessions with Barbara helped me as the team leader to process and apply practical steps that enabled us to re-find unity as a team and discern what God's will is for our corporate ministry in the year that lies ahead.*

## Conclusion

Barbara has been on the frontline for the Lord for about fifty years, going back to her school and university days and the work that she did in Grangemouth, and then going into her many years with KKI and YWAM mobilising young people for mission and training current and future leaders. Prayer has been a fundamental part of her life, as she cast herself on the Lord to seek his will and to pray that God would open the eyes and hearts of those she was trying to reach. As she did so, she sought to hear God speaking to her and, through Scripture or an inner conviction, she has felt led by the Lord and protected throughout.

This does not mean that things have always been easy. Leaving South Africa and later closing the Leadership Retreat Centre were hard decisions, but in each case she knew that this was how God was leading. We have seen how her health has been a major issue from her bronchiectasis in the late 1980s to more recently developing other illnesses such as osteoarthritis. God answered her prayers and those of her supporters to allow her to continue in her ministries.

Barbara has influenced so many people across the world by her godly living and vibrant witness to the truth, following her calling from the

Lord. But her work is not yet finished. Before her sixtieth birthday, she was asked if she would be retiring from missionary work. She gave a resounding '*no*' in response. The nature of her work has now changed '*from mobilising teams of young people for short-term missions, preaching the gospel in the streets and other public places, sleeping on the floor and travelling in dusty Land Rovers on bumpy dirt tracks*' to influencing people indirectly through leadership training, mentoring and coaching.

> *Paradoxically, as I've spent an increasing number of hours behind my computer, I've seen that my indirect involvement, in coaching and mentoring younger leaders and new missionaries, is ultimately influencing a much greater number of people than those I could reach personally during my decades of more direct involvement.*

# Chapter 20: Donald Curry

Donald Curry - or to give him his full title, Baron Curry of Kirkharle, CBE - is one of those men who can make people of all backgrounds feel very comfortable in his presence, whether they be local farmers, Whitehall bureaucrats, government ministers, peers of the realm or the heir to the throne. Born into a Northumberland farming family, rising to run his own tenant farm, representing farming interests at the highest level of public life, dealing with national agricultural crises and becoming a member of the House of Lords, he has been consistently highly respected as a man who knows what he is talking about, who cares about people and who wants to make the world a better place.

What matters most to Donald, however, is that he wants to serve Jesus, his Lord and Master in all areas of his life. In June 2018, I invited him to speak to the Mid-Northumberland Christian Vision for Men group (the group that I mentioned in chapter 18), on the subject 'A Lord in the Lords for the Lord'. The pub in which we were meeting that Saturday morning was packed out as men clamoured to hear about the workings of the Upper House and about Donald's testimony as a Christian serving there.

I learned more about Donald's life and how he was able to contend for truth by having Zoom conversations with him, reading his contributions to parliamentary debates in Hansard, and talking to three men, Andy Cowan, Ben Cadoux-Hudson and Gordon Gatward, about the influence that Donald has had in their lives.

## Early life

Donald was born towards the end of the Second World War into a Christian farming family in the Coquet Valley in Northumberland. For Donald, growing up on the farm was a marvellous experience with tractors, horses and the beautiful countryside around him. He was the eldest of five children, who enjoyed the security and stability of being brought up by loving Christian parents. They belonged to the Christian Brethren, and worshipped in an assembly in the village of Thropton, now called Armstrong Hall. As a youngster, Donald found his life '*a great experience, with Christian parents, Christian families, all of the friends we had were Christians, and we were part of a large family network*'.

It was important, however, for Donald to find his own faith, and not simply rely upon the faith of his parents. During one particular Sunday service when he was thirteen, Donald felt that God was speaking to him directly, and so he made a personal commitment to Christ.

> *God spoke to me that night and the message hit home, even though I had heard it week after week after week. It is amazing how at one point in time the Holy Spirit was at work, and I suddenly for the first time thought that I had to do something about it – this was for me – I need to make a personal commitment. I did, and it was absolutely a life-changing experience.*

After he left school, Donald was determined to continue working in agriculture, despite the fact that his father tried to dissuade him from doing so. He went on a day-release basis to Kirkley Hall, the local agricultural college, where he particularly enjoyed farm management and accounting, which would be of great use to him in his future career. In 1966, he married Rhoda, with whom he has spent over fifty years of happy married life, supporting each other as they raised their family, which, as we shall see, was not without difficulty, and together trying to serve the Lord. After trying to secure a tenancy for two or three years, in 1971 Donald and Rhoda were successful in obtaining the tenancy of their own farm at Kirkharle in mid-Northumberland, which was a major step for them.

Part of his Christian service in his late teenage years and into his twenties involved working with others of his generation to organise youth events, which were called 'squashes' in the 1950s and '60s. Christian young people wanted to come together to seek fellowship and support in Christian meetings beyond the normal church programme. These squashes were held in the homes of Christian couples, where Christian young people would come together for Bible study and prayer.

Demand was such that these meetings outgrew homes, and so events were organised in village halls. Donald and other Christians took responsibility for organising youth rallies at Hedgeley Village Hall, near Alnwick. About a hundred young people attended these meetings regularly, which was an amazing turnout for a rural community. The programme had singing, testimonies, talks, and food to be shared afterwards. Many young people became Christians, as it was a safe environment in which to bring non-Christian friends to hear the message of the gospel.

These events had a major influence on Donald himself, as he felt blessed that he was able to serve in this way. It also led to preaching opportunities across a number of fellowships, where he attempted to expound Scripture as God led him. He also later joined a Christian Male Voice Choir, organised by Mrs Lizzie Cowan, and he sang at about twenty concerts in churches and village halls each year. This was a wonderful opportunity to proclaim the love of God to audiences. He and his friend Ozzy Johnson shared responsibility for giving a gospel message at these popular events.

One of the members of the choir was Andy Cowan, one of Lizzie's sons. Even though he supported his mother in the choir, Andy was at that time not a Christian. Lizzie earnestly and persistently prayed that her sons would come to know the Lord. For Andy, that happened on August 7th 1976. When the choir sang 'How Great Thou Art', a hymn that he had heard so many times before, Andy was on this occasion absolutely overwhelmed when he realised how much God loved him, in that he sent his Son to die on the cross for his sin.

At the end of the concert, Donald spoke about God's great love for us by sending Jesus to die for us, so that if we believe in him, we would have eternal life.[195] He explained that Jesus has done it all for us on the cross, and that there is something missing in our lives until we accept Jesus. Donald said, '*Tonight is your opportunity to receive the Lord.*' Andy explained his response: '*The Spirit of God just came down upon me like never before. I quietly asked Jesus to enter my life.*' As you can imagine, Lizzie was overjoyed when Andy told her that he had made a decision to follow Jesus. In the weeks to come, Donald and Rhoda became good friends with Andy (and his wife Joan) and nurtured him as a young Christian. Andy, now in his eighties, is still living powerfully for the Lord today.

## Family tragedies

Donald and Rhoda had a family of three children, Jonathan, Jane and Craig. Sadly, Jane died in 2013 at the age of forty-two.

When she was born, their daughter Jane had difficulty breathing, initially being starved of oxygen, and then, in order to try to compensate for that, she ended up being given too much oxygen. The overall consequence was that she suffered brain damage, and so after birth she failed to develop as a child normally would. Her severe learning disability meant that Donald and Rhoda had to give her a lot of time and attention, and it was tough for both of them. For example, she could not feed herself or dress herself. She did not walk until she was nine, and even then, because her leg muscles had not developed properly, she required calipers on her legs.

By the time she was fourteen, Donald and Rhoda felt that they needed more help, as they found it increasingly difficult to meet her needs as

195. John 3:16 was the main text that Donald used in his talk.

she grew bigger and heavier. They managed to obtain a place for Jane at Stelling Hall near Stocksfield, one of the National Children's Homes. This organisation had originally been founded by Reverend Thomas Bowman Stephenson, a Methodist Church minister, and it still had strong links with the Methodist Church. As a result, the home had quite a strong Christian ethos. She was well cared for there, but by the time she reached her early twenties and was deemed to be an adult, Donald and Rhoda had to find another solution for her.

There were a number of parents who were facing the same situation as Donald and Rhoda. Together they learned of a Christian charity called Prospects, which tried to support adults with learning disabilities by providing residential accommodation linked to a local church. The group contacted David Potter, the founder of Prospects, in the hope that he would set up a branch of the charity in the north-east. Unfortunately he felt that he could not help them as Prospects was working at full capacity, and so he told the group that they should set up their own organisation.

This was of course not the response that Donald, Rhoda and the others wanted to hear but, nonetheless, the challenge appealed to Donald's entrepreneurial spirit. He and other Christians eventually felt inspired to form a charity, At Home in the Community, based in the north-east. Its aim was to provide houses for up to five residents with learning disabilities and their carers, who would ideally be Christians. With support from the Social Services Department of Newcastle City Council, they opened their first home in the Walker area of the city. This led to a number of other homes being opened across the city and Northumberland, and Jane joined the home that opened in Hexham in 1992.

Donald chaired the board of the charity for twenty years, until it finally merged with Prospects. By the time he stood down from the chair, there were forty-five people living in the homes and the charity employed 130 staff. The charity had filled a gap in the provision for adults with learning disabilities and had a major impact on the lives of those it was trying to help, along with their parents, demonstrating the love of Jesus in practical ways.

Jane herself was well cared for by the brilliant staff in the Hexham home where she lived for over twenty years. Towards the end of her life she contracted pneumonia, after which she was very vulnerable to infections, and had difficulty feeding. After another bout of pneumonia, she sadly passed away in 2013. Donald and Rhoda had been on holiday, but they were able to get back in time and spend twenty-four hours with her in hospital before she died. Death is always sad, and the person who goes leaves a great void. The void is even greater when the person who goes has been so dependent on you. Donald and Rhoda, however, knew that God's timing is perfect, and trusted Jane into his loving care.

Although Jane had severe disabilities, she had nevertheless an amazing personality. Donald had this to say about her:

> *When Jane was in a humorous mood, she could influence a room. She had the ability to make everybody laugh, because she was laughing. Conversely, if she threw a tantrum, she could have an impact, and nothing was safe, and stuff could fly off the table. Anything in reach was at risk. She could grab some unsuspecting person by the hair.*

When Jane was born, Donald and Rhoda had asked themselves the question that most parents who were facing similar circumstances would ask: '*Why is this happening to us*?' Friends of theirs had a baby about the same time, and they announced it in the local newspaper with the verse '*Every good and perfect gift comes from above*.'[196] This made them wonder whether Jane was an imperfect gift, and although it took them a while

196. James 1:17

to work through the issues, they understood that everyone is created as an individual with a special place in God's heart. They knew that God does not make mistakes, and that Jane's life would have a lasting legacy. For example, it is very unlikely that At Home in the Community would have been formed as a Christian charity had it not been for the situation that Donald and Rhoda had found themselves in with Jane. Individuals were affected in different ways. As a result of looking after Jane, Donald and Rhoda drew on reserves of patience and tolerance that they did not know they had. Friends and family were also affected by Jane, and, as they met her, they learned to understand the nature of Jane's disability and became more tolerant people. Indeed, one of their nieces made a career choice to work with people with disabilities as a result of being with Jane.

One person who has been more recently influenced by Donald's testimony in looking after Jane is Ben Cadoux-Hudson, minister of St Oswald's Church in Newcastle. Donald has been acting as a mentor to Ben, providing him with encouragement and advice in his Christian ministry. It is most appropriate that Donald is Ben's mentor, as he and his wife Valentina also have a child, Nathan, who has serious disabilities. Ben and Valentina came under great pressure from the medical authorities to have the pregnancy terminated because of his disabilities. They refused on the grounds that this baby was a gift from God and had all the dignity of someone created in the image of God, and so deserved to live. From his and Rhoda's experience, Donald has been able to encourage them in their care of Nathan. He also encouraged them to write a book on the subject of abortion, which they have done together, along with Chris Richards, a Christian paediatrician who is also director of the Christian charity, Lovewise.[197] Donald encouraged Ben to have a

197. Chris Richards and Ben and Valentina Cadoux-Hudson, *Thinking About Abortion: Where Do We Begin?* (Evangelical Press, 2021).

real ambition for this book, that it would be used by God to help people who are struggling with the issue of abortion.

Jane's death, however, was not the only family tragedy to hit Donald and Rhoda. In May 2000, Donald lost his brother Stuart in a tragic farming accident at the age of forty-six. Stuart was crushed by a four-wheel-drive loader, the brakes of which had failed. As Donald expressed it, '*It was such a tragic experience. Stuart was such a lovely guy, very dedicated, very caring. We all asked why this had happened, because he was needed by his family. He was such an important, stable figure for the family. It was a devastating time.*'

The family came through this, supporting each other, and showed themselves to be very resilient. It was Stuart's son Matthew who released his father's body from the loader. He went through a rebellious period in his teens, but his faith was restored, and he is now a strong Christian. He works in the agricultural sector and also helps in leading Christian adventure camps.

Another tragedy was yet to come, however, this time affecting Donald's sister Sheena's family, who lived in Edinburgh. On May 30th 2007, Sheena's daughter, Rachel, was coming back home from collecting the children from school and nursery when a four-by-four car tore out of a junction opposite their house, failed to turn the corner and crashed into Rachel and four-year-old Olivia. Tragically, Olivia was killed, and Rachel had to have her leg amputated. The car just drove off, but the driver was later apprehended by the police, and was discovered to have been high on drugs.

This was an indescribably difficult time for Sheena's family, who were faithful, committed Christians. They had to ask God spiritually searching questions, such as why he allowed this tragedy to happen. This third tragedy, of course, brought great sadness to Donald as well. As he reflected on it, he was able to say:

*Everyone goes through dreadful, emotional sadness. It's awful having to face up to these issues; they are never ever forgotten, but are always there. There are reminders all the time of these tragedies that have taken place; whether it's the date in the calendar or birthdays or family gatherings, there is always the sense that these people are missing. I have to rationalise it, and we talk about it as a family. This is a fallen, sinful world, and the tarnishing impact of sin affects every aspect of life, and Christians are not immune from drug-fuelled drivers. We are not given a special cordon of protection around us. We are subject to the same influences as everybody else in this fallen world. Brakes fail, and Christians are not exempt from the tragedies of life. We need to see ourselves as transitioning through this sinful world, and our destination is more important than the journey. God's will is something we have to accept and subject ourselves to, no matter if it seems that it is an irrational, illogical, tragic waste of life when you experience these things. This is part of God's eternal plan, and where we are going is so much more important than where we are now.*

What Donald is saying is just what Paul wrote in Romans chapter 8: '*I consider that our present sufferings are not worth comparing with the glory that will be revealed in us.*'[198]

## Agricultural politics

Donald and Rhoda worked hard on their farm at Kirkharle, with Rhoda also opening a farmhouse bed-and-breakfast business that generated some more income for the family. Donald was a member of the local branch of the National Farmers' Union (NFU) at Cambo, and he was so respected by local farmers that he was elected chairman. He became more

198. Romans 8:18

widely known as he represented the Cambo branch at Northumberland branch meetings. He was later to be propelled into being a national figure at a time of crisis in the agricultural sector.

In 1985, he was appointed as a delegate to the NFU in London, and sat on subcommittees for livestock and cereals. He was later offered a place on a government body, the board of the Meat and Livestock Commission. In 1992 he became deputy chair of the board, then acting chair in 1993 and finally permanent chair nine months later, until he stepped down in 2001.

Donald becoming chair was at the peak of the BSE crisis that engulfed the livestock sector. BSE stands for 'bovine spongiform encephalopathy', a disease that affects the neurological systems of cattle, and has been commonly called 'mad cow disease'. Over four million head of cattle had to be slaughtered in the 1980s and '90s, causing great hardship to the agricultural community. There were other diseases which affected livestock during Donald's time as chair, including e-coli, salmonella and swine fever. His period as chair, however, culminated in 2001 with the outbreak of foot and mouth disease, which required the slaughtering of six million cows and sheep in a successful attempt to contain the outbreak.

He described his experience of being chair as '*fascinating, as here was a country boy from Northumberland operating at national level amidst the most serious period of crisis that the farming industry had experienced for decades*'. Donald had to use his massive knowledge of the industry and skills of diplomacy as he navigated his way through media interviews, meetings with government ministers and scientists, and reconciling differences of opinion in what he described as '*a complex matrix of interests*'. Although the experience for the industry was dreadful, Donald learned a whole new set of skills; for example, living in Northumberland he could never have imagined himself spending a day going round television and radio studios in London, giving interviews on the progress that was being made in dealing with the crisis.

He also had contact with Prince Charles, who provided a lot of assistance during his time on the board. For example, he was deeply concerned about the impact of BSE on beef farmers through tumbling prices, falling home demand and closed export markets. He took the initiative of inviting top chefs from across Europe to come to Britain to find out how safe British beef was. He and Donald hosted a meeting of these top chefs, and this turned out to be a great success, helping to restore confidence in British beef. They later worked together on a series of initiatives to provide support and advice to small family farms. Prince Charles set up the Prince's Countryside Fund in 2010, with Donald as one of the founding trustees and latterly as chair, with the aim of helping these small farmers.

Donald knew amidst all these crises that it was power from his Christian faith that enabled him to undertake these major responsibilities. He could say as David declared, '*Surely God is my help; the Lord is the one who sustains me.*'[199] He learned to rely more and more on the power of the Holy Spirit, as he himself did not have the resources to cope with all the issues that he had to deal with. Through it all, he experienced the peace that Jesus promised to his followers, '*Peace I leave with you; my peace I give you. I do not give to you as the world gives. Do not let your hearts be troubled and do not be afraid.*'[200]

After he retired from the Meat and Livestock Commission, he was asked by Tony Blair to chair a commission looking at the future of farming and food in England in order to report to the Secretary of State for Environment, Food and Rural Affairs. The Curry Commission, as it was called, received evidence from individuals and organisations from within the industry and beyond, and published its report with many

199. Psalm 54:4
200. John 14:27

recommendations in January 2002.[201] This report had a lasting impact on the farming sector.

Donald is the last person who would seek honour and glory for all of his work, but he was recognised through the honours system for what he had achieved. In 1997 he was made a Commander of the Order of the British Empire, and he had the pleasure of taking his mother to Buckingham Palace when he received his award from the Queen. In 2001, after he had retired from the Meat and Livestock Commission, he was knighted by Prince Charles on behalf of the Queen. Ten years later, he was approached to see if he would like to apply to become a cross-bench peer in the House of Lords. He was not initially sure about this, but he prayed that he would know God's will, and subsequently completed the application form, went for interview, and was finally created a cross-bench life peer. He took the title Baron Curry of Kirkharle, referring back to the farm he loved in Northumberland.

Donald was so grateful for these honours, but what was more important to him was being known as a Christian. He does admit that there were times when he did miss opportunities to speak for the Lord, but he was nevertheless respected as someone who lived for Jesus. For example, at the many grand dinners that he had to attend as chairman of the Meat and Livestock Commission, he was often asked to say grace because he was known to be a Christian. Donald took this very seriously, and gave thanks to God for all the blessings that he had bestowed on us, as well as praying for the specific needs of the livestock industry. This was greatly appreciated by many who were present.

## A Lord for the Lord in the Lords

Donald found it incredible that he was now a member of the House of Lords. As he himself put it, '*Every time I walk into the House of Lords,*

201. Policy Commission on the Future of Farming and Food, 'Farming and Food: a sustainable future' (Archived documents, 2002).

*and look around the walls, I ask myself, "Why I am here?" It's amazing.'* He knows, however, that the reason that he is there is because God had put him there. Thinking of his life in Northumberland, he could never have imagined being there if it had not been part of God's greater plan. God places his people where he wants them to serve him. For Donald at this time, it was the House of Lords, and it was all through the grace of God. He knew that he had to pray daily that he might contend for the Lord in that place.

From his first day in the Lords, Donald was determined that people should know that he was a Christian, and that he would take opportunities to speak for the Lord wherever possible. That did not mean that he would speak only on specifically Christian issues, but rather that his Christian integrity would shine through in whatever topic he was talking about. This could be related to agriculture, the proposed high speed (HS2) rail line, the national school breakfast programme or any other issue he felt called to speak on. He wanted to be seen as a rounded person, who was not only concerned with religious or socially conservative moral issues. In this, God gave him success, as he is greatly respected across the political spectrum in the Lords.

His sense of humour and general affability have helped him enormously in being accepted by others in the House. For example, in a debate on HS2, he followed the Labour peer, Lord Adonis, and used humour to lighten the proceedings. He began his speech saying, '*My Lords, it is a privilege to follow the noble Lord, Lord Adonis, whose commitment to HS2 is very well known. I must say that I am impressed with his tie. I have a pair of socks which I clearly need to donate to him to match.*'[202]

Early on in his career in the Lords, he nailed his colours firmly to the mast in a debate on religion in the United Kingdom. He made it very clear where he was coming from when he declared:

202. Lords Hansard (UK Parliament, November 30th 2020).

*The UK is constitutionally Christian. It is explicitly not a secular state. The monarch at her coronation swore an oath to God, not to a secular philosophy. Thank God for her continuing faithful, godly service. History has shown that this Christian constitution provides for a tolerant society in which people of all faiths or none are free to worship or not as they please. It has provided the basis for the kind of stability, peace, prosperity, happiness and individual freedom that still eludes a great many countries in the world that have not had this important influence. It is why many of us are so proud of our heritage.*

He went on to express concern at how some Christian charities have been treated by funding authorities.

*A homeless charity run by a Baptist church was told that it would lose its funding unless it stopped allowing people to say grace before meals. Pilgrim Homes, a charity providing homes for elderly people, was denied funding by Brighton Council because it could not in all conscience comply with the diktat that all its Christian residents had to be questioned about their sexual orientation every three months. I find it difficult to believe that this is happening in Britain. I am sure that we are all aware of NHS nurse Caroline Petrie who was disciplined for making a kind, gentle offer to pray for a patient. The banning of prayers and the news last week about the demotion of Adrian Smith, who expressed a personal view about gay marriage, are further worrying challenges.*

He ended his speech very forcefully saying:

> *The prevailing political attitude that I am concerned about was succinctly expressed in the famous statement by Alastair Campbell, 'We don't do God'. We all want to live in a society where people, regardless of their religion, can make a full contribution to public life and be respected for it. We should not make compliance with some sort of secularist state orthodoxy a precondition for full participation in society. The power of God can change lives and influence communities and society. It has done so in the past. Doing God and doing good is what millions of people in Britain want the freedom to do today.*[203]

Donald has had to speak on many difficult subjects in the Lords. The one that caused him most upset was same-sex marriage, which was pushed through Parliament by David Cameron's government in 2013. To Donald, it seemed completely contrary to his Christian beliefs, and he could not understand why there was either complete ambivalence or absolute enthusiasm regarding this cause. It even made him wonder what he was doing in the Lords at all, as it seemed that a line had been crossed. God, however, kept him there, and he did make two important speeches on freedom of conscience in churches and schools in the final stages of the bill's passage.[204]

He spoke from his own experience on many occasions, and for example in the debate on the Domestic Abuse Bill in 2021, he mentioned his experience with Jane, emphasising the need for people with disabilities to be protected from abuse from carers.[205]

Again from his experience with Jane, but also from his understanding of what God says about the sanctity of life, Donald has spoken out against abortion. Most recently, this has been to try to prevent the government

203. Lords Hansard (UK Parliament, November 22nd 2012).
204. Lords Hansard (UK Parliament, June 19th and July 8th 2012).
205. Lords Hansard (UK Parliament, March 8th 2021).

from pushing through regulations that would allow the termination of babies with disabilities in Northern Ireland. In a speech in April 2021, he expressed concern for the lives of the unborn, and in particular those with disabilities. He felt that this was something that should not be imposed on Northern Ireland, as abortion was a matter that had been devolved to the Northern Ireland Executive. Furthermore, he was concerned that freedom of speech would be restricted by preventing peaceful protest by those opposed to abortion.[206]

A significant and very long debate took place in the House of Lords on October 22nd 2021, when the Second Reading of Baroness Meacher's Assisted Dying Bill came before the Upper Chamber. This bill, if passed, would make it legal for doctors to prescribe lethal drugs to adults who are believed to have less than six months to live. Many were concerned about the ramifications of the bill if it became law, and many peers spoke against it, including Donald, who used his own experience of Jane to warn peers of the danger of passing this bill. Jane had a terrible bout of pneumonia with severe complications six years before she actually died. At that stage she was not expected to survive. He and Rhoda sat day and night watching Jane battle to survive. Donald told his colleagues in the debating chamber, '*If someone at that time had offered an assisted dying – assisted suicide – option, I firmly believe that in our heightened emotional state, not thinking rationally, we may have been tempted to agree to her premature death. Had we done that, it would have troubled us for the rest of our lives.*' Miraculously, Jane pulled through enriching the lives of hundreds of people in the ensuing six years. As Donald declared in his speech, '*I fear that this country will become a society that terminates the lives of its old people and its sick and disabled people because they fear they are being a burden to their loved ones and because of the time and the cost of their care.*' So many peers like Donald spoke against it that the

206. Lords Hansard (UK Parliament, April 28th 2021).

proposers of the bill decided not to put it to a vote, as they realised that they would surely have lost.

As a footnote to his speech, he was able to bring in a point of clarification about the death of Christ. Another peer, Lord Vinson, a supporter of the bill, said, '*On the cross, Christ was put out of his agony by a kindly Roman centurion, who pierced his side with a sword. His death was assisted.*' Donald was able to correct Lord Vinson's theology by declaring, '*Christ's death was not assisted. He voluntarily offered up his life and it was the purpose for which he came.*'[207]

Donald's Christian concern goes well beyond the United Kingdom, with a passion that he has for those who are downtrodden and persecuted. Since 2010 he has been a trustee on the board of Anglican International Development (AID), a Christian charity, '*working to relieve poverty in the name of Jesus Christ through long-term sustainable solutions which empower and enable citizens*'.[208] It operates mainly in South Sudan, although it has also started to work in Kenya and Uganda.

Donald has used his influence in the Lords over issues related to South Sudan, which continues to suffer severe famine and healthcare problems, largely as a result of a ruinous civil war. He is careful in each contribution that he makes to declare his interests as a trustee of AID. In one of his earliest speeches, he described the economic crisis faced by the people of that impoverished country saying, '*South Sudan is stuck at the bottom of global development indices and by most measures it is still going backwards*.' He concluded his speech by pleading with the government as follows:

> *South Sudan is a high priority. We must not relax our efforts to assist and to help to influence the transition from civil war to independence, to stable and sound governance with good*

207. Lords Hansard (UK Parliament, October 22nd 2021).
208. https://anglicaninternationaldevelopment.org/about-us/ (accessed 17.12.21).

*healthcare and education facilities and economic stability. I hope that our Government will seriously address these issues. We have a huge responsibility.*[209]

Members of the House of Lords have a key role in scrutinising government bills and trying to bring about appropriate modifications. In his time as a peer he has played his part in this, sometimes with success and sometimes not. He has, however, endeavoured to have an influence for Christ in his speeches and in the way that he conducts himself in the role that God has given him.

## Conclusion

In the eyes of the world, Donald has come far; from being a tenant farmer in rural Northumberland to being a prominent national figure dealing with agricultural crises, and from there to being a member of the House of Lords. For Donald, however, what is important is serving Christ and contending for truth. He may be a lord of the realm, but he knows who his ultimate Lord is; it is the Lordship of Christ that is of paramount importance to him and the driving force in his life.

He is particularly aware of the humility of Christ, who '*being found in appearance as a man, he humbled himself by becoming obedient to death – even death on a cross!*'[210] Donald feels that for him Philippians chapter 2 '*is the most important chapter in Scripture*'. Knowing the amazing love that Christ showed upon the cross keeps him absolutely grounded, realising that he is where he is only by the grace of God. He tries to follow the command of Paul in that same chapter when he says, '*Do nothing out of selfish ambition or vain conceit. Rather, in humility value others above yourselves, not looking to your own interests but each of you*

209. Lords Hansard (UK Parliament, October 17th 2012).
210. Philippians 2:8

*to the interests of the others.'*[211] This means that when he is working in the Lords, he tries to make time for all the people that he meets, regardless of their position in the organisation. He does not wish to be seen to be aloof and above others who are also doing highly important jobs.

One of his friends is Gordon Gatward, who is an agriculturalist and a Methodist minister. He was, until his retirement, head of the Arthur Rank Centre, which supports rural churches and trains Christians working in rural settings. Gordon sees Donald as his prayer partner and mentor, and whenever he had an issue to share he would call Donald. They have worked together in different forums, and even in secular meetings he sees Donald as *'someone who is so open about his faith, and he won't be afraid to say what Jesus has done for him'*. Gordon invited Donald one year to speak at the Sunday service at the Royal Show, and in Gordon's words, *'He gave a strong evangelistic message, which would speak to many who had come to hear a national figure in agriculture speak, and who found that he was an evangelist as well – that was very powerful.'*

Gordon sees him as being *'the most humble of men'*. He listed many other qualities that Donald has, which of course he would never mention himself.

> *He has tremendous compassion – he genuinely cares for others. He has a Christ-like character. I have never heard anyone call his integrity into question. I have never heard him get ratty, even in difficult meetings. He was a good person to turn to in adversity.*

Gordon's words are very powerful. They do not of course mean that Donald is perfect, as nobody but Christ can be. Donald is aware of his weaknesses; that he has 'feet of clay' and that he always has to battle against the wiles of Satan. Nevertheless, his Christian character

211. Philippians 2:3-4

and values shine through as he tries to make the world a better place, promoting Christ as he does so. He is indeed one of God's men to whom we can look up and from whom we can learn.

# Chapter 21: David Holloway

A previous interviewer of Vicar of Jesmond, David Holloway, described him thus:

> *He is medium height with wavy hair, gold rim specs, secular suited with eyebrows in the Denis Healey class. He's warm and direct and you're not long in his company before you realise that the speed and thoroughness of his speech is a direct result of trying to deliver the results of a mind whose perceptions and connections are turbo-charged. If I had to record all Holloway's table talk my battery of pens would have expired and I would have burnt a hole in my pad. I defy anyone to be bored in his company.*[212]

That was written almost twenty-five years ago (when people could still remember the eyebrows of the Labour Chancellor of the 1970s), but that remains an apt description of David Holloway today as he continues to minister into his eighties. I was fortunate to be able to make Zoom recordings as he talked to me; otherwise I would not have been able to take down by hand all that he said, and I would have lost many golden nuggets. His mind is as sharp as ever and is indeed '*turbo-charged*'; he is able to see the big picture of what is happening in both the church and the world today, as well as having a firm grasp of the details of particular events.

He is someone who has consistently contended for truth by proclaiming Christ so that people might come to faith and grow in their knowledge of him. Church growth has been a continuing theme of his ministry, and he has seen Jesmond Parish Church grow from a relatively

212. Robbie Low, *Interview with David Holloway* (Trushare, May 24th 1998).

small church to a flourishing fellowship that has planted two other churches in Newcastle and Gateshead.

For David, however, contending for truth also includes rebuking error. In his instructions to Timothy, Paul said, '*Preach the word; be prepared in season and out of season; correct, rebuke and encourage – with great patience and careful instruction.*'[213] Preaching the word, where the truth concerning Jesus can be found, has been the cornerstone of David's ministry, and this has included rebuking error. If error is allowed to grow through false teaching, people will stop seeing the truth and not find the real Jesus of the New Testament. The stand that David has taken over issues has won him much respect, as he is seen as someone who contends firmly for what he believes. It has also, of course, brought him into conflict with those who disagree with his views, but he has continued to stand firm for the sake of the truth of the gospel. David has had to be thick skinned as he has had to deal not only with disagreement but even insults from national journalists.[214]

Let us now look at some of the main events in his life as he followed his calling to share God's love with a world that so desperately needs it.

## Beginnings

David grew up in a strong Christian environment in Stanmore in north London. He attended the local Brethren assembly Sunday school as a child, and learned the basic facts of the gospel. His father was lay pastor at Stanmore Free Church, and on Sundays he would hear discussions round the lunch table with people who had come to speak at the church. Under these and other influences, including a couple of his teachers at school, David built up his knowledge of the Christian faith.

---

213. 2 Timothy 4:2

214. He was described as '*repulsive*' in an opinion column by Andrew Brown 'This latest Church of England schism has an unexpected source' (*The Guardian*, May 10th 2017), although Brown did also describe him as '*intelligent, energetic, legalistic and strategic in his thinking*'.

He realised, however, that knowing facts was not sufficient. He also had to agree that these facts were true. David was very struck by John 7:17 where Jesus said, '*Anyone who chooses to do the will of God will find out whether my teaching comes from God or whether I speak on my own.*' He came to agree that the teachings of Jesus as recorded in the Bible were indeed from God and so were true and worthy of following. Even intellectual agreement, however, was not enough; he knew that he had to commit his life to Jesus, and this he did publicly at a Tom Rees evangelistic meeting. After this, he was invited to join the school Christian Union, where he heard other notable speakers such as John Stott, who would become probably the most prominent Anglican evangelical clergyman of his time, and Raymond Turvey, whom David would later work alongside in Leeds.

After school, David went to study Classics along with Philosophy Ancient and Modern at University College, Oxford. He loved the academic study, but he also loved the sporting life, especially rugby and cricket. He went to Christian Union meetings, but did not fully commit himself to the CU until his third year when he became the representative for his college. One of the events that he was involved in as college rep was in 1961, helping to organise a university mission led by Dick Lucas with evangelistic meetings every night of the week. One personal spin-off for David was that there was a reading list included in the booklet *Henceforth*[215] that was given out at the mission. David read each of the books, and as he said later, '*That was the start of my theological education.*'

The long summer vacation between his third and fourth years was significant for David in a number of ways. First of all, very sadly his mother died suddenly in her forties, which was a major blow for the family. Secondly, he went to help on a beach mission in Ireland where he met a young lady who was later to become his wife. The circumstances were that he was on kitchen duty, but he and other young men were

215. Hugh Evan Hopkins, *Henceforth* (Inter-Varsity Fellowship, 1951).

standing around chatting when Joy, the lady in question, came in and said, '*You are meant to be doing the washing up*', and thrust a tea towel in his hands.[216] Thirdly, he went hitchhiking to Greece with a friend who was planning to enter the Church of England ministry. These three events made him realise that he, unlike his friend, did not have a clear plan for his life. On coming back home, he went to Edgware Parish Church and prayed to God for guidance. The answer came during the service, first from Psalm 65:4: '*Blessed are those you choose and bring near to live in your courts! We are filled with the good things of your house, of your holy temple.*' Immediately afterwards, the first verse of the hymn 'Be Wholly Thine' spoke to him:

*My faith looks up to thee*
*Thou Lamb of Calvary*
*Saviour divine!*
*Now hear me while I pray*
*Take all my guilt away*
*O let me from this day*
*Be wholly thine!*[217]

The psalm and the hymn really struck David, and he believed that this was God calling him into full-time Christian ministry.

Unfortunately, however, the following year, he failed to obtain a grant to continue at Oxford to study theology. This made him begin to doubt whether God was calling him into ministry after all! God, however, was about to make it clear that he did want David in ministry. During the summer after he had completed his classics degree, David and a friend went on another European hitchhiking holiday, this time to Rome. They went to St Andrew's Church of Scotland in Rome, where the psalm that

216. Some might well see this as a foretaste of things to come!
217. 'Be Wholly Thine' written by Ray Palmer (1830). Public Domain.

was read was again Psalm 65, and once more followed by the hymn 'Be Wholly Thine'. This was no mere coincidence, but rather it was God teaching David to trust in him. He did finally receive a generous grant to continue studying at Oxford and subsequently at Cambridge.

David enjoyed his study of theology at Oxford. The course involved study of the whole of the Old Testament, the whole of the New Testament and the teachings of the Early Church Fathers. He found many of his teachers very helpful, but there were also liberal teachers at Oxford, some of whom, like David Jenkins, would later become bishops in the Church of England. His biblical foundation was so strong, however, that he was not swayed by the liberal theology of those teachers. Indeed, he gained a deeper understanding of the flaws and shortcomings in liberal theology.

The same was true when he later went to Ridley Hall in Cambridge to train for the Anglican ministry. This was the time when John Robinson, the Bishop of Woolwich, caused a storm by writing *Honest to God*, which attacked traditional Christian teaching.[218] David felt that in the light of this attack on the teaching of the Bible, he should go to a somewhat liberal college to understand better the thinking of this new wave of liberal theology and thus formulate counter arguments against it. It would also give him a better understanding of the new, seemingly pernicious influences at work in the Church of England.

Before going to Ridley Hall, however, he felt that he needed a break from academic study and so he looked for the opportunity to serve the Lord in a totally different environment.

## Adventures in the Sudan

To try to plan out what to do in his 'gap year', David contacted a Church Missionary Society (CMS) worker called Douglas Webster. Through him he became a short-term CMS missionary in Omdurman in the

218. John A.T. Robinson, *Honest to God* (SCM Press, 1963).

Sudan for a year from the autumn of 1964, although mainly seconded to the American Presbyterian Mission to teach Scripture and English in its Commercial High School. This seemed to be an ideal job for David, as he wanted to see how the Christian faith worked out in a different context. By October, however, David got concerned because other people had gone back to university, but he did not yet have a visa to go out to the Sudan. As has been the case before, and would be after, God was testing David's faith by keeping him hanging on, and so finally his visa came through. He was all set to fly out for a new experience teaching in the Sudan.

New experiences, however, took place well before he got to the classroom. As their plane approached Khartoum airport, they were told that they could not land because '*there was a revolution going on!*' They had to fly on to Aden where they had to wait in blistering heat until it was relatively safe to fly back to Khartoum. They eventually landed in Khartoum where a car was waiting for David to take him to his accommodation in Omdurman. To get there, however, they had to drive through tear gas and the rioters who were aiming to overthrow the government, which would seem to be a common occurrence in Sudan. This was an exciting start, although David would experience yet more excitement in the weeks and months to come.

He enjoyed his teaching in the school, including all of the sport in the afternoon. During this time, however, political troubles continued. The country was plagued by strikes. University students in one college, for example, were reported to have been on strike for about a year, simply not turning up to classes. The headteacher of the American school, however, refused to allow the students to go on strike. One day, out to get revenge for this non-compliance, large numbers of young people scaled the perimeter wall of the school to capture the headteacher and to run riot through the school. David remembered it well: '*I was teaching Mark Anthony's speech from Julius Caesar, and I suddenly saw the perimeter wall and a huge number of these guys, sixteen or seventeen year olds, climbing over. I was just mesmerised.'* As it happened, the headteacher and other staff members were not harmed, but much of the school was destroyed. David ended up doing individual tuition with the students from his little house to help them in their exam preparation.

Another rather frightening and violent episode that David witnessed was when he was on his way by taxi to a baptismal service in Khartoum at the headquarters of the American mission. As he travelled by taxi, he found himself in the middle of a huge crowd, many of them armed with sticks and other offensive weapons. The taxi driver told him that there were rumours that the South Sudanese were rioting. These rumours spread. A football match was halted at half time and a large cinema was closed, resulting in even more people joining the throng on the streets. David's taxi turned round to take him back home and to relative safety. It was just as well, as David's original destination, the American mission headquarters, was attacked. The South Sudanese were forced to scale the walls for protection and then had Molotov cocktails thrown at them. It was totally destroyed and the following morning looked like a bombsite.

With much of his teaching in disarray, David took the opportunity to take students from Khartoum and Omdurman to a conference organised by the Pan African Federation of Evangelical Students in Uganda. This cost a lot of money, but English-speaking Christians in the Sudan provided the financial support that was needed. The students enjoyed the conference, and it certainly broadened their horizons.

After taking the students back, he did some travelling in Uganda and Kenya. Both through the conference and his subsequent travels, he met a number of Christians who would later call on him in Cambridge, Leeds or Newcastle. David felt that it was a privilege to maintain these friendships across cultures and geographical distances. The unity that comes through the gospel allows this to happen!

He felt that the northern Muslim Sudanese that he had worked with were such lovely people, but they so needed the gospel. At the same time, he was encouraged by their willingness to study the Bible. He recalls one employee of Sudan Airways who wanted to go to a British university, but he had to pass a Cambridge qualifying examination. He was a Muslim and he chose to take Christian religious instruction as one option with David. He had to read and study Mark's gospel, and as a result he came to faith in Christ. As David said, '*He was converted through his A level course!*'

The whole Sudanese experience was so uplifting for David. He learned to trust God, whether it was in matters of obtaining his visa or for his personal safety against rioters. He saw God at work in individuals' lives by bringing them to faith or growing as Christians. He also saw the bigger political picture in a country that was so divided between north and south, along ethnic lines and between Muslims and Christians. Officially it was a democratic country with everyone having a vote, but where there are so many divisions, he learned that democracy would only work within a Christian framework; those in minority groups, such as Christians in the south, were underrepresented and treated very much like third-class citizens. It was no wonder that there was constant unrest and civil war.

South Sudan, which is Christian-dominated, finally obtained independence in 2011, but it has continued to be racked by civil war and poverty since then. One long-term effect of David's experience in Sudan in 1964-65 was that he was led along with others in 2008 to establish Anglican International Development, a Christian humanitarian charity that would provide healthcare, microfinance, agricultural support and church strengthening, initially in South Sudan and later in Kenya. In the previous chapter, we have seen how Donald Curry has been involved with AID and South Sudan, both as a trustee and through his work in the Lords.

## Ridley Hall, the Keele Congress and abortion

David took up his place at Ridley Hall in 1965 to train for the Anglican ministry. It was a time of upheaval. The charismatic movement was making an impact. Although not agreeing with all aspects of the movement, David learned much from those who had a more charismatic leaning than he had, including Dennis Bennett, author of the influential book *Nine O'Clock in the Morning*[219] when he visited the college. Of great concern, however, was the influence of the 'new morality'. When he presented a paper, for example, on sex and sexuality, his traditional biblical views that sexual intercourse should be reserved for marriage seemed to be too much for his tutor and others.

In April 1967, David was able to obtain a student place as the college's representative at the first National Evangelical Anglican Congress at Keele University. The congress was led by prominent Anglicans such as John Stott and Jim Packer, with the aim of bringing evangelicals out of the woodwork in order to have greater influence in the Church of England. In many ways this happened. An article in the *Church Times* commemorating the fiftieth anniversary of the congress made the statement, '*The Church of England was slowly being "Evangelicalised"*'.[220] David, however, was not so sure, thinking that many evangelicals have not maintained their standards and have '*gone native*'. He later wrote: '*Evangelicals at Keele sought to participate fully in Anglican structures in order to capture the Church of England for the gospel, but, instead, they became ensnared by the institution and rendered ineffective*.'[221]

One issue at the congress that incensed David and brought him to his feet in protest was abortion. This was the time when David Steel's abortion reform bill was going through Parliament. Many evangelicals

219. Dennis Bennett, *Nine O'Clock in the Morning* (Bridge-Logos Publishing, 1970).
220. Andrew Atherstone, 'Evangelicals exit their ghetto' (*Church Times*, March 31st 2017).
221. David Holloway, 'Discussion Paper Number 1' (Reform, 1995).

were either supportive of the bill because it would reduce the need for back-street abortions or they were completely passive, not thinking that it was their place to interfere in political issues. Also, many, including John Stott, believed that the foetus in the womb was 'a potential human being', not yet an actual human being.[222]

Although David was brought to his feet at the suggestion that the foetus was only potentially human, he was initially prevented from speaking because it was argued that he was only a student. (The person who finally gave him permission to speak was Raymond Turvey, the congress secretary, and who would later offer him a job in Leeds.) When he was finally allowed to speak he caused uproar by disagreeing with Norman Anderson, the chair of the session, and other leading evangelicals such as Stott by claiming that life began at conception and that the foetus was a person with potential, rather than a potential human. This was a clear case where David was prepared to stand his ground and contend for truth against the views of the powerful majority.

Attitudes amongst leading evangelicals were to change, however, as a result of a number of influences. The Abortion Act was leading to many more abortions than were expected, and it was more like abortion on demand than abortions to save the mother's life. As advances in photography in the womb took place, more people could see clear human features in the foetus. Probably the most significant influence in changing evangelical views, however, was the visit to the United Kingdom in 1980 of Francis Shaeffer, an American theologian, and Everett Koop, later Surgeon-General of the United States, with their film series, *Whatever Happened to the Human Race*? These films very powerfully argued the case against abortion.

David also had further discussions with John Stott, Jim Packer and others in the years after Keele. By 1984, the change in attitudes was

222. I am grateful for access to Sharon James' PhD thesis 'Evangelical response to the reconfiguration of family in England 1960-2010' (2012) for background information.

evident when Stott published his seminal book *Issues Facing Christians Today* where he argued very strongly that life began at conception. He referred to verses in Psalm 139, such as verse 13, '*For you created my inmost being; you knit me together in my mother's womb.*' His argument centres on our personhood coming from God knowing us before we were even in the womb, and thus he writes:

> *For God our Creator loved us and related himself to us long before we could respond in a conscious relationship to him. What makes us a person, then, is not that we know God, but that he knows us; not that we love God but that he has set his love upon us. So each of us was already a person in our mother's womb, because already then God knew us and loved us.*[223]

What a change in attitude on the part of the leading evangelical statesman of the time! What role David's brave stand at Keele had in this change of heart we shall never know, but it was so right for David to make that stand. It would not be the last time that David would go against the flow.

## Joy, Leeds, Wycliffe Hall and on to Jesmond

After they first met in the kitchen on the beach mission in Ireland, David and Joy got to know each other better, particularly after Joy came up to Oxford to read medicine. They eventually got married in the summer after David completed his Ridley Hall course. The questions for David were of course where they would live and where he would be working at the beginning of their married life. He had expected to become curate at a church in Bristol, but that fell through. Nevertheless, David put that to the back of his mind, and after the wedding and official honeymoon, they spent six weeks on a motor scooter travelling across Europe.

---

223. John Stott, *Issues Facing Christians Today* (Marshall, Morgan & Scott, 1984), p. 288.

They went back home, with David still not having any immediate prospects of employment, until out of the blue Raymond Turvey phoned him up and offered him a curacy at his church, St George's in Leeds. This was again God providing for him at the last minute! David was initially not very keen to go to Leeds, because he saw himself as being very much a southerner, and his one previous visit to the bus station in Leeds had not left a very good impression on him. David realised that this snobbish attitude was wrong, and he followed God's leading to Leeds. As it turned out, he found Leeds to be a very pleasant city to be living and working in.

He learned his craft of working in a parish, carrying out the responsibilities expected of a curate, including preaching, conducting marriage ceremonies, teaching in the parish primary school, and being chaplain to a female probation hostel, as well as playing for the diocesan cricket team. He was also involved with helping those who were sleeping rough in the Crypt. The Crypt under the church had been established by Don Robins, vicar at the height of the 1930s depression, as a soup kitchen and night shelter for the destitute and homeless. Now at the height of the drug culture of the late '60s and early '70s, over two hundred gathered there and received ministry support from David and others in the church.

One area in which Raymond Turvey wanted David to specialise was the work with students. In a large university city such as Leeds there were lots of students who came to St George's, and David got to know them and worked with them.

Student work also involved being a missioner on university missions in Leeds and elsewhere. One such mission that was a highlight in David's memory was held in Oxford in 1970, when he worked alongside the evangelist David MacInnes. On the evening of February 2nd, the union debating hall and an overflow room were packed out with hundreds of students, most of whom would have heard the news that had just been announced of the death of Bertrand Russell, the veteran atheistic philosopher and anti-nuclear campaigner. Russell had had no respect for the Christian faith, including the fundamental truth of the resurrection of the dead. David persuaded MacInnes to read the words of despair that Russell had written before his death:

> *The mental night that has descended upon me is less brief and promises no awakening after sleep . . . But now all this has shrunk to be no more than my own reflection in the windows of the soul, through which I look out upon the night of nothingness . . . There is no splendour, no vastness, anywhere; only triviality for a moment, and then nothing.*

There was total silence as the full passage was read out. David MacInnes then preached on the resurrection and the glorious hope that could be found in Jesus. This was in complete contrast to the despair expressed by Russell who had completely rejected that glorious hope. Many students responded to the gospel message that the mission team presented.

In 1971, David had come to the end of his period of curacy, and it was time to move on from Leeds. Once more, however, he had nowhere to go to, until again at the last minute he received a phone call from Wycliffe Hall, the Anglican theological college, asking him to take up a post lecturing on Doctrine and Ethics there. David agreed to go for a year and did his best to ensure that his students achieved good exam results.

At the end of the year, again he had no definite employment to go to, having tried unsuccessfully to obtain various posts. At the same time, Jesmond Parish Church, an evangelical church in Newcastle, had been looking for a vicar for almost a year after the previous incumbent, Roger Frith, left, but they could not find anyone suitable. Time was running short, and if the church patrons did not find anyone suitable, the bishop would make an appointment, and this appointee would not necessarily be an evangelical. Raymond Johnston, churchwarden at the time, was prayerfully determined that an evangelical should be appointed. Jim Higginbottom, principal of Wycliffe Hall, contacted David and asked him to consider going to Jesmond. David was not very keen as, after all, it was even further north than Leeds! He did, however, accept the post at the very end of 1972. It was not just in desperation that he took the post; he realised again that this was where God wanted him to be.

## Jesmond Parish Church: Godly Living, Church Growth and Transforming Britain

The origins of Jesmond Parish Church go back to the mid-nineteenth century, when a large number of members of St Thomas' Church in the centre of Newcastle felt forced to leave their church and establish a new church elsewhere in the city. The circumstances were sad. Richard Clayton, chaplain of St Thomas', had a powerful gospel ministry there, but when he died in 1856, the replacement who was appointed by the church authorities failed to preach the truth of the gospel as Clayton had. As a result, the church planned to establish '*a church in the memory of the late Richard Clayton, in which evangelical truth shall be declared and which would form a central point for the maintenance and promulgation of sound scriptural and evangelical truth in a large and populous town*'. And so Jesmond Parish Church opened in 1861.

David was very much aware of the historical roots of the church and saw his role as continuing in the tradition of Clayton's congregation. He believed evangelical truth to be the truth of the Bible, particularly in the need to understand the sinful nature of our humanity, the need to be redeemed by Jesus as our Saviour and receiving new forgiveness and new life through the Holy Spirit. He called these fundamental truths the 'three Rs': ruin, redemption and regeneration. It was his calling to ensure that these truths were 'maintained' by not allowing false teachers from either within or beyond the church to distort these truths. These truths, however, also had to be 'promulgated' so that the truth of the gospel would go out into the wider world. Contending for truth was at the heart of David's ministry at Jesmond.

Later, David formulated a mission statement for the church to summarise its calling: 'Godly Living, Church Growth and Transforming Britain.' Godly living required a commitment to God through the Lord Jesus Christ that was total. It meant submitting ourselves to him and letting him live through us as we respond to him. As he works through us, we should be transformed into the likeness of Christ. Godly living should then see us desiring church growth so that other people become Christians and join the church. Evangelism and drawing people to a living faith in Jesus has to be at the heart of the church's mission. This also involves teaching new converts to grow in Christ that they become disciples, and not just converts. We also want our society to change so that it reflects God's standards. This will involve showing love to the people around us and making a public stand against injustice and corruption and whatever violates God's standards.

These ideals have kept David going throughout his ministry, but on taking up his post at the beginning of 1973, with the church much smaller, the question David had was how to start. Raymond Turvey at Leeds had given him simple advice: '*Be careful of women, be careful of boys, be careful of money, and have a crèche.*' Basically, he was being told to avoid sexual temptation, both heterosexual and homosexual, and financial temptation. So many church leaders have fallen foul of these particular temptations. What Turvey was saying in very practical terms was what Peter warned in his first letter: '*Be alert and of sober mind. Your enemy the devil prowls around like a roaring lion looking for someone to devour.*'[224] No such scandal has tainted David's long ministry.

He was also given practical advice by Turvey to get more people into church, especially young married couples, by starting a crèche. Joy, of

224. 1 Peter 5:8

course, was an expert in this area, being a paediatrician, and so she started the crèche in the church building and continued to organise it for the next forty years or so. Also, when Turvey moved on from Leeds to his next church, he painted the doors of his new church yellow to show that it was under new management. David did the same, and yellow doors still remain a feature of Jesmond Parish Church.

He introduced other changes, many of them from his time at St George's in Leeds. Through time, the work of the church expanded, attracting more people to join the congregation and to hear gospel truths. Children's and young people's work was developed with a wide range of activities, attracting large numbers of children and youth from the church along with their friends. Music was diversified, with a balance between traditional hymns and more contemporary Christian songs. Various courses were introduced, such as Christianity Explored, to explain the gospel to those who were seeking answers to questions that they had. Celebrate Recovery provided a safe, confidential environment for those who needed help with particular issues. Like Leeds, Newcastle had a large student population, and David from his Leeds experience knew how important it was for the gospel to reach students and for Christian students to grow in their faith, with the particular needs of international students being specially catered for. At the heart of all of these activities was prayer; David knew that all of this work would be fruitless effort unless it was grounded in prayer.

Early on in his ministry David took a keen interest in the church growth movement. He was fascinated by the work of Donald MacGavran, a missionary in India from before the Second World War, and whom David regarded as '*the pioneer of the church growth movement*'. MacGavran tried to identify what caused some missions in India to be very fruitful, while others were much less so.[225] He discovered a key principle in looking at people movements in India when masses

225. Donald MacGavran, *The Bridges of God* (World Dominion, 1955).

of people came to Christ; it was that *the Christian faith usually spread along lines of existing social networks*.'[226] Therefore, it is important in evangelism to see what these key networks are in terms of family, work relationships, cultural ties and so on. As David later wrote, '*Evangelism is not preaching the gospel in a vacuum, but in a social context*.'[227]

MacGavran later, along with Peter Wagner, a colleague at the Fuller Theological Seminary in California, ran courses for clergy on church growth based both on biblical principles and evidence from around the world. David was desperate to learn more from these 'church growth gurus' and so during a sabbatical in 1979, he took a course at Fuller where he learned the theory as well as undertaking practical research in looking at growing churches in the Los Angeles area. He came back to Newcastle with a burning desire to put these principles into practice.

One important lesson that he learned was to plan for growth. For example, in terms of premises, he realised that unless the premises were adequate for a growing congregation, including an increase in the number of children, young people and students, growth would be stifled. Therefore, David believed that if growth is part of God's plan for the church, then the church needed to plan its premises requirements in advance. Changes were made to the main building as well as purchasing vacant apartment and office blocks.

David also had a vision for the church to grow across Tyneside, as so many in the region needed to hear the gospel. Church planting had long been on his agenda, and then God miraculously provided new opportunities. The first was in Gateshead, where land was available from a small Christian fellowship that asked if Jesmond Parish Church could help. Through sacrificial giving from the Jesmond congregation, in 2008 a modern church was built called Holy Trinity, Gateshead. The second was in the Benwell area of the city, where the Roman Catholic

226. David Holloway, *Ready, Steady, Grow* (Kingsway Publications, 1989), p. 24.
227. David Holloway, *Ready, Steady, Grow*, p. 24.

diocese had a redundant church called St Joseph's. The Jesmond Trust was able to buy this building for a nominal £1 in 2013, although a lot of money was required to refurbish the church. In both cases, members of the Jesmond congregation moved across to be the core congregations in these church plants. Both churches have seen growth as they serve their particular communities.

David also had a burning interest in education. In the late 1980s, the Thatcher government wanted to reform education, to ensure higher educational standards through a national curriculum, a market-driven approach to school places and giving schools greater freedom from local authority control. David and others wanted to ensure that the Christian faith had a prominent place in these reforms. A group from the church and beyond lobbied government ministers to ensure that assemblies and religious education should be wholly or mainly of a broadly Christian character. This requirement was written into the legislation that became the Education Reform Act of 1988, and it is still legally in force today, although it is not particularly stringently enforced. Having a Christian basis to education was part of the mission statement of the church: transforming Britain. Out of that also came the Christian Institute, of which David was one of the founder members. The Institute has become a powerful national force in standing up for Christian values in the public square.

## Contending for truth: the bishops

Early in his ministry, David was elected to the General Synod, the national assembly of the Church of England, remaining a member of the Synod for fifteen years from 1975 to 1990. There was much that he found frustrating about the bureaucracy of the organisation, but perhaps none more so than with the appointment of bishops. The appointment of David Jenkins as Bishop of Durham in 1984 was a particular shock.

As he later wrote, 1984 was a significant year for the church in England. In March there was a memorial service in York Minster for the Anglican preacher and evangelist David Watson, whose preaching had a lasting impact on so many people, including large swathes of the student population. It was the year that Billy Graham came to preach the gospel during Mission England. David recalls Roker Park in Sunderland being full, with many coming forward to respond to the evangelist's message. Sadly, it was also the year of '*the consecration of David Jenkins as a bishop in the Church of England after denying or doubting fundamental doctrines of the Creed*'.[228]

Earlier in 1984, David had been at an address to the Synod's Board of Social Responsibility given by David Jenkins, and on the way out he and Bishop Hugh Montefiore discussed what they had just heard. They felt that it was incoherent and lacking meaningful sense. Imagine David's shock and horror when the following week he found out that Jenkins had been appointed Bishop of Durham. This was just to be the beginning. In a series of interviews, Jenkins made a number of controversial statements doubting the historicity of the virgin birth and the bodily resurrection of Jesus, and whether historical claims in the Bible could be trusted as such. For example, in a Radio 4 interview, he made the astounding claim in reference to these events recorded in the Bible: '*There is absolutely no certainty in the New Testament of anything of importance*.'[229] Ironically, this interview was broadcast the morning after Billy Graham had proclaimed the truth so powerfully at Roker Park.

David felt that he had to respond, and so he wrote a letter to *The Times* which was published on June 19th 1984. He refuted the claim that Jenkins made about the lack of certainty about historical events by saying that his claim was '*sheer nonsense. There are commonly agreed*

228. David Holloway, *The Church of England: Where Is It Going?* (Kingsway Publications, 1985), p. 11.
229. BBC Radio 4, *Sunday* (May 27th 1984).

*criteria that can give us sufficient certainty about the past*'. David asked the fundamental question, '*For these reasons, is it right that David Jenkins should allow himself to go forward for consecration? We can't have bishops whose teaching undermines the truth of the resurrection*.' David admits to being nervous about sending this letter, as it was questioning the authority of bishops and that of the Archbishop of York who would carry out the consecration. The issue was so important that he decided to deliver the letter by hand when he was in London, but he did pace up and down outside the newspaper offices before he actually delivered it. David knew, however, that he had done the right thing.

After this, David did a number of interviews explaining the heretical views of David Jenkins, explaining why it was wrong for the consecration to go ahead.[230] He had hoped that the Archbishop of York would listen to the group of northern clergy on the Synod and then defer the consecration. Unfortunately, the Archbishop refused to do so, and the consecration went ahead in York Minster on July 7th 1984. Two days later, a lightning bolt hit the south transept of the minster, destroying its roof and causing over two million pounds' worth of damage. Whether there was any connection between the two events is mere speculation, but Christians do not often believe in 'coincidence', rather preferring to see the hand of God in events. As the then Register-General said to David in York the day after the fire, '*It makes you think, doesn't it?*'

In subsequent years in his preaching and writing, David has made it abundantly clear that all the evidence pointed to an empty tomb and that Jesus had bodily risen from the dead and appeared to his followers. The resurrection is at the heart of the Christian faith. Likewise, with regard to the virgin birth, David contended for the biblical truth, as, for example, found in Matthew's gospel: '*His mother Mary was pledged to*

230. The author's first contact with David Holloway was listening to him in a radio interview on this subject before he and his family moved to the north-east. See Jim Cockburn, *All by Grace*, pp. 32-33.

*be married to Joseph, but before they came together, she was found to be pregnant through the Holy Spirit.*'[231] This fulfilled what was prophesied in Isaiah 7:14: '*The virgin will conceive and give birth to a son, and they will call him Immanuel (which means "God with us")*'.[232] David wrote an article which was published in *The Times* on December 20th 1986, where he explained clearly why the Bishop of Durham's views were erroneous, and that we can trust what God says and what he has done in history.

A decade later, David was going to have difficulty with another bishop, Martin Wharton, who was appointed Bishop of Newcastle in 1997. This time the issue was sexual ethics. In 1987, there had been an important debate at the Synod on homosexual relationships. A motion was passed by a 98 per cent majority affirming traditional biblical sexual ethics, including the affirmation that homosexual acts fell short of God's standard and required repentance and the exercise of compassion.

This clear view of the sinfulness of homosexual acts was, however, watered down by the House of Bishops in their report 'Issues in Human Sexuality' released in 1991. There was no call for repentance from homosexual activity, and so this led to some degree of confusion over the church's position on this issue. David, however, was quite clear that homosexual activity was a contravention of God's standards as set out in Scripture. For example, in Romans chapter 1, Paul talked about sin in these terms:

> *Because of this, God gave them over to shameful lusts. Even their women exchanged natural sexual relations for unnatural ones. In the same way the men also abandoned natural relations with women and were inflamed with lust for one another. Men committed shameful acts with other men, and received in themselves the due penalty for their error.*[233]

231. Matthew 1:18
232. Matthew 1:23
233. Romans 1:26-27

It was inevitable that David's traditional views would come into conflict with the more liberal views of certain bishops such as Martin Wharton. Before coming to Newcastle, Wharton had been a bishop in the diocese of Southwark, and had taken part in a celebration of the twentieth anniversary of the Lesbian and Gay Christian Movement in Southwark Cathedral. Not long after his appointment as Bishop of Newcastle was announced, he gave television and newspaper interviews. In the *Evening Chronicle* report of June 18th 1997, he said, '*homosexuality within a loving, permanent relationship is no sin*'.

The Jesmond Parochial Church Council had made it clear in 1996 in their advice to the vicar that any bishop who refused to subscribe to traditional biblical sexual ethics should not be involved in confirmation services in the church. This meant that Martin Wharton should not be invited to these services and that the church would be in impaired communion with the bishop. In an article published on November 4th 1997 in *The Journal*, the leading north-eastern daily newspaper, David wrote: '*Jesmond Parish Church must follow the Bible . . . That is why we also believe that sex is to be reserved for heterosexual monogamous marriage.*' In that article he argued that the church's disagreement with Martin Wharton meant that they would be asking the Archbishop of York for alternative oversight.

Since then, the church has continued to be in impaired communion with the bishop. Evangelical bishops from elsewhere in England and abroad, including Martin Morrison, Bishop of the Reformed Evangelical Anglican Church of South Africa, John Ellison and Rod Thomas have provided oversight and have presided at confirmation services. The move away from traditional sexual ethics has of course continued unabated, as we shall see in the next chapter, and David has continued to speak and write on these issues.

Reading this chapter in the 2020s, many might ask the question as to why David got so involved in the issues surrounding sexual ethics.

Are they not just secondary issues, like the vestments that clergy wear to conduct services? Should not more effort be put into preaching the gospel so that more might come to faith? For David, however, these are not secondary issues, but rather they are concerned with godly living and preaching against the sin that offends a holy God as declared in his word. Of course, sexual immorality is not the only – or even the worst – sin that offends God. Nevertheless, David would see the Church of England as needing to repent from sin in order to preach the gospel more effectively. A true picture of the awfulness of sin, including sexual sin, points to a greater need of the Saviour who hung on the cross for our sin.

Furthermore, David believes that it is his sworn duty to rebuke error. When he was ordained, he had to make promises according to what is called the 1662 Ordinal. This included the bishop asking: '*Will you be ready, with all faithful diligence, to banish and drive away all erroneous and strange doctrines contrary to God's Word?*' To which David replied, '*I will, the Lord being my helper.*' Given this promise that he had made at the beginning of his ministry, David felt compelled to rebuke error, even when it came from bishops and archbishops.

## Christian broadcasting

Throughout his ministry, David has displayed a passion for broadcasting as a means of spreading the Christian message. Indeed, when he was looking for posts at different points in his career he did apply for some in broadcasting, but he was not successful in finding anything suitable.

When he was at Leeds, however, broadcasting did play an important part in his ministry. The BBC was at this time establishing local radio stations, and BBC Radio Leeds was one of the first to be set up. This new station was keen to include a weekly religious broadcast, with St George's producing the programme every third week. Seeing its tremendous potential, David jumped at the opportunity of presenting this programme.

During these programmes he would interview people to discuss their Christian faith or to discuss current issues from a Christian perspective. One of the people that he interviewed was Denis Healey (of eyebrows fame), who was Member of Parliament for Leeds East and at the time Secretary of State for Defence; some of this interview was transcribed and included in *The Listener* magazine published by the BBC. He also got to know Nigel Goodwin, a Christian actor, writer and co-founder of the Arts Centre Group, a group bringing together Christians involved in the arts. Nigel alerted him to interview Cliff Richard for the BBC about his faith and how it impacted on his career in show business after his performance at the Batley Variety Club. He also dabbled a bit in television production and managed to interview Peter Hain (now Baron Hain), the anti-apartheid activist, for Associated Television on the 'Stop the '70 Tour' campaign which disrupted the tours of the all-white South African cricket and rugby tours of 1970.

An opportunity arose to be involved in television broadcasting in the late '70s when Independent Television franchises were being redistributed. David saw that this could provide a Christian voice in television broadcasting, and so established a consortium to bid for the franchise for the north-east. This consortium called Tele Vision North (TVN) had powerful people on its board, although not all were Christian. One committed Christian on the board and the potential head of television for TVN was former BBC producer Andrew Quicke, the first producer of BBC's flagship current affairs programme, *Panorama*. He also co-wrote Jackie Pullinger's autobiography about working with gangs and prostitutes in Hong Kong called *Chasing the Dragon*.[234]

234. Jackie Pullinger and Andrew Quicke, *Chasing the Dragon* (Hodder & Stoughton, 1980). Andrew actually put a lot of the manuscript together in David's home as they worked on the TVN bid.

This would not be a specifically Christian television company, as the law at the time did not permit that, but as David later wrote: '*It was a modest attempt by those of us who were Christian at social responsibility. It was a piece of social leavening, not Christian witness.*'[235] The aim was to produce better quality television programmes for the north-east. Unfortunately the bid was only partially successful. The three consortia that had placed bids were each offered a third of the franchise, but TVN felt that this would not be appropriate and so declined the offer.

Although this bid was unsuccessful, David worked with other Christians to form a group called Christian Choice in Broadcasting to campaign for the right for Christians to own local and regional broadcasting stations. This was achieved in the Broadcasting Act of 1990. As a result, Premier Christian Radio, which now has a national and international reach, won the franchise for the London region.

Working on Radio Leeds, submitting a bid for a television franchise and campaigning for Christians to be allowed their own broadcasting stations, David saw the power of the media to promulgate the gospel. He also saw that if Christians were not involved in broadcasting, there would be no social leavening, and what would be broadcast would be far from Christian truth. He had enough foresight to see that in terms of technology, computers and television were coming closer together. David saw the potential of establishing a library of Christian material that could be fed onto people's televisions and computers.

Thus Clayton TV was born. As it says on its website, '*Clayton TV – broadcasting excellent, free, Bible teaching, music and courses for Christians around the world. New programmes and live content weekly.*'[236] David's daughter, Zoë Earnshaw, a television producer and editor, was the original brains behind setting it up, and its materials are now accessed from people across the globe. Sermons and other material from

235. David Holloway, *A Nation Under God* (Kingsway Publications, 1987), p. 125.
236. https://www.clayton.tv/about/0i0/2924/ (accessed 17.12.21).

Jesmond Parish Church were included in the bank of resources, but in 2018, the church went one step further by live streaming its evening services, so that those anywhere in the world who could not get to church for whatever reason could take part in a service from home. Therefore, when churches were closed as a result of pandemic restrictions, the church was in a strong position to live stream its services; without this, many Christians would have suffered spiritually by not being able to attend church.

In terms of maintaining and promulgating the gospel, the church has now got a much wider reach. It has been estimated that two-thirds of those who regularly tuned into the Jesmond services on Clayton TV at the height of the pandemic came from beyond the normal membership of the church. David's vision of the power of Christian broadcasting has borne much fruit.

## Conclusion

In October 1999, the front walls of Jesmond Parish Church were daubed with obscene graffiti including drawings and words such as '*Holloway Out*' and '*Gays OK*'. In an interview with journalists, David was quoted as saying in response:

> *All I stand for is orthodox Christian values . . . Political correctness almost forbids or prevents the traditional morality of the majority in this country from being expressed. But this vandalism will not stop me from saying what I and many others think is right.*[237]

David has been consistent in contending for truth, whether it was over the virgin birth and the empty tomb or sexual ethics, and has stood his ground, despite the opposition that he has received. When events such

237.https://www.theguardian.com/world/1999/oct/23/religion.uk2 (accessed 17.12.21).

as the graffiti incident mentioned above take place, David bounces back, not prepared to give in to the '*madness of crowds*' (as we saw Douglas Murray describing it in chapter 4). Contending for truth, including rebuking error, does give rise to opposition, but there are also many who will follow in support behind brave leadership. The growth of Jesmond Parish Church, including its church plants, is testament to the support that faithful preaching of the gospel by David and others bears fruit.

David has not sought success or plaudits. What he wants is for people to respond to the truth of the gospel and the light that it brings, and for himself to be true to the calling that God has given him.

# Chapter 22: Julie Maxwell

In May 2021 an extraordinary case was reported by the Daily Mail: a school chaplain employed by the independent Trent College near Nottingham, a school affiliated to the Church of England, had been disciplined following a sermon he had preached in one of the regular chapel services in 2019. Not only had Dr Bernard Randall been disciplined by the college, but his case was reported to Prevent, a government strategy to combat any radicalisation that could lead to a terrorist threat. Fortunately, the police decided that there was no case to answer and so no further action was taken. The school did, however, tell Dr Randall that they would censor future sermons, and he was finally made redundant in December 2020.[238]

This situation was devastating for Dr Randall. But what was so contentious about his sermon? The answer seemed to lie in the fact that the school had commissioned an organisation called Educate and Celebrate to promote issues related to gender identity and sexual orientation within every aspect of school life. Bernard Randall was simply responding to a question that a student had asked him to speak on: '*How come we are told we have to accept all this LGBT stuff in a Christian school?*' He felt that was a reasonable question to ask, particularly as it was concerned with a conflict of values. Included in his sermon were these words:

> *So, all in all, if you are at ease with 'all this LGBT stuff', you're entitled to keep to those ideas; if you are not comfortable with it, for the various, especially religious, reasons, you should* ***not*** *feel required to change. Whichever side of this conflict of ideas you*

238. Ian Gallagher, 'Fee-paying boarding school reports its chaplain to anti-terror unit Prevent' (*Daily Mail*, May 8th 2021).

> *come down on, or even if you are unsure of some of it, the most important thing is to remember that loving your neighbour as yourself does not mean agreeing with everything he or she says; it means that when we have these discussions there is no excuse for personal attacks or abusive language. We should all respect that people on each side of the debate have deep and strongly held convictions.*[239]

All sorts of questions arise from this case. Why has a church-affiliated school brought in an organisation with completely non-biblical values to permeate school life? Why are students not allowed to think for themselves as to why this is right or not? Why does a chaplain, who encourages students to think for themselves and show love to those they disagree with, get hauled over the coals for doing so? Why do the school authorities consider that this same chaplain has committed such a crime that he should be reported to the police under the Prevent strategy? Why has this man's life and career ended up in tatters?

Another case involving education came to light in March 2021, when a new website was launched called 'Everyone's Invited' which invited young people who had been sexually assaulted at school or elsewhere to come forward and share their experiences. Over five thousand anonymous testimonies had been uploaded on to the website.[240] *The Guardian* reported:

> *Each account is achingly raw, personal and unique. But when they are collected in one place online, a pattern emerges. Girls are being constantly touched and molested by boys at school. Their days are punctuated by sexual remarks, casual degradations and*

239. Bernard Randall, 'A School Sermon: Competing Ideologies' (Christian Concern, May 10th 2021).
240. https://www.everyonesinvited.uk/ (accessed 17.12.21).

> *explicit photos and texts from their male classmates. And outside school, they are being raped and sexually assaulted at parties, often when they are drunk and particularly vulnerable.*[241]

The school inspectorate, Ofsted, undertook a review in schools and came up with similar findings, saying, '*It is concerning that for some children, incidents are so commonplace that they see no point in reporting them.*'[242]

It is very easy to blame poor discipline or bad teaching of relationships and sex education in schools, but the problem must go deeper. As a result of what they see in the media and the poor examples that are given to them by politicians and others in authority, young people have been led to believe that all that matters is their own sexual gratification.

Since the 1960s there has been a massive change in the moral climate with regard to sexual ethics. The traditional Christian view of the primacy of marriage between a man and a woman is mocked in many progressive circles. The erosion of an institution that has been the bedrock of societies for generations has resulted in moral confusion, social instability and the rape culture evidenced by Ofsted. Even churches have added to this confusion. In June 2021, the Methodist conference passed a motion allowing same-sex weddings to take place in Methodist churches and to be conducted by Methodist ministers. This followed the example of some other denominations in the United Kingdom, but takes it out of line with most denominations that continue to follow the Bible's teachings. The confusion is made worse by the holding of two completely contradictory views: '*Within the Methodist Church this* [marriage] *is understood in two ways: that marriage can only be between a man and a woman; that marriage can be between any two people. The Methodist Church affirms both understandings and makes provision in its*

241. Donna Ferguson, 'How schoolgirls finally found voice to tell of sexual abuse' (*The Guardian*, March 28th 2021).
242. Ofsted, 'Review of sexual abuse in schools and colleges' (June 10th 2021).

*Standing Orders for them.*'[243] How can it possibly be that marriage can *only* be between a man and a woman, and at the same time between *any* two people? No wonder there is moral confusion.

In addition, the competing claims of various groups vociferously promoting different lifestyle choices have often prevented those with more conservative views from speaking out and proclaiming the truth. In particular, young people may well be confused by these different philosophies and lifestyles. They need to know that the Christian faith offers a radically different approach to sexual ethics, with an emphasis on men and women being created in the image of God, created different from each other, and God's gift of sexual intimacy to be enjoyed in marriage.[244]

One organisation that has tried to spread this message largely against the prevailing trend, is Lovewise, a charity founded in 2002, based in Newcastle, and of which I have been privileged to be a trustee. Over the years they have produced high-quality resources to be used in schools and churches, promoting the biblical view of sexual ethics, including the importance of marriage. Lovewise representatives have spoken in schools in different parts of the country.[245]

One of the Lovewise representatives who has worked very effectively in schools in the Basingstoke area is Dr Julie Maxwell. Julie has worked in community paediatrics in that area for over twenty years, and through that role she has developed strong relationships with families. As a result of the respect that she has gained as an NHS professional and the contacts that she had developed, Julie has been able to teach Lovewise materials in relationships and sex education sessions.

I have heard her give an excellent presentation at a Lovewise conference, attended meetings with her and interviewed her for

243. Hattie Williams, 'Methodists agree to same-sex weddings in church' (*Church Times*, June 30th 2021).
244. Genesis 1:21-24, quoted by Jesus in Matthew 19:4-6.
245. https://lovewise.org.uk/ (accessed 17.12.21).

the purposes of this chapter. I have also watched her give interviews for Coalition for Marriage and a Truth for Science DVD entitled *The Transgender Agenda*.

## Early life

Julie was born in rural Herefordshire in 1971. Her mother provided a strong Christian input, although her father was not a Christian, and Julie attended a small Brethren-based assembly. She became a Christian at the age of nine at a special anniversary service held in a marquee, and from there became an active member of the church youth group.

After school, Julie went on to study medicine at Cardiff University for five years. During her time there, she worshipped at Heath Evangelical Church and involved herself with the Navigators organisation, leading student Bible studies, as well as leading the Christian Medical Fellowship. She also helped on Word of Life camps during her holidays. In her fourth year she met her future husband, Alistair, whom she later married in 1997. After qualifying, she spent a year in Cardiff, and then moved to Basingstoke in 1996, which has been her home ever since and where she and Alistair raised their family of three children. Julie is currently an associate specialist community paediatrician, with particular interests in special needs, language disorders and autism.

In her years at university, in training and at work, she has never hidden the fact that she is a Christian. She did recall on one occasion how her colleagues in a coffee room in Portsmouth were '*absolutely gobsmacked*' that she was not living with Alistair before they got married, but rather that she was lodging with a family from the church in Basingstoke and he was sharing a flat with a friend from church. In her role as a paediatrician, she is able to talk with parents about the effects of family breakdown – for example, having a stepfather in the family – from a Christian moral stance, without being judgemental. She is very much accepted by the families with whom she works.

## Work in schools

Julie first came across Lovewise at a sex education conference run by Anglican Mainstream that she attended in her role as a school governor in 2010, and took some leaflets from the Lovewise stand. At that conference she also met Liz Jones, a retired paediatrician, who along with another paediatrician, Chris Richards, originally founded Lovewise. This initial contact was going to be very important, as a crisis soon arose over the sex education programme at the school that one of her children attended. When she saw the material to which her children were going to be exposed, she was horrified, and started to make a noise about it, believing that she would get support from other parents. This unfortunately did not happen, and so she decided to withdraw her daughter from the programme. She researched alternative programmes and came across the Lovewise material, which she and another parent started to use at home with a group of children from their church, St Mary's Basingstoke. These teaching sessions with children from the church have continued each year since.

Julie met Liz Jones again at a Lovewise conference a year later. When she heard what Julie was doing, Liz asked her if she would be interested in doing some presentations for Lovewise. Liz and Chris were keen that the message of Lovewise should be delivered in different schools across the country, and so it was ideal to employ someone with Julie's knowledge, experience and Christian commitment to do presentations in Hampshire. Julie agreed to take this on, and she soon built up a number of schools in the Basingstoke area that she was able to visit, comprising a mixture of primary, secondary, special, faith and non-faith schools.

On the whole, the reaction to her visits has been positive, with teachers, parents and pupils being supportive, even in many cases enthusiastic, and appreciating the opportunities to ask questions. What helped was that Julie often had contacts with people in the schools who paved the way for her, and she was seen to be a professional who knew what she was talking about. Julie was always careful to ensure that parents had the opportunity to find out what she was presenting to their children, and so she held parents' meetings about two weeks in advance of her visiting a school; these meetings tended to be positive, with parents coming away feeling reassured about Julie and her message. They were also pleased that Julie was willing to share her materials with them, something that other organisations were reluctant to do.

Roman Catholic schools were particularly welcoming, especially if Julie's visit coincided with a special mission week that they were having. Indeed, she was able to have an influence on the policy of one particular Roman Catholic secondary school, with regard to their relationship with the lobbying organisation, Stonewall. Julie was a regular visitor to this school making presentations on topics such as marriage and pornography using Lovewise materials.

If only the Church of England had been as supportive! Several Church of England primary schools were welcoming, until some parents looked at the Lovewise Online website, which had been set up to give biblical answers to questions on sexual ethics for Christian young people.[246] The local Anglican diocese decided that Lovewise should not be endorsed to go into schools in the diocese. Julie and her friend Sarah, who helped her with presentations, arranged to have a meeting with the Diocesan Director of Education, who said, '*It's not necessarily what you are teaching that is the issue, but just like if someone went into a school, and we found out that they were a racist, we wouldn't be able to have them in.*' Julie rather taken aback replied, '*So you are comparing our biblical views on marriage to racism?*' Very embarrassed, he had to deny actually meaning that, but nonetheless his policy remained in force.

In her work in schools, Julie wants to provide a balance to the prevailing approach of what she calls 'sex positive education'. In an

246. https://lovewiseonline.org/ (accessed 17.12.21).

interview with Tony Rucinski of Coalition for Marriage, she described sex positive education thus:

> *You just give children a whole load of information, and the trend is sex positive education where you just teach them how good sex is (which it is in the right context), and you give them this information and say that as long as everyone is consenting, it is fine.*

She then went on to explain that the reality was far from fine.

> *But what is consent? How can you consent to something that you do not fully understand, because you are not old enough to? Schools are not giving all the information. They are not explaining the impact of casual partnerships on the stability of future marriage. They are not telling them about the emotional impact of casual sex. They are not telling them about potential issues if they get pregnant and have to have a termination. So they say that they are giving all the facts, but actually they're not.*[247]

## Marriage and parenthood

One of Julie's strong messages when she visits schools concerns the importance of marriage. She believes in this because of what the Bible teaches about a man and a woman coming together, and about how marriage is a picture of our relationship with Christ.[248] She has also seen the devastating consequences in her own family and in her professional work of marriages falling apart.

One particularly sad example of marital breakdown that she saw at an early stage of her life took place when she was at university. A couple

247. https://www.youtube.com/watch?v=XFt4EGf1hSg (accessed 17.12.21).
248. Ephesians 5:22-33

who organised the Word of Life camps that Julie helped on, and who were very influential in her life, decided to end their marriage. To make matters worse, another couple was split up by each taking one of the partners for themselves. This rocked the faith of many who helped on the camps, and they had to support each other to get through it.

An example closer to home, however, was when in 2002 she discovered, as a young mother herself, that her own father, who was not a Christian, had been having a clandestine affair with a woman for eight years. Her mother, who was a Christian, Julie and her sister were devastated by this revelation. Sixteen years later in 2018, Julie posted an article on Lovewise Online to give advice to Christian young people who find themselves in the same situation when their parents' marriage falls apart. She makes a number of points, but two are worth emphasising here:

> *No marriage is perfect and marriage needs protecting and constant work to keep it healthy. Relationships take a lot of work and we need to work hard at our own relationships and support others who may be struggling. Marriage is a wonderful gift from God but it isn't always easy and must be taken very seriously.*

How important it is that married couples and young people looking forward to the day when they are married follow Julie's advice. Likewise, with God's help, we can forgive those who have wronged us.

> *We can forgive even when we have been hurt very badly. That relationship may never be quite what it was before, but it can continue and we can still love someone who has let us down because God loves us (and them)!*[249]

249. https://lovewiseonline.org/when-my-family-broke-down/ (accessed 17.12.21).

In the interview referred to in the previous section, Julie gave advice to married couples with their children. The first piece of advice was to prioritise their marriage, so that they had time for each other to nurture their relationship. Many couples concentrate so much on the welfare of their children that they neglect each other. By prioritising their marriage, parents will be good role models for their children. The second piece of advice was simply to be there for their children. Parents need to make sure that they have time for their children, ensuring that they lead them in the right direction and listen to their concerns.

In that same interview, she was asked if it mattered if children grew up with their biological parents as long as they were loved. Julie agreed that love was very important and admitted that even with biological parents they might not experience love, which will significantly affect their lives. Nevertheless, Julie emphasised:

> *Biology is hugely important. You only have to look at children who are adopted, for example, or who never know their biological father, which is quite common, and those children, no matter how much they are loved, they always want to know where they came from. They always want to know who their parents are, and so clearly biology is hugely important, as well as love.*

She was also asked about the stability of families and whether it really matters how many times one of their parents changes partners. Julie drew on her experience from her clinics. Here she had seen so many children suffer in their development as a result of a lack of stability in the family home with different partners coming in and then moving on.

Proponents of marriage, such as Julie, who work with children and young people are often criticised for making the children feel bad because their own parents are not married. In the interview, Julie made it clear that that was not the case. When asked that sort of question by, say, a single parent at a parents' meeting before one of her school visits, she would reply, '*It's not like that. It's about teaching them what they can have.*' She then went on to explain that usually the parents will say that they want their children to get married and to have a happy marriage.

Julie is so right in wanting to present the best, indeed God's ideal, relationship in her work with children and young people. She has seen the damage that the breakdown of family life can do to children and young people, and the evidence in society points to the need to give marriage the place that God intended it to have. The Bishop of Manchester might consider adultery as only '*a middle-aged man having a bit of a fling*', as he depicted the affair that ultimately led to the resignation of Health Secretary, Matt Hancock on GB News on June 27th 2021. God, however, sees marriage as a covenant made between a man and a woman, something that he has instituted as part of his common grace given to all people, with adultery seen as breaking a commandment against his holy law. That is the message that Julie and others are trying to promote.

## Transgender issues

Wide-scale discussion of transgender issues is something that has appeared relatively recently, but it is a controversy from which we cannot escape. It is everywhere, and news items, such as the cancelling of J.K. Rowling that we mentioned in chapter 4, show how prevalent these issues are. Not only do they demonstrate how widespread they are, they show how damaging they can be. If you use the wrong pronouns, support someone who makes the traditional binary distinction between male and female, argue that a man who has allegedly made the transition to being a woman cannot compete in women's sporting events or use women's changing areas, you might find yourself under pressure. You might experience bullying from the transgender lobby, disciplinary procedures or being investigated by the police as a perpetrator of a hate crime. It is no wonder that people are reluctant to say what they believe.

All of this adds to the confusion as to what is right and wrong, and what is truth and what are lies. Children are particularly vulnerable when it comes to this confusion, as it seems that from an ever-earlier age they are taught that they can change gender if they wish. After the BBC produced a relationships and sex education video for children in 2019 which amazingly claimed that there were over a hundred genders,[250] Celia Walden, a *Telegraph* columnist, wrote, '*All of which is likely to leave us with a generation of lost, confused and angry young adults asking a question we will find it very difficult to answer: "How did you let this happen?"*'[251]

Julie Maxwell is one of those, however, who does want to contend for the truth to prevent children and young people in particular from being confused. For her, truth is based on the Bible's teaching that God created us male and female,[252] which is backed up by scientific evidence that there are only two genders which are assigned at conception, when either an X or a Y chromosome is fused with the X chromosome in the egg.

In 2017, she began to take an interest in this area, as she became increasingly worried about what even young children were being taught about gender. She attended a couple of seminars run by the Tavistock Gender Identity Disorder Clinic, and was concerned by the messages presented. Gender dysphoria was seen as a mismatch between what a person felt was their gender identity and what was their biological sex. The Tavistock approach was that medical intervention in the form of, for example, puberty blockers or full-scale surgery were appropriate solutions for those who had diagnosed themselves as having gender dysphoria. Julie felt that these solutions were totally inappropriate, and

250. https://www.youtube.com/watch?v=r6Cu0JdBDtQ (accessed 17.12.21). This video was removed by the BBC in January 2021 as a result of the criticism it received.
251. Celia Walden, 'How dare the BBC teach children that there are "100 genders"?' (*The Telegraph*, September 9th 2019).
252. Genesis 1:27

it was better to treat gender dysphoria as a mental health issue, where a person can receive help to become compatible with the biological body that they had been given.

In the DVD *The Transgender Agenda*, she made this statement to show how the Tavistock approach was so wrong:

> *I think that one of the things that bothers me about the whole transgender issue is that we treat it completely differently from any other similar condition such as anorexia or body dysmorphia. We would not seek to alter a person's body to fit in with what they think or feel. We would always seek to help them to fit with what they are, the reality of what they are, and it seems in this whole transgender issue, we are throwing* [medical science] *out of the window. We are using experimental treatments and we are using them completely differently to any other illness particularly in children.*

In the same video, Dr Peter Saunders, Chief Executive of the International Christian Medical and Dental Association, talked of '*a huge unregulated experiment being carried out with children*'.[253]

Julie is passionate about the long-term wellbeing of children, and is desperate to see them protected from well-meaning adults who want to give them the freedom to choose their gender identity. In the video, she spoke about the need to guide and protect children and young people.

> *Children are vulnerable. They need guiding. They need protecting. Children if left to their own devices would happily eat chocolate all day, watch television all day, but we are considered poor parents*

253. 'The Transgender Agenda: a scientific and compassionate response' (Truth in Science, 2020).

*if we let them do that. But in this situation, children are being given puberty blockers because they feel that they are a different sex. We have no idea what the long-term outcome of this is, and children need protecting from this experimental treatment.*

In 2018, Julie, along with Chris Richards and Noel McCune, a retired paediatrician from Northern Ireland, wrote a letter to the journal of the Royal College of Paediatrics and Children's Health, in response to material published by the Tavistock Clinic. In the letter they expressed their concern about puberty blockers being used on children to suppress the normal changes in puberty. To their surprise (as this journal does not normally publish letters in response to previous articles), their letter was published in January 2019.[254] As Julie commented on its effectiveness, '*Chris' brilliant phrase "use of puberty blockers for gender dysphoria: a momentous step in the dark" has been widely quoted by many people and eloquently sums up what has now become a widely held view that medicalising children with gender dysphoria is experimental and damaging*.'

Certainly, there was a lot of positive follow up to their letter. Almost immediately, a psychiatrist from Winchester contacted Julie and springboarded her into a network of secular clinicians who were generally like-minded in their concern about the transgender movement from a medical point of view. She has learned a lot from this group, and it has been good to find other people to fight the battle with. She is known as a Christian and they have had interesting discussions about the nature of identity, with Julie believing strongly that our identity can only really be found in God. She also believes that she has been a positive witness to the group, by saying that although she does not believe in same-sex

254. Christopher Richards, Julie Maxwell and Noel McCune, '*Use of puberty blockers for gender dysphoria: a momentous step in the dark' (Archives of Disease in Childhood, January 2019).*

marriage, that does not make her homophobic, in the sense of hating individuals who profess to be gay.

One event which gave Julie great encouragement was the case of Keira Bell. This brave young lady took the Tavistock Clinic to court because of the treatment that she had received from it. As a teenager she had believed that her feelings about her body were not in line with being born female. The Tavistock encouraged her to make the transition to allegedly becoming a male and provided her with puberty blockers. As an adult she later received surgical treatment to supposedly make her male, which ultimately Keira regretted. Upon later feeling that she had been pressurised into this, and believing that it was a mistake, Keira decided to detransition to live as a woman. She still, however, bears the marks of this process as her breasts have been removed, and she has a deep voice and facial hair. She brought a lawsuit against the Tavistock, which resulted in a judicial review of the practices of the clinic. In her evidence to the judicial review, she stated:

> *I started to realise that the vision I had as a teenager of becoming male was strictly a fantasy and that it was not possible. My biological make-up was still female and it showed, no matter how much testosterone was in my system or how much I would go to the gym. I was being perceived as a man by society, but it was not enough. I started to just see a woman with a beard, which is what I was. I felt like a fraud and I began to feel more lost, isolated and confused than I did when I was pre-transition.*[255]

The judges ruled against the Tavistock in December 2020. They argued that the decision whether to take puberty blockers was very complex,

255. Royal Courts of Justice, 'Bell v Tavistock Judgement' (December 1st 2020), paragraph 81.

and children under the age of sixteen would find it very difficult to weigh up both the immediate and long-term consequences of such a decision.[256]

A sinister development in making the ability to help children and young people much more difficult is the proposed ban on carrying out conversion therapy on those who identify as gay, lesbian, bisexual or transgender. At the time of writing, the British government has carried out a consultation on the issue. Probably all are agreed that suspect medical practices are cruel and should be outlawed. The issue arises when people with same-sex attraction or gender dysphoria seek counselling or prayer because they want God to deal with such feelings, or when pastors preach on biblical sexual ethics. It is to be hoped that Christian preaching, prayer or counselling are not included in the proposed ban, but activists, including those who profess to be Christians, want such activities to be banned in order to celebrate the lifestyles of the LGBT community. The state of Victoria in Australia has already outlawed all prayer and counselling on sexual ethics, with offenders facing up to ten years in prison. Indeed, anything but absolute affirmation is seen to be conversion therapy. Such a law is frightening, at one stroke overriding two thousand years of Christian teaching and practice![257]

Clinicians, whether Christian or not, are placed in a difficult position in trying to help children and young people who approach them for treatment in this area. Julie puts it thus:

> *You can already see that even though there is not yet a ban in this country, people are afraid of being accused of conversion therapy. People are afraid to question or even engage with these children*

256. Royal Courts of Justice, 'Bell v Tavistock Judgement', paragraph 151. This decision was, however, overturned in the Court of Appeal in September 2021. Keira Bell hopes to appeal to the Supreme Court.
257. The Christian Institute, 'Banning conversion theory or banning the gospel?' (November 2020); 'Conversion therapy update' (May 2021).

*and young people a lot of the time. That's what I see at work. All people are prepared to do now is to refer to the Tavistock. People just don't want to get involved with it, and a number of work colleagues say to me, 'You're very brave.' But at the end of the day, there are children who are hurting, who are very distressed and who need help. Just palming them off and throwing medication at them is not the answer.*

For Julie, transgender is not just an issue, but rather it is about people who need help. By supporting a number of Christian families who have children struggling with gender dysphoria, she has seen at close hand the pain experienced by children and their parents. Young people and their parents facing such a situation need loving Christian support.

## Conclusion

Julie has consistently contended for what she believes. As a parent, for example, she tried to take on Hampshire County Council, her local council, over their sex education policy. This resulted in her meeting local councillors, her local member of parliament and the Head of Children's Services. Some of those she met disagreed with Julie's position; there were others, however, who seemed to understand, but did not feel strong enough to go against council policy.

She and a group of other parents are currently challenging the council on their LGBT guidance to schools. Some of the group are Christians, while others are not believers, but all are in agreement over transgender issues. Julie has been very open about her faith within this group and has had interesting conversations, particularly with the members of the group who claim to be atheist. The official letter of complaint from the group may result in a judicial review and court case.

Julie has a passion for the wellbeing of children and young people. This is seen in the way that she undertakes her professional role as a paediatrician, her work in schools with Lovewise, her campaigning work, and the work that she and Alistair do with the children and young people in their church. All of this flows from her Christian faith which lies at the heart of her life. She knows that God has created us to live in a particular way, and following that path is what is best for society.

The way that Julie contends for truth is a very brave one, going as it does against much progressive thinking on sexual ethics. Yet she believes strongly that she is doing what God wants her to do, and as such she feels that she has no option but to take the stand that she does. As she takes this stand, she does it in such a way that shows the love and compassion that God has for his people. It is God at work through Julie that allows her to be accepted by many people who hold quite different views to her. It is God at work in her that has enabled, for example, an atheist lady to take Lovewise material from Julie to use with her child because there was nothing else suitable to use – and who knows how that story will end?

# Chapter 23: Charles Price

There are some Christians who continue to have an influence on your life many years after you have first met them. For me, one such Christian is Charles Price. I had not met with Charles in over thirty years, and so it was a tremendous pleasure to carry out a series of Zoom interviews with him in order to write this chapter.

Charles and I first met in August 1973 when I joined the mission team that he was leading in Muirkirk, a small former mining village in Ayrshire. Charles was a student at the time at the Bible Training Institute in Glasgow, and had accepted the invitation to lead the team to reach out to children, young people and adults in the village. It was a privilege to work with Charles, to learn from him and to see people of all ages respond to the claims of Christ as he and members of the team proclaimed the gospel message. It was actually an even greater privilege to meet Ella (she suggested that I say this!), who lived in the village and was a member of the team, and whom I married three years later in the parish church in Muirkirk.

Since that first meeting in Muirkirk, I took the opportunity to invite Charles to speak at a number of meetings in different churches with which I was involved. This included speaking at an evangelistic youth club in my home church in Grangemouth about his experiences of Bible smuggling to Christians living on the other side of the Iron Curtain; speaking at a young people's Bible Class residential from that same church; leading a week-long mission in St Neots in Cambridgeshire; speaking at a residential weekend in the Lake District for members of a church in Bedlington in Northumberland. Ella and I also took the opportunity to go and hear him speak if we knew that he was ministering in a town close to where we lived.

The main reasons why we invited Charles to be involved in speaking at these different events were that he had a living faith which was evident for all to see and that he was an exceptionally clear presenter of Christian truth – people listen to what he is saying and many respond by taking that initial step of faith. His preaching also reaches the hearts of Christians, God clearly speaking to them about how he desires we should live. I can still vividly remember him when he spoke at the 'Huntingdon Keswick Convention' in May 1984. God spoke directly to me when Charles said, '*You can be as spiritual as you want to be. Don't blame your church, your pastor or anyone else for your spiritual condition. It is only between you and God*.' That hit home to me, as I am sure that it did to others.

One aspect of Charles' speaking that was very powerful was his ability to make use of vivid illustrations. One illustration that I remember him using (and which I have used many times myself, although attributing it to 'a friend') was to explain the nature of faith. His point was that it did not matter how much faith that you have, it is who you put your faith in that is important. He recalled his first flight, and how he was a bit nervous about making it. He sat between a very relaxed businessman who had made the flight on many occasions and an old lady who seemed terrified. The three of them, all with their different degrees of faith in the pilot of the plane, got to their end destination at the same time. It is putting our faith in God that matters, not how much faith we have, and he will see us through to the end of our lives. Yet, the person who enjoyed the flight most was the relaxed businessman and the one who enjoyed it least was the terrified old lady. The businessman had more experience of safe flying and, as a result, he had far greater faith in the process. It is the same with God; the more we get to know God the more we will trust him and the more we will enjoy living the Christian life with him beside us.[258]

---

258. When I originally heard Charles tell this story, he used much more dramatic flair than I have used here. To read the illustration in more detail, please refer to Charles Price, *Christ for Real* (Kregel Publications, 1995), pp. 128-132.

Since that initial flight, Charles has spent much time circling the globe to preach God's message in over a hundred countries (and is no longer nervous!). The travel restrictions resulting from the pandemic have of course curtailed much of that. In his family newsletter of January 2021 he wrote, '*For 24 consecutive weeks in 2020 I slept in my own bed every night – the longest period of time since I was in school! I didn't board a flight for 7 months, my longest time on the ground since 1975.*'

Charles is a highly popular Christian speaker across the world. He has ended up living in Canada where he has been Lead Pastor of the People's Church in Toronto and, since his retirement from that post, he is Minister at Large with that church. His story and his dedication to contend for the Lord Jesus Christ should be an encouragement and challenge to all of us.

## From country lad to city student

Revival spread through Wales in 1904 when the Spirit of God touched men and women in a fresh way as they met in large numbers in churches and chapels. People repented of their sin before God, often in tears, and gave their lives afresh to the Lord Jesus Christ. As a result, lives were transformed, relationships were renewed, crime rates plummeted, heavy drinking, gambling and the use of foul language almost disappeared, and productivity in the mines and other workplaces rose.

The Spirit of God did not just come down in places of worship, but in other places such as pubs. One man to experience that in Monmouthshire was a farm worker called Edward Price. He had scoffed at the whole idea of revival and mocked those who were caught up in it, until he experienced God for himself one night in the pub. He came home excited, although not drunk as he often was. He told his wife what had happened, and the whole family over the next few weeks were converted. This man was, of course, Charles' great-grandfather, and thus the Christian roots of Charles' family were established.

The family moved across the border into Herefordshire, where Charles was born in 1949, and where he grew up on the farm on which his father worked. His parents were both Christians, and Charles, one of six children, had a secure family upbringing, although always just on the edge of poverty. The family went to the local Brethren assembly and Charles heard the gospel message many times. It was, however, not until he was twelve years old that he had complete assurance of salvation. He attended a Youth for Christ event in Hereford Town Hall one Saturday evening. A Billy Graham film was shown, and Charles felt drawn to God in a new way, realising that he had to make a decision. At the end of the meeting he prayed that God would make him a Christian that night. As he later wrote, '*I went home that night with an assurance that I had not known before, and which I have never doubted since. I was a Christian*.'[259]

He attended weekly youth events in the church, grew in his knowledge of biblical truth and tried to live for the Lord, but he felt frustrated, feeling a failure in the light of his struggles during his teenage years. A significant event took place, however, when Charles attended a series of meetings in 1962, again in Hereford Town Hall, led by Major Ian Thomas, the Christian who had more influence on his life than any other.

Major Thomas invited the young people at the meetings to come up to Capernwray Hall, a Christian conference centre he had founded, to take part in the Bible programme that the centre ran for a week that summer. Charles knew that neither he nor his family could afford the cost of going there, but Major Thomas was insistent that Charles should go and he even paid for Charles and his brother to go at his own expense. Later, the major's wife would tell Charles that God had prompted him '*to get to know that boy*'. Charles was to go there for a week in 1962 and again in 1963. In the summer of 1965, at the age of sixteen, he spent six weeks there, working on the estate and also as a steward in the evening

259. Charles Price, *Christ for Real*, p. 12.

meetings where he could hear the talks each night for six weeks. This particular year was to be life changing for Charles.

In many ways, Ian Thomas' testimony was similar to that of Charles. He also became a Christian at the age of twelve, and for the next seven years he busied himself in Christian activity. By the time he was nineteen, he was absolutely exhausted as a result of his whirlwind of activity. One night, God spoke to him in his despair:

> *You have been busy trying to do for Me all that only I can do through you. Now supposing I am your life, and you begin to accept it as a fact, then I am your strength! You have been pleading and begging for that for seven years. I am your victory in every area of your life, if you want it! I am the One to whom it is perfectly natural to go out and win souls; and I know precisely where to go and find them. Why don't you begin to reckon upon Me and say 'Thank you'?*

Ian Thomas realised that Jesus was there all along and that he wanted to run his life. The next morning Ian was able to say: '*Lord Jesus, I thank You for the first time in my life, this is Your day! I no longer have the burden of running my own life.*'[260]

Charles was to learn that same lesson from Major Thomas particularly in the time he spent working at the conference centre over the summer of 1965, where the message of Christ living in you was constantly reinforced. Charles was later to describe the difference in experience as like trying to mow the lawn with a motor mower but without engaging the clutch, which meant '*manually operating something that was meant to run on its own power*'.[261] In other words, we achieve nothing when

260. https://deeperchristian.com/major-ian-thomas/ (accessed 17.12.21).
261. Charles Price, *Alive in Christ* (Kregel Publications, 1995), p. 9.

we live our lives using our own strength rather than letting Christ live through us.

After he left school, Charles worked on the farm, which provided him with much satisfaction but he also knew that he wanted to go to Bible college. God had also put on his heart that he wanted to travel and see the world. He got the opportunity to travel when he took on the role of a farm assistant in Southern Rhodesia (now Zimbabwe) working for a Christian farmer. He took up this appointment on the proviso that it would only be for two years before going to Bible college, and so he took his flight as described earlier in the chapter. Charles loved his Rhodesian experience; the outdoor work in a different environment was very fulfilling, and the family with whom he lived were godly people who taught him much.

In 1970, Charles went back to Capernwray to study on their year-long Bible school before beginning his three-year course at the Bible Training Institute (BTI) in Glasgow, situated in the heart of the city. Studying in Glasgow was an excellent opportunity for Charles for all sorts of reasons. For one thing, he had little experience of city life, and so working in Glasgow broadened his horizon and made him consider how to communicate the gospel to urban dwellers. He took whatever opportunities God gave him, such as serving on the month-long Don Summers Tent Hall campaign in 1973 and leading the missions in Muirkirk in 1973 and 1974. Study at BTI was academically rigorous, and it provided him with the necessary tools to study Scripture in a structured way.

He used his summer holidays from college to gain new experiences to share the message of the gospel and in so doing to trust in God in different ways. This included travelling with a friend, smuggling Bibles into Eastern Europe, which under the Communist regimes of the time were officially closed to the gospel. God protected them during their travels taking Bibles to believers in different countries. They concealed their 'contraband' in secret compartments in their car, in the hope that border guards or other officials would not find them. On one occasion, waiting at the Romanian border to be let through, they realised that they might be in serious trouble, as the car in front was thoroughly searched by the border guards with their belongings being strewn across the road. If the same sort of search happened to them, they were likely to be arrested. The border guard approached them and asked them where they came from, and when they replied that they had come from Britain, he said, '*Bobby Charlton is the best footballer in the world*.' He then let them through. It could be argued that because the guards only thoroughly searched cars at random, and the car before had been searched, it was unlikely that their car would be searched. Charles and his friend, however, were convinced that the protecting hand of God was upon them. The pastors and their congregations were overwhelmed at meeting western Christians who had brought them much-needed Bibles in their own languages.

## To Capernwray and the wider world

Immediately after he left BTI in July 1974, he volunteered as a host and usher at the International Congress on Evangelisation held in Lausanne in Switzerland, headed up by American evangelist, Billy Graham, and leading evangelical Anglican minister and theologian, John Stott. Over 2,300 evangelical leaders from more than 150 countries attended and drew up the Lausanne Covenant that provided new direction for world evangelisation. Charles was catapulted into the centre of evangelical life by looking after a number of these leaders and by having one of the best seats in the house for the main meetings as he ushered them to their seats. He made contacts with key leaders in Lausanne that would be fruitful in years to come. This was all of God's doing; Charles could not have manipulated this himself.

In the summer and autumn months after Lausanne, he fulfilled a number of speaking engagements, teaching Bible truths to both Christians and non-believers. Although he enjoyed these months of being an itinerant speaker, he realised that he needed to be part of an organisation, rather than simply being a freelance preacher. By the end of the year, he had six offers of jobs from different churches and organisations, but none really struck Charles as the one that God wanted him to take up. He sought advice from a friend, Bill Galyer, who was an open-air evangelist. Bill suggested that it sounded as if none of them were suitable for Charles, as he did not really know what he wanted to do; in other words, he lacked vision. Bill told him that he needed to spend time alone with God and find the vision that God had for him.

Charles spent three days on his own with God in a Christian conference centre in Herefordshire, walking, praying, reading, meditating and taking notes on his different thoughts. He found a key verse, Psalm 37:4, that was to provide the fundamental promise that would uphold his vision: '*Take delight in the Lord, and he will give you the desires of your heart*.' Too often we see God as someone who is going to spoil our enjoyment of life and give us the opposite of what we really want. In this verse, Charles learned that the contrary was true: if we align ourselves with God, delighting in him, then he will give us his desires, so that God's will and our desires become one.

As a result of spending three days in retreat with God, Charles came up with six aims for his life, a six-part vision. None of the six job offers really fitted with his vision, and so he wrote back declining them. As he put the letters in the post box, he felt a terrific sense of relief, as if a huge burden had been lifted from his shoulders. He still, however, did not have a job, but he was trusting God completely to show him the way forward.

He did not have long to wait, as only a week later he stayed overnight at Capernwray, on his way to take a speaking engagement in Scotland.

Alan Redpath, a well-known and influential speaker and pastor, was due to be speaking at the morning meeting, but had taken ill with a bout of flu. Charles was wakened during the night and was asked to take Alan Redpath's place. When Charles asked the messenger why Major Thomas could not do it, he was told that Major Thomas had specifically asked that Charles should do it. For Charles, this was both a privilege and a challenge, as Redpath was one of Charles' 'Christian heroes'.

After the service, Charles met up with Major Thomas, who asked him what his plans were, and of course at this stage he had no definite plans. Only fifteen minutes into the conversation, however, he invited Charles to join the staff at Capernwray. On receiving that invitation, Charles asked the major what he would be doing. In reply, the major outlined an idea that covered all six parts that Charles had written down only a few days before. Charles explained to the major about his experience on retreat and his six-part vision. It was clear to both of them that this was where Charles was meant to be, fulfilling both the vision that Charles had been given, and the word that God had given the major when he first met Charles at Hereford Town Hall all these years before.[262] Thus began a role for Charles on the staff at Capernwray that was to last and indeed develop further over more than twenty-five years.

In many ways, Charles continued as he had been doing before, travelling across the United Kingdom and beyond, telling others about Jesus, seeing people make a commitment to him and growing in their knowledge of him. He was, however, now doing this as a representative of Capernwray. In addition, he helped with the summer evangelistic youth programme, when about two hundred young people came week by week from all over Europe to take part in the activities that were run. Many young people came to know the Lord as a result of these weeks. In due course, Charles was asked to lead the summer programme and

262. Charles has never revealed to anybody apart from Ian Thomas what these six points were; they were between himself and God.

teach in the Bible school that he had originally attended as a student. Ultimately he became principal of the Bible school that draws students from all around the world.

His Capernwray ministry opened doors in many countries, eventually travelling to over a hundred countries across each continent of the world. He had sensed that, as part of his vision, travel would play a role in his ministry. Charles believes that these opportunities developed from prayer. When he was working in Southern Rhodesia, he had a map on his wall and he started almost randomly praying for countries on the map, without knowing very much about the spiritual states of these countries. As it turned out, he realised much later that many countries in which he had opportunity to preach were the countries that he had been praying for. For Charles there was an important spiritual principle here: a burden for prayer precedes calling and opportunities for ministry. During his years with Capernwray, Charles never went looking for engagements, but rather trusted God to open the right doors and send the right invitations as to where he should go.

He also very much appreciated the prayers of faithful people for his continuing ministry. It was particularly important that those in the community in which he was preaching should commit themselves to regular prayer for his work there. An example of how God answered prayer was during a ten-day campaign in the town of Accrington in the north-west of England. For the four months prior to the mission, the church organised daily hour-long prayer meetings that involved praying for individuals that they might be drawn to God. These names were put up on a chalkboard in the church. From the first day of the mission, Charles sensed that God's Spirit was very much at work. At the end of the first evening meeting, three ladies in their eighties came to the Lord; it seemed that they had been going to that church for most of their lives, but they had never been born again of the Spirit.

The church had also arranged for Charles to go into the local high school to take the morning assembly with a fifteen-minute talk to the students. The headteacher, who was a Christian, actually allowed Charles to talk for forty minutes, which gave him much more opportunity to explain why the students should become Christians. At the end of the assembly, the deputy headteacher, came up to him and asked him if he would go round classes with him to talk further to the students. Charles explained that he would love to do that, but it would mean taking the next logical step of explaining how to become a Christian. Strictly speaking, the law did not allow that to take place in a compulsory setting as it was seen to be proselytising, but the deputy headteacher said that he would take full responsibility. Charles and the deputy headteacher went round a number of classes with Charles explaining how to become a Christian, using A for Admit, B for Believe and C for Commit. At the end of the classroom sessions, the deputy headteacher walked out with Charles to his car, and admitted to him that he had learned that morning that he was not a Christian. He said that he would try to come to one of the evening meetings.

In actual fact, he came that evening, and at the end of the evening, he came forward to speak to Charles. He was clearly upset and explained that fifteen years ago his wife came home and said that she had become a Christian. He persuaded her after a week to give up this newfound faith, and she never mentioned it again. Now he realised that he had done the wrong thing on that occasion; he repented and Charles led him to faith in Christ. His wife came to the meeting the following evening when she recommitted her life to the Lord. On the last night of the mission, another teacher came to the meeting with his wife. He had become a Christian as a result of responding to the message that Charles gave his students in his lesson. His wife also became a Christian during the meeting.

Four months later Charles went back to the church for follow-up meetings, including another visit to the school. He again met the deputy headteacher, who with his wife seemed to be getting on well in their new Christian lives, both being active in their local church. He, along with the headteacher, the other teacher who became a Christian and another Christian teacher, met each morning to pray for the school. As a result, yet another teacher had become a Christian. Charles reported this back to the church. One of the church members had said that the deputy headteacher had been very difficult in the past when they wanted Christian groups to have access to the school, so they had put his name on the prayer list to pray that he would not stop Charles from getting into the school. Someone suggested that they should pray even more than that – that the deputy headteacher would be converted! Of course, that's what happened, and indeed much more besides.

## To Toronto

A major change took place in Charles' life when in 2001 he accepted the post of Lead Pastor at the People's Church in Toronto, having worked for Capernwray for twenty-six years. This meant a major upheaval for Charles, his wife Hilary and their three children, as they moved continents and settled into a new way of life and work. (As we saw in chapter 17, Andy Bannister was also to move to Toronto in 2010, with their paths crossing on a number of occasions.)

In 2000, Charles spoke at the Toronto Spiritual Life Convention, an event sponsored by a number of Toronto churches, but held at the People's Church. During the convention he had a strange sensation that this was where he belonged. When he came home and spoke to Hilary, she told him that she also had a sense that Charles would come back from Toronto and tell her something that would change their lives. Six weeks later, he received an email from a friend telling him that the pastor had resigned. At that point, both Charles and Hilary knew that this meant that they would be going to the People's Church. As he relocated to Toronto to lead the church in 2001, it was with a strong sense that this move was from God and that this was where God wanted Charles, Hilary and their family to be.

Being lead pastor at the church was going to be a major challenge for Charles, as it was such a massive operation. The congregation on a Sunday numbered about two thousand with several dozen people on the payroll of the church, plus those who were employed at the school that was attached to the church. It had a global reach, which was part of the vision of the founder Oswald J. Smith, who believed that it should be a missionary sending church. There was a television programme that was broadcast each week over Canada called *The People's Worship Hour*.

Despite all the seeming activity of the church, Charles reckoned that the congregation was discouraged. The previous pastor had only stayed for a few years, and there was also a massive debt of 5.3 million dollars, though many of the congregation were not aware of the scale of the debt.

He knew that he could not fulfil all of the roles that were necessary to take the church forward, as he had neither the time nor the skills to do so. The board of elders really wanted Charles to focus on preaching and teaching, because this was the primary reason that they brought him across the Atlantic. He was, however, effectively the chief executive officer, appointing his staff, and in particular the various pastors and directors of ministries who were primarily accountable to him. Charles himself was accountable to the board for the overall strategic direction of the church and the setting of the church's budget. With regard to finance, the massive debt that the church had was cleared within three years of Charles taking up his role, which was an amazing work of God moving in the hearts of members to give generously and sacrificially.

By the time that Charles retired in 2016, church attendance had more than doubled to a regular weekly attendance of around four thousand five hundred. There were over ninety on the church's payroll, with about seventy-five being full time (including twenty-five in the *Living Truth* ministry of television and radio) and the rest part time. Charles and the leadership wanted to be sure that there was a strong evangelistic thrust to their work so that growth in numbers came from the addition of new converts. The church ran lots of evangelistic courses across the city, including Christianity Explored and Alpha, resulting in many hundreds of people over the years making a commitment to the Lord.

The overseas mission work also expanded using the medium of television that the church had already developed. In 2003, Charles challenged the television staff to work out how the church could use television to support the mission work abroad. They came up with the idea to support particular projects around the HIV-AIDS crises in Malawi and Tanzania at the time and produce three programmes to show the work that was being done in each centre and appeal for funding. That initial project brought in $350,000, which was more than they had dared hope for. This became an annual event (or sometimes even bi-annual) generating close to, and sometimes more than, a million dollars each time. This work expanded at a massive rate with more and more programmes being made all over the world, generating many dollars for major projects. This work expanded beyond all expectations; as giving grew, the scope of different projects was able to expand exponentially. In this way, schools, colleges, hospitals, medical centres and feeding stations in poor regions were built, and humanitarian needs were met, in parallel with the gospel going forward.

This massive work finally caught the attention of the Canadian Foreign Minister, who came to meet Charles at the church and found out the immensity of the work that the church was involved in. In recognition of the huge sums that had been raised, Charles was awarded the Queen Elizabeth II Diamond Jubilee Services Medal for services to humanitarian need. Although Charles would have preferred it to go to the whole team, the medal could only go to individuals. He gratefully accepted it on behalf of all those who worked so hard to produce these programmes and those who had been its beneficiaries.

*The People's Worship Hour* also developed and grew massively as it changed its format and its name to *Living Truth*. The aim of the programme was to concentrate on evangelism and discipleship, and it saw massive growth internationally. Charles saw this expansion as very much a work of God, and as he explained, '*Whereas* Living Truth *went into about seventy countries, we didn't plan any of them*.' One example was in Australia, which all started with Charles receiving an email in 2005 from a Christian doctor. This doctor wanted to have a weekend series of meetings in his town in New South Wales over an extended holiday weekend, to revitalise the churches that he felt were in a spiritually poor position. It was a long way to go for a relatively short period of time, and there was no assurance that there would be many people at the meetings. He decided to accept the invitation as '*I felt in my heart that it was the right thing to do, although rationally it didn't make any sense*'. As it happened, numbers began very low, with only fifty attending the first night, although they grew to six hundred at the last meeting. Someone from the most influential church in the town claimed (erroneously) that he had heard Charles deny the deity of Christ; he used his influence to prevent other members from coming to the meetings. God, however, worked the situation for good, as one of those attending the meetings was a man who worked for a national television station based in Queensland. He was keen to broadcast some of Charles' material, and so Charles told him about *Living Truth*. As a result, *Living Truth* was broadcast across Australia and New Zealand three times a week for many years. Charles applied what he had learned many years before at Capernwray: '*The right doors open naturally, but not because you go looking for them*.'

Charles retired from his position as Lead Pastor of the People's Church in 2016, although the church gave him an honorary title of

Minister at Large. A factor contributing to his decision to retire related to heart problems that he had had for a number of years, starting from when he was still based in England, although the initial event took place in Canada. In 1998 he was speaking at a conference in Canada and after the morning session he went for a walk in the conference centre estate. As he was walking up a hill, he felt something like a clamp on either side of his chest; he was clearly having a heart attack. In his 1998 newsletter he described it thus:

> *I remember praying, 'Lord, if this is a heart attack, I have nothing to ask you for and no requests to make. I only want to thank you that this does not take you by surprise, for you know exactly what is happening and you are sufficient for any emergency. So thank you.' The result was an overwhelming sense of peace.*

This was what Paul described in Philippians 4:7: '*And the peace of God, which transcends all understanding, will guard your hearts and your minds in Christ Jesus.*'

He got a lift back to the conference centre, and was told by one of the staff that he had had a phone call from a certain Michael Bentley-Taylor. Michael was a leading cardiologist in Canada who came from a village close to where Charles had lived in Herefordshire, and whose family had hosted youth events in the barn attached to their house. This staff member also knew Michael, through her parents, and so after Charles was taken by ambulance to the local hospital, she contacted Michael to let him know that Charles was on his way to hospital with a suspected heart attack. The following day Michael arranged that Charles should be taken to his hospital in Toronto where he would treat him. He recommended that Hilary and the children should fly from England as the heart attack was serious. After Charles was discharged, he and the family stayed in Michael's house for six weeks. The involvement of a leading cardiologist he had known since boyhood was all part of God's amazing providential plan for Charles and Hilary.

Three months after they got back to England, Charles was contacted by a Christian private cardiologist based in Liverpool, who offered to examine Charles free of charge. His advice was for Charles to change his lifestyle, so that he would preach shorter sermons, no more than thirty-minutes long, and only once a day. Charles accepted that he might have to do that. It did not, however, quite work out that way, as Charles explained:

> *The first time that I preached at Capernwray, I prepared a message that I could exit at twenty minutes or thirty minutes if I needed to. But at thirty minutes, I felt stronger than I was at the beginning, and so I went for forty-five minutes, full whack. I was never limited. God was very gracious to me.*

This meant that Charles felt free to continue with his work for Capernwray, and then later take up his new role at the People's Church.

Nevertheless, his heart had been badly damaged, but he was able to continue carrying a heavy workload until a serious incident took place in 2014 in northern Iraq. He was speaking to a group of pastors, when towards the end he felt all energy drain out of him. He had to sit down, feeling weak and frail. He was taken to the airport to fly back to Toronto, and on his way he phoned his cardiologist, who told him to come to his hospital on landing. A week after putting Charles under a battery of tests, he told him that he was a '*candidate for sudden death*', as his heart was enlarged and inflamed. He had several periods in hospital going through various procedures that gave him back some strength and energy.

Michael Bentley-Taylor was very definite that Charles should not preach more than once a day. The church had grown so much that they needed to have three repeat services on a Sunday, and so they recorded Charles preaching live at the first service, and then showed that recording on cinema screens at the subsequent services, with Charles coming in to close the service. This seemed to work well, and the elders and congregation seemed to be happy with the arrangement. Charles, however, felt that the rapport with the second and third congregations was missing. Therefore he planned to retire in June 2016, when in any case he would be sixty-seven.

This was a major step for Charles, but he still continued to travel and preach as and when doors were opened to him, but without having responsibility for the People's Church. Many people passed on their best wishes on his retirement, including the Canadian prime minister, Justin Trudeau, who sent a personal video message played at his final service, and the former prime minister, Stephen Harper, who also sent a personal letter. Charles' ministry in Toronto and beyond was greatly appreciated.

## Contending for truth

When Major Thomas invited Charles to join the staff of Capernwray, he said, '*I'll give you a job description that is two words long, "Preach Christ." If you stop doing that, we'll not be interested in you. Don't preach Christianity. Don't preach techniques to live the Christian life. Preach Christ.*' That, of course, is what people the world over have wanted him to do, including the board of elders at the People's Church when they appointed him to the post of Lead Pastor. For Charles, contending for truth is pointing people to Jesus that they might begin a relationship with him and continue in that relationship allowing him to live his life through them. As he would say: '*Christ in you, Christ for you and Christ through you.*'

Charles is a powerful preacher, but what is amazing is that as a young teenager, he was so shy and withdrawn that he was exempt from debating and drama classes because he could not stand up and articulate ideas very well and nor could he act. Some people in Herefordshire, who knew him as a boy, would sometimes comment that he would be the last person they would have expected to stand up and preach as he did. Things fell into place for Charles, as we have already seen, in the summer of 1965 at Capernwray. There he learned about Christ working in him and through him, and so when people saw him preach they thought that he was confident in his natural ability, whereas Charles saw it as Christ at work in his life enabling him to be confident in God's ability to draw people to Jesus. As Paul said, '*it is God who works in you to will and to act in order to fulfil his good purpose*'.[263] That has been the cornerstone of Charles' Christian experience.

If you listen to his preaching you will see that God has given him wonderful gifts for communicating Christian truth.[264] He is able to put his message across in an exceptionally clear and coherent way so that there is no possibility of not understanding the message that he is trying to convey. All of it is rooted in biblical truth, but with a practical application that listeners can seek to put into practice with God's help in their own lives. He knows how to pause so that his audience can take time to see the significance of what he is saying. He knows how to use hand gestures and to turn his head to face in a different direction if he wants to show that he is taking part in a conversation with a biblical character. He uses humour in a completely natural way. He is a master of using illustrations that came from his own experience, gained particularly from travelling over different continents. We have already seen his illustration regarding faith, which came from his first flight to Africa.

Another illustration from his travels was one that he used when preaching about David's courageous heart in fighting against Goliath

263. Philippians 2:13
264. His sermons can be found on this website:
https://www.youtube.com/c/CharlesPriceMinistry/videos (accessed 17.12.21)
and also on the website: https://charlespriceministry.org/ (available in 2022).

in 1 Samuel 17.[265] He explained that fear comes about when you face some threat that has bigger resources than you have, such as when Saul's relatively small Israelite army faced the might of the Philistines and their fearsome giant, Goliath. Charles had been speaking at a conference centre in India that was set in the grounds of a large game reserve where the animals were allowed to roam freely. Elephants could be particularly dangerous and were known to attack humans. He went out for a walk in the grounds along the bank of a river when he came round a bend and saw in his way was a huge female elephant. When the elephant saw Charles, its ears went out and its trunk went up, which Charles knew were danger signs. It seemed for an instant that his heart had stopped and his feet froze to the ground. He then decided to take his chances with the crocodiles and so jumped into the river and swam to the other side. He made it, and to his amazement, he realised that the elephant had received such a shock having seen him jump into the river that it turned back and ran in the direction from which it had come. Once he had got back to the conference centre, he told people his story and as a result they called him 'the one of whom elephants are afraid'. This nickname stuck, and he was introduced by this name at the next church at which he spoke. Despite his new nickname, Charles had been terrified seeing the elephant that was much stronger and more powerful than he was. In the same sermon, he contrasted that experience with seeing another wild animal in a house in New Zealand, but this time it was much smaller as it was only a mouse (although the lady of the house who first spotted it shrieked and jumped up on the chair that she had been sitting on). Charles, however, was not frightened, and he set about trying to catch the mouse. Because the mouse was so small, he had no fear of what it might do to him.

As he told these stories, he used dramatic gestures, such as how the elephant would raise its trunk, how the elephant might end up sitting

265. https://www.youtube.com/watch?v=4qHK6_sCZv0 (accessed 17.12.21).

on him, how he swam across the river and how he went about trying to catch the mouse. Humour came throughout his stories, which was appreciated by the audience who laughed as he told them.

There was, of course, a serious point to the stories. Saul was terrified of the massive power of the Philistines, despite the fact that God promised him that the Philistines would be subjugated.[266] Saul had started off well as a God-centred man, but he failed to believe and follow God's promises, and so his power was eventually lost. He was terrified of the giant Goliath, even though he himself was physically tall. In chapter 17, David came on the scene, prepared to fight the giant, because he had seen what God had done before in his life, and he trusted in his promises. David approached Goliath saying, '*You come against me with sword and spear and javelin, but I come against you in the name of the LORD Almighty, the God of the armies of Israel, whom you have defied.*'[267] The power of God was greater than that of Goliath, and God working through David won the battle. Charles applied this to us today. We need to be aware of the danger of living using our own resources, and ending up just as an empty shell, even using spiritual language, but not knowing the reality of a relationship with Christ. We can end up living for Christianity, rather than for Christ. Or we can be like David. '*And David stepping out in that obedience and trust, became the one who gained victory.*'

Charles has preached many other sermons based on Old Testament passages, not simply because they are good stories, but because they point to Jesus and the victory we can have in our Christian lives. Some of the passages may seem difficult, but as he prepares a sermon, he constantly asks himself whether a twelve-year-old would understand it. Simplicity does not equal superficiality, for great communicators like

266. 1 Samuel 9:16
267. 1 Samuel 17:45

C.S. Lewis, Billy Graham and others have portrayed profound truths in simple language that anyone can understand, and this is his aim.

## Conclusion

Charles has had a long and fruitful ministry. He has been greatly supported in this by his family. Charles and Hilary were married in 1980, and Hilary has been involved in his ministry as well as her own speaking and writing over these years. (She probably deserves a chapter of her own!) They have three children, Hannah, Laura and Matthew, and five grandchildren. From their annual newsletter you can sense how important their family is to Charles and Hilary.

Charles will have a tremendous legacy from his many years of ministry in terms of people won for Christ, and those who have grown in their relationship with him. But Charles has never felt apparent 'success' to be the 'be all and end all' of ministry. He thinks of the prophet Jeremiah who had very little success in his ministry, and who instead was maligned and ignored by those he was trying to reach. Jeremiah, however, was completely faithful in the call given to him by the Lord, even though he experienced hardship and seemed to accomplish very little. Likewise, Charles consistently wanted to be faithful to God's agenda for him, living for him and pointing people to Jesus, and the power for living that he provides.

# Chapter 24: The Class of 61

'*Vellore Christian Medical College – it was the best medical school in Asia.*' So said Graham Morritt, my friend and prayer partner, with great pride about his alma mater. He talked glowingly about his time there, about the Christian fellowship that he enjoyed, the quality of the medical teaching in the college and the opportunities he experienced to develop his many skills and interests.

The college is part of a campus situated in the city of Vellore in the state of Tamil Nadu in southern India, comprising a medical school, hospital and medical research institute. Its origins go back to 1900 when it was set up by a very determined young American missionary, Dr Ida S. Scudder, who saw the great need for high-quality medical training in that part of India in order to alleviate the suffering that was so evident there. Ida's plans were originally to finish her education in America and probably marry some rich young man. God, however, had other plans for her.

Her father was a missionary doctor in India, as were all his brothers, and indeed her grandfather was the first missionary doctor to leave America for India way back in 1819. She was writing letters in her father's Indian house one night when there were three separate knocks on the door during the evening from three young men. Each had the same plight, that their wives were dying in childbirth, and they were desperate for Ida to come and save them. Ida had to explain that she was not a medical doctor, but rather it was her father who should go and treat their wives. They each refused, as it was against their religion for a man outside their family to enter the private quarters of a woman, even if it was to save the woman's life. Ida felt that she could not go, and the following morning she heard the mourners in the funeral processions grieving the loss of these young women, all because there were no female doctors to treat them. This was God's call to her: to go back to America and train as a doctor, and then return to India to meet the needs of the suffering.

She graduated from Cornell University Medical College at a time when women were only just being accepted for medical training, and came to Vellore to follow her calling there. She started dispensing medication from a room in her father's house to ever-increasing queues of patients. Her vision, however, was to run a medical school and hospital for the glory of God, and through tireless determined fundraising, particularly from American churches, over time her vision was realised. She saw this as God's provision for the people of Vellore. Ida was much loved, because of how she poured herself out for her people, in the same way as her Lord poured himself out for her.

She died in 1960 at the age of ninety, but her work continued to flourish after she had gone. She had managed to surround herself with very eminent medical teachers, who would influence generations of students and meet the physical and at times spiritual needs of countless people. One of the most prominent was Paul Brand, a man of tremendous Christian faith, who was a leader in the treatment of leprosy. He pioneered tendon transplant surgery to restore function to damaged hands and feet. Paul understood the necessity of pain, as leprosy made limbs numb and thus not feel pain, leading to serious damage to body parts. Paul provided practical help to those who suffered in this way.

In the providence of God, pain plays a vital role in maintaining bodily wholeness. As Paul said to the renowned American Christian writer, Philip Yancey:

> *Most people view pain as an enemy. Yet, as my leprosy patients prove, it forces us to pay attention to threats against our bodies. Without it, heart attacks, strokes, ruptured appendices and*

> *stomach ulcers would all occur without any warning. Who would ever visit a doctor apart from pain's warnings?*[268]

Graham Morritt started at this prestigious Christian medical college in 1961, the year after Ida Scudder had died, but when eminent Christian practitioners such as Paul Brand were still there to influence young students like Graham. He joined what was called 'The Class of 61', a very able group of mostly Christian medical students who went on to practise medicine and be influential in different walks of life, not only in India but across the world. Graham keeps in touch with members of the class and he has organised group Zoom calls for class members. We have chosen three class members, Chitra Bharucha, Kalpana Krishnamurthy and the late P.S. Peter, plus Graham himself, to be included in this chapter. I was privileged to have video calls with Chitra and Kalpana, with Graham's assistance.

I would like to have talked to Dr P.S. Peter, but sadly he passed away in 2021. I have been able to obtain information from the secretary of the Alumni Society of Vellore Christian Medical College, as well as from a friend of his from 'The Class of 61', Alexander Thomas, who described him as a '*spiritual giant*'. Therefore, I have included a short section on P.S. Peter.

## Chitra Bharucha

Chitra sees her life as being '*one unplanned series of miracles*'. God had opened doors for her unexpectedly, from the way in which she joined 'The Class of 61', to serving the Lord in hospitals and holding high positions of trust in the National Health Service (NHS) in Belfast, as well as being Acting Chair of the BBC Trust, the governing body of the British Broadcasting Corporation. God had brought different people

268. Philip Yancey, *Soul Survivor* (Hodder & Stoughton, 2001), p. 69.

into her life at the right time, and had led her in the direction he wanted her to go.

She was born in 1945 in the city of Madurai into a family who provided Chitra with a degree of Christian influence. Her maternal grandmother was very important in this regard. She was a very strong Christian who wrote commentaries on books of the Bible, and told Chitra many Bible stories that would stand her in good stead in the years to come. Chitra also enjoyed going to the local Sunday school, run by Australian missionaries.

Faith, however, was not really important to Chitra in her childhood and early teenage years. It was at the age of fourteen when she really saw how different Christianity could be when she and her friends attended a Billy Graham rally. She was captivated by the Christian message as presented by the dynamic American evangelist, and went back each night. On the final night she responded to the altar call, and gave her life to Christ.

Looking back, she realises that people had been praying for her to come to faith. Her grandmother would certainly be praying for her. The secondary school that she went to was mixed in terms of religion, and most of her friends were Hindus. The headteacher and assistant headteacher, however, were very strong Christians, and at break times when the girls were out on the yard these two godly ladies would sit on the grass, read their Bibles and pray. Later, Chitra realised that they were praying for her.

Chitra had always wanted to study medicine, and so she prepared her application for entry to Vellore Christian Medical College, albeit at the very last minute. It was a five-hour bus journey to Vellore, and Chitra arrived at the reception desk and handed her application in just before the deadline. Several thousand young people applied and took the written exam, but only a hundred were called for a three-day assessment; Chitra was one of them. There were to be fifty applicants selected, and Chitra remembers everyone gathering round the lily pond at the end of the three days, as the names of the selected candidates were read out. Chitra was not on the list! She was devastated. Those selected remained to begin their course, while the others, including Chitra, had to go home.

She did nothing for the next week, and in fact she did not even unpack. She was completely demoralised because she believed in her heart that God wanted her to become a doctor. Then totally out of the blue, a telegram came from the college saying that she had been given a place after all, as one of the students had dropped out. This was another miracle in her life, and so Chitra went back to Vellore and joined 'The Class of 61'. She excelled in the college, enjoying the high-quality teaching and the academic challenges of her studies. She was impressed by the good example set by Christian staff, and the way in which they welcomed students into their homes for discussion. She also met her future husband, Hoshang, a pathology student, in Vellore and they got married in 1967.

Chitra's first job after graduating was in Vellore as a haematologist, working under an American missionary doctor, Bob Carmen. Bob was a wonderful mentor to Chitra and gave her opportunities to teach medical students as well. She was initially a bit reluctant to do this, but under Bob's guidance ('*you know more than they do, and so just tell them*') she quickly grew in confidence. Unfortunately, however, during her time in this post she suffered a number of miscarriages, which made her think that she would never have a baby.

Hoshang was offered a post as a pathologist in Ludhiana Christian Medical College in northern India, and so they moved there. Here she met an obstetrician from New Zealand, Beryl Howie, who befriended her and gave her a strict instruction that if she felt that she was pregnant, she should contact Beryl immediately. Chitra did just that, and Beryl confined her to bed for seven months and looked after her until her '*miracle baby Anita*' was born in June 1972. For Chitra this was an example of God bringing a key person into her life at just the right time.

During the time of her confinement, she was only fifty miles from the India-Pakistan border where fierce fighting continued for two weeks in December 1971, and which finally contributed to the formation of the new state of Bangladesh. Bombers flew overhead, and indeed one was shot down not far from their home. Chitra, Hoshang and baby Anita were, however, about to move to another war zone; this time Belfast at the height of the Troubles in Northern Ireland in 1972, as Hoshang had been offered a pathology job there. The initial contract was only for six months, but the family (including Tara who was born in January 1974) stayed there for over thirty years.

Belfast was of course a divided community between Protestants and Catholics, but Chitra felt that because their family was different from others through their colour, they did not pose a threat, and so their home was seen as an open house where all were welcome. People from opposing factions, who knew everything about each other but who had remarkably never spoken to each other, came and met in Chitra and Hoshang's house and formed lasting friendships. Christian reconciliation was taking place in that house.

The minister of the local Presbyterian church, Reverend Lowery, came and visited Chitra and her young baby, as did other members of the church. When Chitra went to the church herself, she was overwhelmed by the welcome that she received. Over time, she joined the choir, the two girls joined the Sunday school and youth group, and Chitra herself later became an elder.

It was Mrs Breakey who put the church in touch with Chitra after she arrived in Belfast. This lady was a contact from Ludhiana, as her son and daughter-in-law were missionaries at the medical college and knew Chitra and Hoshang from there. When he knew that Chitra was going to Belfast, Bill Breakey gave her a tape recording to be passed on to his mother. Again Chitra saw this as part of God's hand directing her life as she started her new adventure in Belfast.

In 1974, she started her long career with the NHS in Northern Ireland as a researcher for a haematologist. She took on more positions of responsibility as her skills and integrity were increasingly recognised. She was asked to become deputy director of the Northern Ireland Blood Transfusion Service, but only agreed to do this if she could still do clinical work with patients as well, which she did at Belfast City Hospital. In her role, she dealt with all of the general practitioners in Northern Ireland, and was responsible for all blood donation and the safety of all blood donors.

The 1980s saw the beginning of a new crisis for the medical profession, the AIDS epidemic, and Chitra treated the first AIDS patients in her unit. In her professional work with these and other patients, she wanted to show her caring concern for them as people, who were special in the eyes of God. She would go the extra mile by delivering prescribed drugs to patients' homes, and if they ended up in the Marie Curie hospice, she would visit them there, sometimes taking the children as well, which greatly cheered up her patients.

As her reputation grew, she was given increasing responsibility at a national level. For example, in 1999 Chitra was elected to the General Medical Council, in her own words, '*against all odds, much to everyone's surprise, and a few people's horror*'. In 2002, she received a phone call from the Food Standards Agency, asking her to sit on the Advisory Committee on Animal Feedingstuffs. Her first reaction was, '*I am a doctor. I know nothing about animals*.' She might not have known about animals, but she had become an expert in regulation standards, and she was appointed chair. So much of the legislation that we now have on labelling came out of the work done by Chitra's committee. She was appointed a Member of the Order of the British Empire for her work in this area.

She was also approached to serve on various media councils. Again she did not seek these positions, but she felt in each case that God was opening new doors for service. From 1996 to 1999, she was a member of the BBC Broadcasting Council for Northern Ireland, followed by a period from 2001 until 2003 when she was the Northern Ireland member of the Independent Television Commission, and then a member of the Advertising Standards Authority from 2004 to 2007. In all these positions, she tried to ensure that the highest standards possible were achieved in the media.

In 2006, the BBC formed a new trust as its governing body with the aim of ensuring that the corporation provided the best service possible for licence payers. Out of the blue, Chitra was asked to apply for a position on the trust board. She obtained this position, and soon became vice chair as the previous holder had stood down. This was a complete surprise to her because, as she said when she was appointed, '*You don't normally appoint people of my colour or my gender to this sort of position.*' Michael Grade, the chair, resigned after only a month in post, to become chief executive of Independent Television. This catapulted Chitra into a position that she did not expect, and did not really want, as acting chair of the trust for a few months.

Her service on the trust board from 2006 to 2010 was not an easy time for Chitra, as she faced a great deal of personal hostility. She did, however, stick to her principles, and did her best to lead a disparate group of people in the roles that they had been given. As we mentioned in the first section of this book, there was a high degree of opposition to the Christian worldview within the BBC. Some of the executives wanted to remove the religious slot *Thought for the Day* from the flagship Radio Four *Today* programme. When this was discussed, Chitra looked down the table, and in a stern voice worthy of an old-school headmistress, said, '*Do you not realise that this is a Christian country, and so what is all the fuss about?*' The slot is still there, although it is now more open to other faith contributions.

Chitra and Hoshang moved from Northern Ireland to Wiltshire in 2003 because most of her work was now in mainland Britain, although she still misses Northern Ireland. She still believes in trusting God to open doors for his people, and she encourages others to do the same. For example, she is currently praying for and counselling a Christian Indian lady living in Canada over various issues, and part of the advice that she has given her is, '*God has a purpose for you, and he will open doors for you. Just walk through.*' That is what she has found to be true in her walk with the Lord.

## Kalpana Krishnamurthy

Kalpana, another member of 'The Class of 61', was born in 1945 to Christian parents. Her father was the first Christian in his family and converted from Hinduism while studying in college. Kalpana's mother came from a Christian family, and so the influence of Christ was very strong in her life. As she grew up, she developed a strong Christian faith and an excellent knowledge of the Bible, encouraged by her family and the local church and Sunday school. She was able to share her faith with her friends, who would come to the family home and experience Christian love as shown by Kalpana's family. Even now, Kalpana keeps in touch with some of these ladies who found Christ as young girls through the family's witness. This is how she recollects it:

> *They would ring me up and say how my mother and I influenced them as children. When they came to our home, the first thing that they said was about the love they received, and through that love they came to know Christ. They wanted to bring their children up in the same way in faith, truth and love.*

Kalpana had always wanted to become a doctor. Her motivation was very similar to that of Ida S. Scudder who had originally founded

Vellore Christian Medical College. Both ladies understood that female patients in India did not want to see a male doctor, and so it was vital that women studied medicine and trained to be doctors. Unfortunately, Kalpana's school did not teach science to its students, believing instead that girls should be taught to be homemakers. As a result, she had to take pre-university cramming courses in maths, physics, chemistry and biology. Nonetheless, she was successful in the selection process and obtained a place in the college at Vellore.

Medical school was not always easy for Kalpana. It was a very competitive environment, and she looked round and saw how clever the other students in her class seemed to be. Indeed, at one point she wanted to give up and go back home. The Lord, however, spoke to her through various Bible verses, such as in Psalm 23: '*Even though I walk through the darkest valley, I will fear no evil, for you are with me; your rod and your staff, they comfort me.*'[269]

Kalpana felt that the Lord was telling her to persevere. He also reminded her about faith from Hebrews 11: '*Now faith is confidence in what we hope for and assurance about what we do not see.*'[270] God had led her to study medicine, and so she needed to hold on to the promises that he had given her. Kalpana stuck at it and ended up loving her time in Vellore, describing it as '*one of the best times in my life*'.

In 1968 her husband-to-be, Kittu, previously a Hindu, became a Christian just as they were about to qualify from medical school. The following year, they married, but sadly Kittu's family who were high-class Hindus did not attend the wedding because he had rejected their Hindu faith. Eventually the family accepted Kalpana, as she humbly showed Christian love to them. They were soon to be blessed with a baby daughter.

---

269. Psalm 23:4
270. Hebrews 11:1

After further studies in Bombay (now Mumbai) and Varanasi, they both ended up working at Moorshead Memorial Christian Hospital, Kalpana as an anaesthetist and Kittu as a surgeon. This was quite a culture shock for them both after training with high-quality equipment in Vellore. The hospital had originally been started by English missionaries but over time they left, and although it had a hundred beds, the hospital had effectively closed down. Kalpana's uncle was the local bishop, and he very much wanted the work revived, believing that Kalpana and Kittu were the right people to lead the team.

On arrival, they could not believe that buffaloes, cows and dogs wandered down the hospital corridor. Equipment was archaic, and Kalpana wondered how she could perform anaesthetics in such a squalid environment with such poor facilities. There was very little money available and staff went unpaid for six months. Because the hospital was in a remote area and there was no other medical facility nearby, they felt that they had to make it work, despite the seemingly overwhelming difficulties that they faced, including the fact that the local tribespeople did not trust doctors.

Kalpana was greatly encouraged by what God said to her through the Scriptures. Verses such as: '*Be strong and courageous. Do not be afraid or terrified because of them, for the* LORD *your God goes with you; he will never leave you nor forsake you.*'[271] They prayed that God would provide for them. Within a year they started to get the hospital functioning properly. Improved security kept the animals and other intruders out, facilities were modernised and the reputation of the hospital grew. The local people now trusted the doctors and were willing to travel for two days to receive treatment.

Prayer was key to the work of the hospital. The majority of the staff were Christians, and they joined together in prayer for their patients, including at the beginning of each operation. Some of the patients were

271. Deuteronomy 31:6

Christians, and they appreciated prayers for their lives and health. Even some of those who were not Christians wanted to pray to Jesus, and indeed some of them became Christians through the ministry of the Christian team that Kalpana and Kittu led.

God blessed the work that they were doing, but Kalpana believed that he was moving them elsewhere. They were concerned about their daughter's education, and also for their newly born son as they were living in such a remote area. God was to use an English surgeon, Frank Tovey, and his wife who visited them to see the work that they were doing to lead them into the next stages of their lives. Dr Tovey invited them to come and work at his hospital in Salisbury. Kalpana knew that this was of the Lord and so the family moved to Salisbury in March 1977.

The timing of the move was absolutely right as there was a strong anti-Christian movement growing in the state of Orissa in north India where the hospital was based. The government took over some of the land owned by the missionary societies, and eventually took control of the hospital. Hindu organisations felt that Christians had too much influence and that too many people had converted to Christianity. Christians began to suffer much persecution, even to the point of losing their lives.

One of the most tragic cases took place over twenty years after Kalpana and Kittu had moved to England, but it involved a missionary whom they knew personally and had often entertained in their home. Graham Staines was an Australian missionary who came to work as a leprosy doctor in India in 1965. In 1983 he married Gladys, who was a nurse, and together they had three children. The tragedy happened in 1999 when after conducting a jungle camp for tribal children, Graham and his two young sons, Philip and Timothy, returned to their jeep to sleep for the night. As they slept, a hate-filled Hindu mob, knowing that Graham had been involved in Christian missionary work, approached the jeep and set it on fire. Graham and the boys had no chance of escape, and they cruelly perished in the blaze. The country was shocked at this horrific act of violence. Once Gladys had recovered from the trauma of losing her loved ones, she appeared on national television to say that she forgave the killers because that is what her Christian faith taught her to do. This brave act from a young widow and mother made a huge impression on the hundreds of thousands of people who saw the broadcast. In 2004 *Christianity Today* described her as '*the best-known Christian woman in India after Mother Teresa*',[272] and in 2005 she was awarded the Padma Shri, a civilian award, from the president of India.

Kalpana, Kittu and the children settled down to their new lives in England, working initially in the hospital in Salisbury, Kalpana in obstetrics and gynaecology and Kittu in plastic surgery. They later moved to Essex, where in 1983 Kalpana trained to become a general practitioner, and was a partner in the practice in Witham in Essex from 1985 to 2010. She found that she could share her faith freely with her patients who were very receptive to her gentle manner and loving Christian care. There were other Christians in the practice, and people realised that it was effectively a team of Christian doctors, and most responded well to that. Kalpana enjoyed the challenge of the more difficult patients such as drug addicts.

During their time in England, Kalpana and Kittu did not forget India and the needs there. They of course had family there and took what opportunities they could to spend time with family and friends. This was not just a holiday, however, as Kalpana would work in outreach clinics, particularly with women, and Kittu would perform plastic surgery. Hepatitis B was a growing problem, and they would help in the vaccination programme. After Graham Staines was tragically killed, they tried to support his work by taking medication, dressings and special shoes to the leprosy colony that he had run. Back in England they raised money that was sent out to India for leprosy patients and

272. Tim Stafford, 'India Undaunted' (*Christianity Today*, May 1st 2004).

hepatitis B vaccines. Many of the leprosy patients became Christians through the love and testimony of Kalpana and Kittu.

They both retired from medical practice in 2010, as Kittu became unwell and they realised that they needed to slow down. He sadly died in 2019. Kalpana, however, is still living her life for her Lord. Over the years she has seen many lives changed through her words and action. God told her many years before that she needed to serve and not to be served, and she has done that faithfully. She continues to look for new opportunities.

## Graham Morritt

Graham, now a retired surgeon living in Newcastle, was born in southern India in 1942. The main Christian influences on his early life were his grandfather, who was a Methodist, and his aunt Blanche, who taught him Bible stories in Sunday school, stories that were to remain with him throughout his life. It was not, however, until he was coming towards the end of his secondary education that the Christian message really came home to him.

For the last two years of his secondary education, Graham was a boarder at Stanes High School in Coimbatore in south India. Unlike his previous schools this was a Christian school, and they had chapel services each morning and evening. They also held a mission once a year, and on one of these missions the main speaker was an English missionary, Reverend Joe Mullins. He had a wonderful testimony of the way in which God worked in his life and called him to the ministry. God spoke to Graham through Joe's testimony.

Joe had become a Christian when he was seventeen. Towards the end of the Second World War, in his twenties, he was an officer in the British Army fighting the Japanese in Burma (now Mynamar). By this time, in his own words, '*I had been a bit of a back slider. You go with the flow so easily in the mess and in the Army*.' His battalion was involved in an operation trying to recapture a village from the Japanese. During the battle he was targeted by a Japanese sniper who, unaware to Joe, fired three bullets at his head.

> *One bullet entered the top of my helmet, ran round and came out the back. The path of the bullet can still be seen in the helmet. I was crouching behind this mango tree and the second bullet in the side of my helmet burst open, ran around inside and came out the other side. So it actually came in near one ear and out near the other. The third one ricocheted off.*

After the Japanese moved on, Joe and the remaining survivors joined the rest of their battalion. Joe realised that he had had a miraculous escape and that God was saying to him, '*Joe, you have no right to be alive. Your only right to live is to give yourself back to me.*'[273]

Joe took that word from God seriously, and so on his return to England, he studied theology at university and trained as an Anglican priest. He felt led to do missionary work in India, where he remained for twenty-two years. Graham saw real live Christianity oozing out from this former soldier, and led by the Holy Spirit he gave himself to the Lord.

As a result of becoming a Christian, Graham felt that God was calling him into medicine to help people in a practical way. He successfully applied to Vellore Christian Medical College, and joined 'The Class of 61'. As a Christian, he felt that this was the right place to go to because of the Christian ethos that permeated the college, including the practical vision of providing modern treatment to people who could not afford it. The college attracted Christians like Graham, but there were also non-Christians in the class who were attracted by the excellent academic

273. Quotes were from a talk given by Joe Mullins at the age of ninety-five and published as *The Joy of the Lord is Your Strength* (The Military Christian Fellowship of Australia, November 2nd 2016).

reputation of the college. Some of them became Christians, and as Graham himself expressed it:

> *When I meet one of them who has become a Christian, I say that this is amazing. As a Christian now, I can see that they were brought there by God himself; it was no accident that they were there. It's really wonderful for me to see how God worked in these people's lives.*

Graham, however, in his very honest way felt that he was not always a good example to his non-Christian classmates, as he tended to drift away from Christianity. He still had a deep conviction, but he tended to let other things take over. He was heavily involved in a range of activities, and these sometimes very easily took the place of attending church. He excelled at sport and won a number of sports trophies as well as plaudits from his classmates, all of which made him excessively self-reliant. Such success and praise from others was great for Graham's self-esteem, but it was certainly not so good for his spiritual growth.

One of Graham's passions was mountaineering, and he absolutely loved the adventure of it. During one expedition, he and two others went up into the Himalayas in what was potentially a very dangerous situation as there was no rescue backup for the three of them. It was also the first time that Graham had seen snow, and God used this experience to make him see himself in a new light as '*only a little black dot in this white expanse*'. The party returned safely, but Graham no longer saw himself as being self-reliant; rather he realised where he stood in this world, that in effect he was nothing and that he needed God to come first in his life.

God reinforced that for Graham during a mission that was held in the college, where the main speaker was again Joe Mullins, the missionary who had made such an impact on him when he was at boarding school.

As he recounts, '*When Joe was preaching it all came home to me again. I had a very strong experience that God was speaking to me in such a powerful way that I could not ignore him. That made a huge change in my life.*'

In the remaining years at college, Graham was able to testify to the reality of Jesus in his life, and he had an influence on other students. One example was when in 2018 he received a phone call from an Indian doctor called Mohan Das who wanted to meet him when he came to Newcastle. When Graham met him and his family, Mohan said to him, '*Oh Graham, you don't remember me, but you don't realise what an influence you had on my life. I heard you give your testimony, and I went back and started thinking and I became a Christian.*' Graham listened to his life story about his work as a Christian doctor in the Kingdom of Brunei, and realised that often we do not know how God is working in the lives of those we have contact with.

Graham graduated from medical school in 1967, along with the rest of his class, and to make it even more special, he married Jennifer, one of his classmates. Graham asked Joe Mullins to perform the ceremony, which he gladly did. From there, the newly married couple worked in the Church of South India mission hospital in Ikkadu.

Graham felt that God was increasingly leading him into becoming a surgeon. It was not possible, however, for him to train in India, and so in 1971, he and Jennifer emigrated to Britain, so that he could achieve his Fellowship of the Royal College of Surgeons. He trained in Newcastle and Edinburgh and ultimately became a cardiothoracic surgeon at the Freeman Hospital in Newcastle. Their two sons, Andrew and Daniel, were born in Edinburgh, and were a great blessing to Graham and Jennifer, as are their seven grandchildren.

Cardiothoracic surgery appealed to Graham's sense of adventure, as he was given the opportunity to save the lives of people who were seriously ill. Prayer was vitally important to Graham as he carried out this risky surgery. If he was, for example, performing a new procedure in the middle of the night, it was reassuring to know that God was in control, and that he and his team were instruments in his hands. '*It was all up to God, and you could always count on God's support.*' If there was a less than five per cent chance of the patient surviving, one knew that it was God who performed the miracle of a successful operation.

God used Graham so much in these years working as a surgeon. There was, however, a problem, similar to that which he had faced in his early years at college. As Graham so honestly expressed it, '*Surgery became my god!*' He spent most of his time working, and so his attendance at Jesmond Parish Church, the church of which he was a member, was not strong; so much so that he was actually asked on one occasion if he was a visitor. Likewise, his Christian witness was not particularly strong, and he regrets now missing opportunities to speak for the Lord.

The change for Graham came in 2005, when he decided to retire. There was a lot of pressure on him from his colleagues to continue working, but Graham stuck to his guns. He believed that God was directing him to retire at this point in time. God has blessed both Graham and Jennifer in their retirement years with good health and time to spend with their grandchildren.

Graham feels that he has grown enormously in his faith since retiring. He has been able to see new horizons in his faith as he gets ever closer to God, and has delved more deeply into his faith through reading God's word and Christian books. He now certainly has time for serving the Lord in church in many ways. He can get alongside other people with his infectious smile and by demonstrating the caring concern that he has for those in need. He has been able to be involved in helping to lead outreach groups such as Christianity Explored, where he is able to share his faith openly with those who are beginning to explore the Christian faith. Members of these groups love Graham for his warmth and for the wisdom and knowledge that he freely shares.

He has many outside interests such as golf and cycling, and he uses them when opportunities arise to share his faith, inviting his friends to special events, such as the sponsored cycle ride he organised for Anglican International Development in 2021.

Prayer is something that has become increasingly important for Graham. He realises how vital it is in developing his relationship with God. It is so encouraging to pray with Graham. He sees answers to prayer in terms of people being healed or being touched by God in some particular way. He finds that God puts people in his path to whom he can speak about Jesus or for whom he can pray.

Graham has made a chart of the spiritual ups and downs in his life. He knows that there have been times when he has let God go, and when he has not testified for Jesus as he should have done. He also knows, however, that God has not let him go. To quote Paul in his letter to the Philippians, '*that he who began a good work in you will carry it on to completion until the day of Christ Jesus*'.[274] The work that God started in Stanes High School and Vellore Christian Medical College is being completed during Graham's retirement years in Newcastle.

## P.S. Peter

Dr P.S. Peter was born on November 4th 1939 in Karimnagar in Andhra Pradesh into a poor family. His father died when he was still young and as a consequence his mother struggled to bring him up. He took a pre-university course followed by a Bachelor of Science qualification at Wesley High School and College in Hyderabad. It was here that he attended a meeting organised by Youth for Christ and committed his life to the Lord Jesus on January 15th 1959. This was to be an absolutely life-changing event for P.S.

He joined 'The Class of 61' at Vellore Christian Medical College, sponsored by the Church of South India mission. His best friend at

274. Philippians 1:6

Vellore, Meshach Kirubakaran, remembered him as a true Christian in every sense of the word who lived a saintly life. He was very gentle, extremely kind to everyone and was a worthy witness to the love of God. His unshakable faith in the Lord was a guiding light to his classmates. He was also actively involved with the Evangelical Union ministry at Vellore.

After graduating, he and his wife Dr Jayaprabhavathi, whom he married in 1970, together served in a number of Church of South India mission hospitals for a few years. He was motivated to work in these hospitals and improve the standard of care and facilities in honour of his father, who had died due to the lack of adequate medical facilities. Though the Church of South India mission had planned to send him to England for advanced studies, he turned down that offer believing that the Lord had given him a vision to move to Metpally, a town in Andhra Pradesh, which was in a very barren district.

In 1978, he and his wife started a private hospital in Metpally. They were the only doctors for about seventy villages, and they were also the only Christians in that area. This was indeed pioneering work, not only medically but also spiritually, as they later started church planting. Though the church had only two families to begin with, it continued to grow and by 2018 God enabled them to reach out to nearly fifty villages and to plant ten churches in the surrounding villages. Despite great persecution against Christians in the area, they stood strong for the Lord and, as a result, many of the villagers came to know Christ, with many also benefitting from their healing ministry.

P.S. and his wife had three children. As a family, things were not always easy for them, particularly when P.S. underwent coronary artery bypass graft surgery in 1995, and the future looked bleak. The Lord, however, spoke to them, promising them that they would come through this and that they would know his blessings. Sure enough, P.S. recovered, and was able to continue his ministry in the church and hospital. His children all studied medicine, and have successful careers. Two of his grandchildren are in fact continuing to serve the Lord in the hospital founded by their grandparents. The blessings that the Lord promised them were indeed bestowed on the family.

P.S. and his wife both died in 2021, within ten days of each other. They left behind a legacy of new churches and a hospital serving the community, and, as a result, many changed lives.

## Conclusion

What Ida S. Scudder established has, under God, had a lasting legacy. The Vellore Christian Medical College has been a place where medical practitioners have been trained to high standards according to Christian principles. Competition was fierce to gain a place with thousands of candidates applying each year, but Aunt Ida prayed consistently that the right candidates would be chosen. The service rendered by 'The Class of 61' demonstrates God's grace in answering her prayers.

God was given his due place in the life of the college, and those Christians who graduated from it knew that they would be serving the Lord using their medical skills. They have also been able to promote Christian truth as they lived out their lives, pointing people to Jesus. People have been healed and spiritually transformed, both on the Indian subcontinent and other parts of the world where Vellore graduates have lived and worked.

# Part Five

## And the Truth Shall Set You Free

Totalitarian regimes seem to have an inbuilt propensity to suppress the truth and allow lies to flourish. Fitzroy Maclean, a British Embassy official in Moscow, saw that when he was an invited guest to Stalin's show trials in 1938. Here top-ranking, loyal Communist Party members, who had held high positions in the Soviet state, were standing trial. They faced the threat of execution, against incredible accusations made against them that were obvious fabrications of the truth. To Maclean's utter disbelief these men confessed to these 'crimes' out of loyalty to the Party.[275]

One man who spoke out against lies in the Soviet state was Aleksandr Solzhenitsyn. In 1945 he was arrested for criticising Stalin in private letters and accused of anti-Soviet propaganda and, as a result, he spent eight years in terrible conditions in a labour camp. He wrote a number of novels and poems about his experiences there, where he also rediscovered his Christian faith. On receiving the Nobel Prize for Literature, he published a lecture calling upon his audience to defeat lies with '*one word of truth*'.[276]Just prior to his exile from the Soviet Union in 1974 he published a pamphlet entitled *Live Not by Lies* where he exhorted the Russian people by saying, '*Let us refuse to say what we do not think*.'[277]

In 2020 Rod Dreher, an American Christian journalist, took Solzhenitsyn's title and wrote about brave Christians in the totalitarian regimes of Eastern Europe who held on to their faith and resisted the lies promulgated by the State.[278] They suffered terribly as a result of their faith, but many of them later became key members of the peaceful revolutions that overthrew the Communist regimes.

The warning that Dreher passes on from these survivors of communist oppression concerns a new form of totalitarianism, what he

275. Fitzroy Maclean, *Eastern Approaches* (Penguin, 1990).
276. Aleksandr Solzhenitsyn, *One Word of Truth* . . . (The Bodley Head, 1972), p. 27.
277. https://www.solzhenitsyncenter.org/live-not-by-lies (accessed 17.12.21).
278. Rod Dreher, *Live Not by Lies: A Manual for Christian Dissidents* (Sentinel, 2020).

calls 'soft totalitarianism'. He gives examples of how this is seen in the West, reinforcing what we have already discussed in the first part of this book: the power of social media, the influence of large corporations in promoting ideological causes, the thrust of identity politics and cancel culture. His claim is that much of it is directed against Christians who take a biblical stance on issues such as sexual ethics and the sanctity of life. His clarion call to us is the same as that of Solzhenitsyn: '*Live not by lies*!'

Is Dreher overdramatising the power of soft totalitarianism? We have already seen examples of it in our assessment of 2020, and there is evidence that it continues to develop in 2021. Many Scottish parents, for example, are understandably deeply concerned at the intention of the Scottish government to impose LGBT ideology across the curriculum in state schools. It would seem that the LGBT lobbying group, Stonewall, has an undue hold on the Scottish government. A podcast produced for the BBC entitled *Nolan Investigates* has demonstrated the influence of Stonewall in cancelling the word 'mother' in official pronouncements. In Nolan's words, '*The Scottish government at the behest of Stonewall, when they are talking about their maternity policies have removed the word "mother" . . . For a word that has so much resonance to be cancelled by a small lobby group is nonsense.*'[279]

If what is happening in Scotland is not bad enough, the erosion of freedom of belief and speech in a liberal democracy such as Finland is absolutely frightening. Christian MP Päivi Räsänen has been charged with a hate crime against homosexuals initially dating back to 2004 when she published a pamphlet on human sexuality, and then to 2019 when she made comments on a radio programme and posted a tweet with biblical texts (Romans 1:24-27), criticising her church for supporting an LGBT Pride event. According to *Evangelical Focus Europe*, however,

279. *Nolan Investigates*, 'Is Government Too Close to Stonewall?' (BBC Sounds, released October 13th 2021).

*'Päivi Räsänen has repeatedly said that she defends the human rights and dignity of LGBT people since this understanding of the value of all people is a central aspect to her Christian faith.'*[280] If convicted, this brave public servant faces up to two years imprisonment. This is a case that could have serious ramifications for freedom of belief and speech across Europe.

Therefore, more than ever we need brave people to contend for truth so that people can find Jesus and live by his standards. Throughout this book, we have looked at the lives and ministries of wonderful Christian people who are in their different ways contending for truth. These people, including Paul in the New Testament, have seen Jesus to be *the* truth, and so are contending for him. Their ultimate aim is that people may come to a knowledge of Jesus as their Saviour and come to know him in a deeper way as they follow him as their Lord.

In the rest of this chapter, for ease of exposition, we shall collectively refer to the Christians whose lives we have examined as 'The Contenders' (hopefully, without making them sound too much like a pop group!).

'The Contenders' all have different approaches to proclaiming Christ, as well as different emphases in their ministries. For David Holloway and Charles Price, it involves preaching expository sermons and writing. For Andy Bannister, it is using apologetics to reach out to non-believers and to train Christians to share their faith. Barbara Connor has had a powerful ministry with children and young people, and is able to train others in this work. Donald Curry is able to speak for Christ in the Lords and at top-level meetings. Julie Maxwell has taken her message into schools and youth groups, as well as being an influence for truth in medical circles. Michael Bushby has a powerful ministry in getting alongside men with the gospel and encouraging Christian men in their faith. Members of 'The Class of 61' have used their professional expertise to provide help and healing in the name of Jesus.

280. Joel Forster, 'Päivi Räsänen case in Finland leads to heated freedom of speech debate both in media and churches' (*Evangelical Focus Europe*, May 5th 2021).

'The Contenders' all have different personalities and character traits, but they all have qualities in their Christian lives that make them powerful under God as they contend for truth. Let us examine the qualities that they have and the qualities that *we* need to cultivate as *we* endeavour to contend for truth. We must of course realise that it is God who provides the growth in our hearts as we seek to cultivate these qualities.

## A passion for God

Paul ended his prayer in Ephesians chapter 3 with these words:

> *Now to him who is able to do immeasurably more than all we ask or imagine, according to his power that is at work within us, to him be glory in the church and in Christ Jesus throughout all generations, for ever and ever! Amen.*[281]

God was at the centre of Paul's ministry, and so he did not want to glorify himself by proclaiming how many converts he had made or how many churches he had established, but rather it was all for the glory of God. Furthermore, he knew that any success that he had had was all due to God '*according to his power that is at work within us*'. Prayer was at the centre of Paul's ministry, but he realised that his prayers were so weak and feeble, as God was able '*to do immeasurably more than all we ask or imagine*'.

Paul had a passion for God, and 'The Contenders' also have at the root of their lives a passion for God. Without this passion and prayerful desire to serve God, their ministries would have been fruitless. Andy Bannister, for example, realises that it is not just his skills that produce fruit, but rather that God is at work and Jesus is at the centre of his ministry. As we have seen, after Michael Bushby tried to commit suicide, he prayed,

281. Ephesians 3:20-21

'*Whatever time I have left, I just want to give my life to you. I just want you to use this bit of life I have left and that some good would come out of this.*' David Holloway responded to the hymn 'Be Wholly Thine' and committed himself to be wholly God's in his ministry. Graham Morritt, in his experience in the snowy Himalayas, realised that he was as only a little black dot in a white wilderness and that God needed to be first in his life.

Prayer is central in the lives of these Christian men and women. In all of Donald Curry's difficult decisions in public life, he knew that he had to throw himself on God and rely on his Spirit to see him through, as he himself did not have the resources to deal with these issues on his own. Charles Price has known throughout his Christian life the power of Christ living within him and that same power opening doors in answer to prayer. Barbara Connor is very much aware of God speaking to her and his protecting hand upon her as she spent time in prayer with him. Julie Maxwell and members of 'The Class of 61' would seek God as they carried out their professional work in clinics and operating theatres for his glory.

## A passion for truth

We have already mentioned that in John chapter 8, Jesus called Satan '*the father of lies*'. In contrast, in speaking to the believing Jews in the same chapter, he said, '*If you hold to my teaching, you are really my disciples. Then you will know the truth, and the truth will set you free*.'[282] Each of 'The Contenders' knows the truth and has, as a result, been set free. They are free in Christ, and so they have been set free from the power of sin, death and Satan. Of course they will do things wrong, and are tempted to do so by Satan, and one day they will physically die. But they are no longer living in the dominion of sin, death and Satan. They have been set free to serve Christ in his kingdom.

282. John 8:31-32

As we have seen, at the heart of David Holloway's ministry is the desire to maintain and promulgate biblical truth about the Lord Jesus. This also includes rebuking error, because if false teachers preach a different message, for example, about the divinity, resurrection and virgin birth of Christ, then others will be prevented from finding the real Jesus. Charles Price also preaches biblical truth, and he has a particular gift in being able to explain even complex truth in a way that people will understand. He wants to see the truth of the gospel change lives and for people to be taught how they may live for Christ by having Christ live in them. Andy Bannister uses apologetics to proclaim the truth as he debates with others, posing questions to encourage people to see the truth of the gospel. Michael Bushby is able to relate the truth of the gospel to ordinary men, and he uses his powerful testimony to show that he has been set free. Barbara Connor has had a long ministry of presenting truth to children and young people and seeing many set free, and then watching them take on the responsibility of telling others the truth about Jesus. Julie Maxwell is able to relate God's truth to young people who have been told lies about issues related to families, marriage, sexuality and gender. Donald Curry is able to use his position in the Lords to stand up for God's standards and proclaim Christian truth.

## A passion for people

Matthew records the love that Jesus had for people in the verse: '*When he saw the crowds, he had compassion on them, because they were harassed and helpless, like sheep without a shepherd.*'[283] His heart went out to them, because he understood their plight that spiritually they were lost with no real knowledge of God and no direction in their lives. He had a desire to help them find their way to God, which he did ultimately through his sacrificial death on the cross. Similarly, one can imagine the late Dr P.S. Peters looking out at the crowds in his own country with

283. Matthew 9:36

great compassion and desiring to help them physically (which he did through his hospital work) and spiritually (which he did through church planting). The other members of 'The Class of 61' also had that desire to help people in need through their Christian faith and medical skills.

Mark records a similar verse to Matthew, except that he added a bit more detail to show what Jesus did immediately as a result of the compassion he felt for the people: '*So he began teaching them many things*.'[284] Teaching was a way that Jesus demonstrated his compassion for people. 'The Contenders' each have a passion for people, and want to use their words to help them. Julie Maxwell, for example, has a great concern for the wellbeing of children and young people, and so in teaching sexual ethics, she wants to lead them in God's direction. She does this, not out of contempt for those with whom she disagrees, but rather out of a love for those who need help. Andy Bannister has spent much time contending with Muslims, not to win debating points with them, but rather because he has a great love and respect for them, and he wants to point them to Jesus. Barbara Connor has a passionate love for children and young people, and is overjoyed when they come to know the Lord.

Their passion is also shown in the practical things that they do for people. The involvement of David Holloway and Donald Curry in Anglican International Development shows their love for the suffering people of South Sudan, and similarly the involvement of the People's Church under Charles Price in humanitarian projects demonstrates Christian love in action. Michael Bushby's work with Lymphoma Action, supporting others with the same illness that he has, and mowing the lawns of his elderly neighbours, all demonstrate his passion for people. Being prepared to go the extra mile for people has been the hallmark of Chitra Bharucha, Kalpana Krishnamurthy and Graham Morritt throughout their lives, both professionally and in their retirement.

284. Mark 6:34

## Awareness of their spiritual heritage

When Paul wrote his second letter to Timothy, he said, '*I am reminded of your sincere faith, which first lived in your grandmother Lois and in your mother Eunice and, I am persuaded, now lives in you also.*'[285] Timothy, now a church leader, had a spiritual heritage going back to his grandmother and mother who taught him the scriptures from infancy.[286] Paul himself was grateful for the service his forefathers gave to God and presumably also the encouragement they gave him in his study of the Scriptures.[287]

Although each of 'The Contenders' had to make their own personal commitment to the Lord, their home and family background played a part, sometimes a very significant part, in their coming to faith. Their background was all part of God's perfect plan for their lives. This also indicates the great responsibility that we, who are parents or grandparents, have for the generations who succeed us.

Charles Price came from a Christian home, but he can also look back to his great-grandfather, Edward Price, who was converted in the Welsh Revival of 1904, a major milestone in his spiritual heritage. Donald Curry is so grateful for his Christian family and friends, and the network of Brethren people that he grew up with in Northumberland. Both David Holloway and Andy Bannister grew up in Christian families. Kalpana Krishnamurthy is very grateful for the Christian influence of her parents as she grew up in a Hindu community, and how their home was such a welcoming place for her non-Christian friends. Julie Maxwell is grateful for the influence of her mother who was a Christian.

In some cases, the family influence for Christ was not as strong, but God brought other people into their lives to pray for them and to point them to Jesus. Michael Bushby, for example, had a difficult home background, and ended up going to London to make a fresh start. Even

---

285. 2 Timothy 1:5
286. 2 Timothy 3:15
287. 2 Timothy 1:3

that did not work out as well as he had hoped, and so he came back to the north-east, where Bob Arkley, a colleague of his, witnessed to him and invited him to church where he committed his life to the Lord. Barbara Connor's parents were church-going, although not yet committed Christians. They encouraged her to go to Sunday school and youth meetings where she heard the gospel, and was influenced by people in the Brethren assembly such as George Wilson and Beth Easton.

Graham Morritt's grandfather and aunt had an influence on him, but it was hearing Joe Mullins initially at school and then later at Vellore Christian Medical College that made him realise that he needed to commit his life to Christ. Chitra Bharucha's maternal grandmother taught her Bible stories, but she also knew that the Christian headteacher and assistant headteacher at school prayed for her, a factor in her responding to Christ at the age of fourteen at a Billy Graham rally. Of course, for 'The Class of 61', the overarching influence was 'Aunt Ida', Dr Ida S. Scudder, who founded Vellore Christian Medical College, and established the Christian ethos that would have such an impact on their lives.

## Awareness of God's calling and guidance

Acts 16 describes how Paul was guided by God to take that momentous step of going across to Europe to preach the gospel there. He was prevented from travelling to the province of Asia or into Bithynia, but he received a vision of a Macedonian man calling for help. Paul responded to that call, and thus began the mission to Europe. Chitra Bharucha knows that experience of being led by God as she describes her life as '*one unexplained series of miracles*', and she counsels others saying, '*God has a purpose for you, and he will open doors for you. Just walk through.*'

Others in 'The Contenders' also know the experience of God's calling and his continuing guiding hand. David Holloway prayed for guidance about his future life during a service in Edgware Parish Church, and received his calling to the ministry, which was reinforced in St Andrew's Church of Scotland in Rome. Sometimes God left it almost to the last minute before providing specific guidance as to where he should be going next, but that guidance always came, as if this was God telling him to keep on trusting him. Barbara Connor had similar experiences as she listened to God's guiding voice; even when God told her that it was time to leave South Africa but did not initially direct her where to go, she still trusted in his kindness. Andy Bannister found that God used previous experiences, for example in schools' work, to prepare him for his future ministries, and that God would bring the right people into his life to lead him on to the next step of his journey.

Charles Price has always been conscious of God guiding him in his ministry. When he was looking for a specific ministry opening after he had finished his training, he was told that he needed to spend time with God to find out God's vision for his life. This he did, and God gave him a six-point vision. Only a week later, he was offered a job at Capernwray which met all six of the points in his vision. He has never sought preaching engagements, as he believed that God would provide the opportunities and direct him where he should go.

Donald Curry is well aware that he is a member of the House of Lords only by the grace of God; it was only God who could have taken him from his farm in Northumberland to serve in top-level jobs in London and end up as a peer of the realm. Julie Maxwell knows that God has brought the right contacts to her at the right time, as she works with young people and serves on committees related to sex and gender. Michael Bushby sees that all the circumstances of his life have been ordered by God, including his recent early retirement, in order that he might reach out to others for the Lord.

## Integrity

Timothy was a young leader of the Ephesian church and about whom at one point Paul said, '*I have no one else like him*.'[288] In his letters to him, Paul gave strong instructions that he should hold on to the faith and lead his church well. He said:

> *Timothy, my son, I am giving you this command in keeping with the prophecies once made about you, so that by recalling them you may fight the battle well, holding on to faith and a good conscience, which some have rejected and so have suffered shipwreck with regard to the faith.*[289]

Others had clearly wandered away from their faith, but Paul was instructing Timothy to hold on, no matter how hard the battle might be. Later on in the same letter, he told Timothy:

> *Don't let anyone look down on you because you are young, but set an example for the believers in speech, in conduct, in love, in faith and in purity. Until I come, devote yourself to the public reading of Scripture, to preaching and to teaching.*[290]

There were clear standards that leaders were expected to maintain, and being young was not an excuse!

Barbara Connor has put an emphasis in her ministry on training Christian leaders who will '*finish well*'. She does not want to see Christians shipwrecking their faith. Sadly, so many prominent Christian leaders have failed to finish well. They have shipwrecked their faith through greed, arrogance, sexual impropriety or teaching false doctrine, and many Christians who have looked up to them have felt let down. They had ceased to hold on to faith and a good conscience, and had stopped being role models in terms of speech, conduct, love, faith and purity.

---

288. Philippians 2:20
289. 1 Timothy 1:18-19
290. 1 Timothy 4:12-13

Andy Bannister, along with Aaron Edwards and Michael Ots, presents a podcast entitled *Pod of the Gaps*, and in one episode, they examined the issue 'When Christian Leaders Go Woke'.[291] Although it might be argued that their use of the word 'woke' is inappropriate, what they are asking in effect is 'Why do some Christian leaders lose their biblical moorings and fit their message and their lifestyle to the way of the world?' Andy Bannister has in fact worked for two organisations whose leaders have later gone that way. He recognises by looking at such leaders that the slide begins '*once you lose your biblical authority, once you no longer trust the Bible, and once you become your own authority. The Bible goes, Jesus goes, and you end up with* [just] *the speaker*'. He has a theory that social media has a large part to play in that leaders are tempted to go for popularity as measured by social media 'likes', and so the self-fulfilment agenda of doing what I want will sadly get more 'likes' than the traditional gospel message.

Going for popularity rather than holding fast to the gospel message and contending for truth is a temptation for all of us, but it is a temptation with God's help that we need to resist. Looking at 'The Contenders', they are very much godly people noted for their integrity. David Holloway's views may not always be popular, but he stands firmly for the gospel, as do Charles Price and Andy Bannister. As we have seen, Donald Curry's colleagues and friends hold him in the highest regard, and Gordon Gatward was quoted earlier as saying, '*He has a Christ-like character. I have never heard anyone call his integrity into question.*' Julie Maxwell has strong views, but because she is recognised as somebody whose motives are pure and who genuinely wants to help people, she is accepted by people in different groups with different worldviews. Chitra Bharucha has been asked to take on a number of different professional roles because she is recognised as a lady with great integrity; this integrity comes from being rooted in Christ.

---

291. https://soundcloud.com/wkop-podcast/episode-20-when-christian-leaders-go-woke (accessed 17.12.21).

That does not mean to say that members of 'The Contenders' are all perfect; they all know that they are sinners saved by grace, and indeed the more they come to know Jesus, the more they realise how much they have fallen short of his standard. Graham Morritt was very honest when he looked at his Christian life over many years. It was like a series of ups and downs on a graph, as there were times when work and leisure activities got in the way of living for Jesus. Now, however, he is 'finishing well'.

Although this was not mentioned in Andy Bannister's podcast, one might wonder whether John the Baptist would have considered taking on a populist message to regain his standing after Jesus appeared. The answer would be a definite 'No!' His view was clearly expressed: '*He must become greater; I must become less*.'[292]If we want to maintain our Christian integrity, we must follow the words of John so that Jesus becomes greater in our lives, and we become less.

## Resilience against opposition and difficulties

Jesus never promised his followers an easy life. Yes, there was the promise of eternal life, but he did warn them that they would face difficulties in this life. Speaking to his disciples, he said, '*I have told you these things, so that in me you may have peace. In this world you will have trouble. But take heart! I have overcome the world*.'[293] 'These things' referred to his death which would cause them great grief, and the fact that they would be scattered in fear. They would face trouble, but despite that, they could have peace. The reason for this peace was the stupendous fact that Jesus had overcome the world. The crucified one overcame death by rising to new life. The risen Lord Jesus had overcome the world system controlled by Satan, and had dealt with our sin so that we could share in this new life.

292. John 3:30
293. John 16:33

There is victory, but nevertheless we face trouble in the world. All of 'The Contenders' have faced difficulties in their Christian lives, some quite serious. Some of them have faced opposition from others as they have contended for truth. David Holloway faced strong opposition from fellow evangelicals at the 1967 Keele Congress when he stood out against them over the issue of abortion, but he felt that he had to make his stand and maintain it in coming years; he was finally vindicated when leading evangelicals came round to agree with his view. Likewise, he faced opposition from many in the church over his stand against the appointment of David Jenkins as Bishop of Durham, and his stance over issues of sexuality, which also provoked reaction from campaigning groups. In all of these issues, he continued to stand firm for what he believed to be biblical truth. Similarly, Julie Maxwell faced opposition when she tried to have Hampshire County Council's sex education policy changed, but she held her ground and, with a group of parents, is currently taking on another battle in challenging the council on their LGBT guidance to schools.

Some have faced serious health issues. Michael Bushby continues to face cancer, and although he almost committed suicide because of it, God has upheld him, and living in faith with terminal cancer has become part of his testimony. Charles Price has faced serious heart problems for a number of years, but God has sustained him in this so that his ministry could continue, albeit in a modified way. Barbara Connor has faced major health problems for most of her adult life, particularly bronchiectasis and later osteoarthritis, but despite these health issues, she has continued in her ministry, amazed at what God has been able to do.

Donald Curry and his family have faced major tragedies in their lives. He knows the pain of losing loved ones, but he also knows God's peace through it all, believing these tragedies all to be part of God's eternal plan. In debates in the Lords on domestic abuse and assisted dying, he was able to talk about his experience with Jane.

Kalpana Krishnamurthy has faced difficulties throughout her long life, initially feeling inadequate at medical college or in trying to establish a hospital in very difficult conditions. She felt the pain of the tragic murder of her friend Graham Staines and his sons, and later went back to India to provide help and supplies to the leper colony where he had worked. She also knew the pain of losing Kittu, her beloved husband. In all of these difficulties, she held on to the promises of God, such as he gave in Deuteronomy 31:6 '*Be strong and courageous. Do not be afraid or terrified because of them, for the* L*ORD your God goes with you; he will never leave you nor forsake you.*'

## Conclusion

'The Contenders' are indeed inspiring people. Their lives, along with the exhortations of writers like Solzhenitsyn and Dreher, should challenge us to make our stand for the Lord Jesus Christ and contend for truth. There is a great need for godly men and women, including *young* men and women like Timothy, to make their voices heard so that the world will know the one who is the Truth.

In a world that is suffering as a result of the global pandemic, and where identity politics has brought confusion and fear, Christians need more than ever to share the good news of Jesus. It is Jesus who offers the blessings of eternal life with victory over sin, death and Satan. It is Jesus who can bring people of different backgrounds together into his kingdom. As Paul said, '*There is neither Jew nor Gentile, neither slave nor free, nor is there male and female, for you are all one in Christ Jesus.*'[294] The gospel is for all, and all who believe on the Lord Jesus Christ will be accepted into his kingdom. And God wants us to take the gospel message to all.

There is moral confusion in the world as Satan has distorted truth and lies; what was once seen as wrong is now seen as good, and what was

294. Galatians 3:28

once seen as righteous is now seen as evil. If people have moved away from God's truth as revealed in the Bible, it is up to Christians to share God's grace and truth in love with the world around.

Most of us, however, might say that we have neither the intellect, the eloquence nor the skills to contend for truth, as 'The Contenders' have done. That may well be true, but each of us needs to go back to God's calling to us as individuals and his equipping to fulfil that calling. If God can take a shy schoolboy who was exempt from drama and debating classes, and later turn him into a Christian preacher renowned worldwide, then who knows what he can do with each of us if we let him? Likewise, if God can take the worst of all sinners who persecuted the fledgling church, and later turn him into his ambassador to the Gentiles, then, again, who knows what the possibilities are for each of us?

God may not want you to fly the globe preaching the gospel, or cross stormy seas to plant new churches. He may, however, be asking you to share your faith with individuals or groups that only you can reach. We need to be open to God, as weak and feeble as we are, but armed with a desire to contend for him, and let him do the rest. As Paul promised the Philippians, '*it is God who works in you to will and to act in order to fulfil his good purpose*'.[295] Let us trust in that promise as we, too, contend for truth.

295. Philippians 2:13

# Acknowledgements

This book is very much about modern-day contenders for truth, and I am very grateful to each one of them who agreed to be the subject of a chapter and to have their Christian ministries shared for the encouragement of others. Each of 'The Contenders' gladly gave up hours of their time to join me on Zoom to share their life stories and answer my questions. They also took time afterwards to check through that what I had written was accurate. Therefore, I am full of appreciation to Andy Bannister, Michael Bushby, Barbara Connor, Donald Curry, David Holloway, Julie Maxwell, Charles Price, Graham Morritt, Chitra Bharucha and Kalpana Krishnamurthy. In addition, Gordon Gatward, Andy Cowan, Ben Cadoux-Hudson, Nigel Moore and Steve also provided me with excellent views on how Donald Curry and Michael Bushby have influenced their lives.

I am also exceptionally grateful to Ella who sowed the original seeds in my mind for this book. Over the subsequent months she very patiently allowed me to have 'yet another Zoom call'. She has also spent hours proof-reading the text, but I have to say that any remaining errors are all mine!

Malcolm Down of Malcolm Down and Sarah Grace Publishing once again provided invaluable support and advice, always with a cheery smile.

Jim Cockburn
2022